The Causal Power of Social Structures

The problem of structure and agency has been the subject of intense debate in the social sciences for over 100 years. This book offers a new solution. Using a critical realist version of the theory of emergence, Dave Elder-Vass argues that, instead of ascribing causal significance to an abstract notion of social structure or a monolithic concept of society, we must recognise that it is specific groups of people that have social structural power. Some of these groups are entities with emergent causal powers, distinct from those of human individuals. Yet these powers also depend on the contributions of human individuals, and this book examines the mechanisms through which interactions between human individuals generate the causal powers of some types of social structures. *The Causal Power of Social Structures* makes particularly important contributions to the theory of human agency and to our understanding of normative institutions.

DAVE ELDER-VASS is a British Academy postdoctoral fellow at the University of Essex. His primary research interests are in sociological theory, particularly the questions of structure and agency, the relationship between realism and social construction, and the analysis and critique of social and political power.

The Causal Power of Social Structures

Emergence, Structure and Agency

DAVE ELDER-VASS

CAMBRIDGE
UNIVERSITY PRESS

CAMBRIDGE UNIVERSITY PRESS
Cambridge, New York, Melbourne, Madrid, Cape Town,
Singapore, São Paulo, Delhi, Tokyo, Mexico City

Cambridge University Press
The Edinburgh Building, Cambridge CB2 8RU, UK

Published in the United States of America by Cambridge University Press, New York

www.cambridge.org
Information on this title: www.cambridge.org/9781107402973

First published 2010
First paperback edition 2011

A catalogue record for this publication is available from the British Library

ISBN 978-0-521-19445-7 Hardback
ISBN 978-1-107-40297-3 Paperback

For Alisa, Hazel, Jasmine and Gerald

Contents

Figures

Acknowledgements

This book has been taking shape for over seven years, during which time I have incurred intellectual debts to a great many people. Perhaps the greatest of those debts is to Jason Edwards, who helped to shape an earlier version of these ideas in his role as my doctoral supervisor. I would like to express my gratitude to him for his constructive criticism, for his positive and supportive attitude, and not least for pointing me towards many key contributions to the debates. I would also like to offer my particular thanks to Margaret Archer, Andrew Sayer, John Scott and Rob Stones, each of whom has gone well beyond any possible call of duty in offering me their thinking and support despite the many other demands on their time.

I also thank Ismael Al-Amoudi, Filipo Artoni, Sam Ashenden, Ted Benton, Roy Bhaskar, Vinca Bigo, David Byrne, Bob Carter, Diana Coole, Phil Faulkner, Steve Fleetwood, David Gindis, Ruth Groff, Martyn Hammersley, Mervyn Hartwig, Stephen Kemp, Anthony King, Clive Lawson, Tony Lawson, Martin Lipscomb, Jamie Morgan, Nicos Mouzelis, Alistair Mutch, Tobin Nellhaus, Caroline New, Wendy Olsen, Andreas Pickel, Doug Porpora, Steve Pratten, Frederic Vandenberghe, Charles Varela, Sam Whimster, Malcolm Williams and Sami Zubaida for their many and various criticisms, comments and conversations both face-to-face and electronic. No doubt I have missed out many others, for which I apologise.

The completion of this book owes a great deal to the British Academy, which has funded my last two years of research as a post-doctoral fellow, and to the supportive environment I have enjoyed in the Department of Sociology at the University of Essex and before that in the School of Politics and Sociology at Birkbeck College. But it has been possible above all because of the constant support of my wife Alisa.

I must also thank a number of journals and their publishers for their permission to reprint material that has appeared previously, though most of these papers also contain additional material that is not used here:

'Emergence and the realist account of cause', *Journal of Critical Realism* 4: 315–38, © 2005 Equinox Publishing (used in chapters 2 and 3).

'Re-examining Bhaskar's three ontological domains: the lessons from emergence', in C. Lawson, J. Latsis and N. Martins (eds.), *Contributions to Social Ontology* (2007), pp. 160–76, © 2007 Routledge (used in chapters 2 and 3).

'For emergence: refining Archer's account of social structure', *Journal for the Theory of Social Behaviour* 37 (2007): 25–44 (used in several chapters).

'Reconciling Archer and Bourdieu in an emergentist theory of action', *Sociological Theory* 25: 325–46, © 2007 American Sociological Association (used in chapter 5).

'A method for social ontology', *Journal of Critical Realism* 6: 226–49, © 2007 Equinox Publishing (used in chapter 4).

'Social structure and social relations', *Journal for the Theory of Social Behaviour* 37 (2007): 463–77 (used in chapter 8).

'Integrating institutional, relational, and embodied structure: an emergentist perspective', *British Journal of Sociology* 59: 281–99 © 2008 London School of Economics and Political Science (used in chapters 4 and 6).

1 | *Introduction*

This book offers a solution to the problem of structure and agency: a new solution, but one that draws on a number of existing traditions of thought, most significantly philosophical theories of emergence and causality, and the sociological debates around structuration theory. This introductory chapter sets the context by explaining the problem of structure and agency and its significance for sociology, and outlines some of the key points of my argument. It also offers the reader some hints on different ways to read the rest of the book and briefly locates it with respect to critical realism, the main philosophical tradition on which I draw.

The problem of structure and agency

Sociology is founded on the belief that our behaviour is causally influenced and in particular that there are *social* factors that influence our behaviour. Karl Marx, for example, famously wrote 'It is not the consciousness of men that determines their being, but, on the contrary, their social being that determines their consciousness' (Marx 1978 [1859]: 4). Émile Durkheim, similarly, argued that 'the individual is dominated by a moral reality greater than himself: namely, collective reality' (Durkheim 1952 [1897]: 38). Conventionally, the social factors that are held to influence our behaviour are known as *social structure*, a concept that even today remains implicit in, and indeed essential to, much of the work done in the social sciences.

Yet there is also widespread disagreement about what social structure really is and how it could affect us. One recent text described the meanings ascribed to *social structure* as 'strikingly nebulous and diverse' (Lopez and Scott 2000: 1). Furthermore, many sociologists mistrust the existing theoretical accounts of its role. Structure, it sometimes seems, is taken for granted, not because the concept is clearly understood and uncontroversial, but because addressing the theoretical issues seems so

1

problematic (see Crothers 1996: 21). This has led some to challenge the very concept of social structure, questioning whether social factors can have a causal effect on our behaviour at all.

Such challenges constitute the core problem of structure and agency: is there something *social* that can be causally effective in its own right and not just as a side-effect of the behaviour of individual people? For *methodological individualists*, the answer is 'no'. For them, there is no place in sociology for explanations of social action that ascribe causal power to social structure. If methodological individualists are correct, then the social sciences cannot study what Durkheim called social facts, nor can they invoke structural forces like Marx's social relations of production. Instead, they can only explain social effects on the basis of the actions of the individuals who make up society. Some sociologists, indeed, give up the attempt to offer causal explanations entirely and concentrate instead on investigating the meanings that are implicit in our actions. Others examine how 'rational' individual responses to different types of situation aggregate up to produce social phenomena.

Individualist accounts like these, in denigrating the role of social structure, privilege instead the role of *human agency* in explaining social behaviour – the capabilities that humans have to act in their own right. Yet agency too is a problematic concept. Some, at least, of the problems are reflections of the problem of structure: some more *voluntarist* thinkers see agency as the exercise of human reflexivity, of conscious decision making about our actions, while other, more *determinist* authors see it as flowing unthinkingly from sets of dispositions that are acquired, equally unthinkingly, from our social context. Individualists about structure, it would seem, must be voluntarists about agency, while it is often believed that those who attribute causal significance to social structure must be determinists about agency. Furthermore, just as there is a tension between explaining social phenomena in terms of social forces or individual ones, there is also a similar tension between explaining individual behaviour in terms of individual agency or forces at a still lower level. Some thinkers – *biological reductionists* – have started to argue that human action is really a product of the neural networks in our brains, for example, or of our genetic make-up, thus introducing an entirely different dimension to the explanation of social behaviour that sometimes seeks to render *both* individualist and structural approaches redundant.

These disagreements over the role of social structure are nothing less than a battle for the heart and soul of sociology; and indeed of the social sciences more generally, since just the same issues arise in *any* discipline that seeks to examine what happens in the social world. The social sciences look completely different through structuralist and individualist spectacles. Are they to be concerned with explaining social phenomena purely in terms of the contributions of individuals, or are there characteristically social forces that affect social phenomena?

Many contemporary authors, however, reject the implication that structure and agency represent a binary choice: that *either* social behaviour is determined by structural forces *or* it is determined by the free choices of human individuals. Indeed, if we look more closely, it is striking that many apparently structuralist thinkers have been unable or unwilling in practice to dispense with agency and apparently individualist thinkers have been unable or unwilling in practice to dispense with structure.

In another famous quote from Marx, for example, he tells us that 'men make their own history, but they do not make it just as they please; they do not make it under circumstances chosen by themselves, but under circumstances directly found, given and transmitted from the past' (Marx 1978 [1852]: 595). Here, the circumstances represent the structural influences on action; yet Marx is at pains to point out that within these constraints, people do indeed make their own history. Indeed, as a communist activist, he was actively involved in inciting them to do so. Though he is often accused of determinism, it seems that for Marx both structure and agency matter. Similarly, although Durkheim may be best known for his advocacy of sociology as a science of social facts, he also insisted on the capacity of the individual to resist collective pressures: 'in so far as we are solidary with the group and share its life, we are exposed to [the influence of collective tendencies]; but so far as we have a distinct personality of our own we rebel against and try to escape them' (Durkheim 1952 [1897]: 318–19). And although Weber is generally known as an individualist, his most famous work theorises the impact of social forces – the protestant ethic and the iron cage of the capitalist market – on social behaviour (Weber 2001 [1930]).

The most characteristic move in recent work on structure and agency has been to recognise that there are good reasons for these apparent ambiguities: they arise because we cannot successfully theorise the social world without recognising and reconciling the roles of *both* structure and agency. Broadly speaking, there have been two alternative ways of reconciling the two: *structurationist* and *post-structurationist* theories (Parker 2000). On the structurationist side, we find most prominently Anthony Giddens and Pierre Bourdieu, who have stressed the importance of both structure and agency, but see structure as something that resides at least in part *within* human individuals – a move that Margaret Archer has criticised as 'central conflation' of structure and agency. On the post-structurationist side, Parker picks out Nicos Mouzelis and Margaret Archer as theorists who also stress the importance of *both* structure and agency, but insist that the two must be understood as analytically distinct: that structure exists *outside* individuals in some sense. The debate between the two schools turns primarily, then, on questions of *social ontology*: the study of what sorts of things exist in the social world and how they relate to each other. I shall be arguing that both structurationists and post-structurationists have something useful to contribute to its resolution, though in ontological terms I shall come down firmly on the side of the post-structurationists.

This book is both a contribution to, and a critique of, this debate. Drawing on the theory of emergence, it argues that instead of ascribing causal significance to an abstract notion of social structure or a monolithic concept of society, we must recognise that it is specific groups of people that have social structural power. As I understand it, the social world is composed of many overlapping and intersecting groups, each of which has the causal power to influence human individuals. But in each case these powers depend on interactions between individual members of the group, and this argument thus depends in turn on the claim that human individuals themselves also possess causal powers – human agency. Social events, then, are produced by the interaction of *both* structural and agential causal power.

Emergence and social structure

The solution that this book offers to the problem of structure and agency is built using the concept of *emergence*. This concept expresses the idea that a thing – sometimes I will say 'an entity' or 'a whole' – can have properties or capabilities that are not possessed by its parts. Such properties are called *emergent properties*. We can illustrate the argument using the case of water – which has been used to make this point since the time of John Stuart Mill (Mill 1900: 243). The properties of water are clearly very different from those of its components, oxygen and hydrogen, when these are not combined with each other in the specific form that constitutes water. We can, for example, put out a fire with water, but the outcome would be very different if we tried to do the same with oxygen and hydrogen (Mihata 1997: 31; Sayer 1992: 119). Similarly, water freezes at zero degrees centigrade, but hydrogen and oxygen would both be gases at this temperature. Water, then, has emergent properties.[1]

The value of the concept of emergence lies in its potential to explain how an entity can have a causal impact on the world in its own right: a causal impact that is not just the sum of the impacts its parts would have if they were not organised into this kind of whole. I shall call the capability of having such an impact a *causal power* of the entity concerned. This is a term that has been developed by a number of realist philosophers in recent times, most notably Rom Harré and Roy Bhaskar (Bhaskar 1975; Harré and Madden 1975).

It is important to distinguish this concept of emergence from the more familiar *temporal* definition of emergence. When we talk about the emergence of something in everyday life, we are not usually referring to emergent properties as they have been introduced above. Instead, the temporal sense of emergence refers to the first appearance of a thing, or its development over a period of time. Anything that exists (unless it has always existed) must have emerged at some time in this temporal sense; but this does not necessarily mean that it possesses emergent properties. Usually in this book, the word *emergence* does not refer to temporal emergence; instead it refers to what we might call *synchronic* emergence, which is a relationship between the properties of a whole and its parts at a particular moment in time.

As we shall see in chapter 2, not all emergence theorists use the concept in the same way, even when they are all talking about synchronic emergence. This book develops a *relational* version of the theory of synchronic emergence. Its value is that it shows how it is possible to reconcile two claims that some thinkers have thought to be in tension: the claim that a whole possesses a causal power in its

---

[1] Advocates of the 'strong' version of the concept of emergence would disagree. See chapter 2.

own right and the claim that we can explain how this causal power works. *Reductionist* thinkers have argued that if we can explain how a causal power works in terms of lower-level forces, the original power itself becomes redundant to any explanation of its effects. By contrast, I argue in chapter 3 that when we explain a causal power, we do not explain it *away*. Emergent powers only exist when the parts concerned are organised into the type of whole that has these powers and hence they are powers of the whole and not of the parts. One implication of this argument is that explaining the *mechanism* behind a causal power does not explain away the power. On the contrary, it may help to justify our belief that it is causally significant.

Chapter 4 offers a method for applying this framework to the social world, preparing the way for the main argument of the book: that there are social entities with emergent causal powers that have the effects commonly attributed to *social structure*. I shall argue that these social entities are causally effective in their own right, with causal powers that are distinct from those of human individuals. But I shall also examine the mechanisms that underpin these causal powers, thus recognising the contributory role that human individuals make to the functioning of social structures. In a parallel argument, chapter 5 develops a theory of human action or agency that shows how human individuals themselves can be causally effective in their own right, with powers that are distinct from those of both their biological parts and their social context. But this also entails recognising the roles of our biological parts in the *mechanisms* that underpin human powers.

While it is relatively easy to accept the argument that human beings are entities with causal powers in their own right – powers that are not possessed by their parts – the claim that there are analogous social powers is more contentious. One reason for this is that discussions of social structure are rarely conducted in terms of entities with powers and hence it is rarely asked what the entity might be that has any particular structural power. The background assumption of many of those who write about structure is that if there is an entity that corresponds in some way to social structural power, then it is *society* as a whole. But the concept of a society has always been rather vague and the implicit assumption that the boundaries of societies map onto those of nation-states makes the concept even less plausible in today's globalising world.

This book argues that there *are* social entities that possess causal powers, but that these entities are *not* whole societies. Instead, there are many different social entities, and indeed a number of different kinds of social entities, that possess social powers. What they have in common is that they are groups of people: people are their parts.[2] This book illustrates the argument by focusing on two kinds of entities with social powers: organisations and *normative circles*. Perhaps the argument is easiest to accept for organisations, as most of us (perhaps even methodological individualists, in their less theoretical moments) are accustomed to thinking of, for example, 'the government' or 'the bank' as social actors in their own right with impacts on the world that are not purely attributable to the personal agency of their employees. I formalise this claim in chapter 7, by showing why it is valid to treat the causal powers of organisations as emergent and how this can be made consistent with explaining the mechanisms by which those causal powers arise from the interactions between their members.

The case of normative circles may be less familiar, but in some ways it is simpler and so it is covered first (in chapter 6). Here the challenge is to explain the power of social norms or rules. In the social structure literature, this power is commonly seen as the product of *social institutions*, but it is rarely clear what a social institution actually is, unless it is the norm itself, or the behaviour produced by it. This book argues that the social power that tends to encourage us to conform to any given social norm is in fact an emergent causal power of a specific social entity, a specific group of people: a normative circle. In order to sustain this claim, I shall be examining the mechanisms by which the members of such groups produce the social power of the group as a whole to affect the beliefs and dispositions – and thus the behaviour – of their members.

If we wish to explain social events, however, it is not enough to isolate particular causal powers, whether human or social. In the realist understanding of cause (elaborated in chapter 3, and based on the work of Roy Bhaskar), actual events are the outcome of interactions

---

[2] More philosophically oriented varieties of this argument have been developed recently by David Weissman and Paul Sheehy (Sheehy 2006; Weissman 2000). I shall suggest that non-human objects may also be parts of some kinds of social structures.

between a variety of causal powers. When a leaf falls from a tree, for example, its path will be influenced by the power of gravity, the power of the wind and perhaps by the power of some animal that interferes with its progress towards the ground. This is what Bhaskar calls multiple determination. Chapter 8 argues that social events are also multiply determined and that in order to offer plausible explanations of them, we need to identify the multiple causal powers that are interacting to produce them, and indeed how those powers interact – how they interfere with each other or reinforce each other, for example. Equally challenging, we must get to grips with the question of how to distinguish different powers empirically, which I will argue is complicated by the fact that human individuals can act as the implementers of both human and social powers. Indeed sometimes both are implemented simultaneously in the very same action, yet despite this I shall argue that we can distinguish between them and, having done so, go on to analyse how they interact to produce social events and larger patterns of such events.

This emergentist solution to the problem of structure and agency, then, recognises the contributions of both social structure and human agency to explaining social events, and also the complexity of the interactions between them. It is therefore distinct from methodological individualist positions, which deny causal effectiveness to social structure, and from methodological collectivist positions, which deny causal effectiveness (at least as regards the causation of social facts) to human individuals. It is also distinct from 'central conflationist' positions, such as that of Giddens, which seek to bridge these other two positions by treating structure and agency as ontologically inseparable. In some respects it leads us to treat the ontology of the social world in similar terms to the ontology of the natural world, with a broad range of causal powers interacting to produce events. But there remain substantial differences between the natural and social worlds. In summing up the argument of the book, chapter 9 looks at some of the similarities and differences between its accounts of the natural and social worlds.

Like Archer's work, this book offers an emergentist account of social structure from a critical realist perspective. Its examination of the nature of emergence, however, leads to the methodological argument that when we postulate emergent causal powers, we must identify the entities that possess them and the mechanisms that produce them. It is primarily in identifying such entities and mechanisms that the book goes beyond Archer's work. In doing so, I have found that despite their ontological weaknesses, structurationist thinkers have done valuable work that can help us understand these mechanisms. This recognition may contribute to the kind of *rapprochement* between structurationist and post-structurationist thinkers that has been advocated by authors such as Rob Stones and Nicos Mouzelis (Mouzelis 2000; Stones 2001, 2005).

How to read this book

Readers of academic books are often in a hurry. They often read introductions to help them decide which other chapters they can omit without missing the main argument. In this book the different steps of the argument are closely interconnected, so anyone dipping in to the book is in danger of misunderstanding, as a result of missing out on a previous step. The best strategy is to read the whole book. However, many readers will not need to, or be able to, so this section provides some signposts for different sorts of readers, pointing the way to potentially viable paths through the book.

The book has two main parts. Chapters 2 and 3 discuss the theory of emergence in terms that are rarely directly related to sociological issues. Indeed they avoid the use of sociological examples to illustrate their argument. Instead, simple and accessible examples from the natural sciences are used, in order to establish the principles of emergence and causal powers without confusing the issue from the outset by introducing the additional difficulties that arise in the social world. This enables them to develop a set of tools that is then applied in chapters 5 to 8 to explain structure, agency and how they interact in the social world. Chapter 4 provides a bridge between the two halves, showing how the argument of chapters 2 and 3 provides a framework that can be applied to the question of social structure. If there is one thing you learn from this section, let it be this: you cannot make sense of the second half without making sense of the first half beforehand. The early chapters provide the foundations upon which the later chapters are built and any effort you make to understand them will be repaid when you get to the later chapters.

The best way to come to terms with the argument of the first half is to read all of chapters 2 to 4, and I would recommend this path to most readers. If emergence as such is of little interest to you and you are prepared to take what I say about it for granted in the later chapters, an alternative is to read only chapter 4. Readers who take this path, however, may find themselves confused about the argument later on, or doubting it, and in such cases I would recommend going back to the early chapters and reading them thoroughly.

It is possible, however, to be more flexible in your approach to the second half. If you are interested primarily in social structure, you could skip chapter 5. If you are interested primarily in agency, you could omit chapters 6 and 7 and read chapters 5 and 8. Readers from outside the social sciences who are interested in this as an application of the theory of emergence will need to read the first half in full, but could then take the 'agency' path or the 'structure' path.

Students might be interested in how the argument here relates to the work of specific thinkers in the structurationist and post-structurationist traditions. Again, reading the first half will help to make clear how my argument differs from others. Beyond this, Bourdieu and Archer are dealt with primarily in chapter 5, while Giddens and Stones are covered primarily in chapter 6.

Inevitably, readers will find that there are important exclusions from the scope of the book. Most significantly, it has not been possible to examine in depth the inter-relationships between issues of structure and agency on the one hand, and the roles of language, discourse and culture on the other, with the consequence that the contribution of post-structuralism to this debate is largely neglected, along with the relationship between realist and social constructionist accounts of the social world. This important set of issues (touched on in chapter 9) is the primary focus of a further research project of mine and hence I hope the subject of a future book.

It has also been necessary to restrict the range of social structures covered to normative institutions and organisations, and I hope in future work to extend this range, perhaps, for example, to more systemic structures such as markets and capitalism. Though these other structures are also important to sociological theory, it is not necessary to consider all kinds of social structure in order to establish the value of the emergentist account of the relationship between structure and agency that is offered here.

Critical realism

This book adopts a critical realist perspective. In particular, it advocates a perspective on emergence and cause that is closely related to that developed by Roy Bhaskar in *A Realist Theory of Science* (Bhaskar 1975) (see Elder-Vass 2005, 2007d). Contemporary critical realism, however, is a somewhat diverse school of thought, and my approach to it is selective. While I strongly endorse his critiques of empiricist and postmodernist thought, I am less than convinced by some of the other strands of Bhaskar's own thinking. I reject his theory of explanatory critiques (Elder-Vass 2010b), I doubt the need for a dialectical turn in critical realism, and like many critical realists I am highly sceptical of the more recent spiritual turn in his thought (see Dean *et al.* 2005; Potter 2006).

Despite my concerns about Bhaskar's treatment of emancipation, however, I remain committed to the need for social theory with an emancipatory intent. This book is not directly engaged with the normative element of social theory, but as Bhaskar has argued, there is an important connection between emergence and emancipation:

> It is only if social phenomena are genuinely *emergent* that realist *explanations* in the human sciences are justified; and it is only if these conditions are satisfied that there is any possibility of human self-*emancipation* worthy of the name. But, conversely, emergent phenomena require realist explanations and realist explanations possess emancipatory implications. Emancipation depends upon explanation depends upon emergence. (Bhaskar 1986: 103–4)

I am rather more cautious than Bhaskar about the claim that 'realist explanations possess emancipatory implications'. For one thing, they may equally well possess the opposite sort. For another, I believe that emancipatory political proposals depend upon combining our understanding of the world with a clearly understood set of values, but that those values cannot be derived rationally and objectively from the facts of the world: they always depend upon our social experience and context (Elder-Vass 2010b; Sayer 2000: ch. 7).

Yet I do believe that we cannot pursue an emancipatory politics without a good understanding of how the social world does work and how it could work differently. It is only if we can provide causal explanations of the social world that we can attempt to predict the consequences of a possible change. It is only if we are able to predict, at least in broad outlines, these consequences that we can assess whether that change offers progress in a normative sense. And it is only if we can do this that we can honestly advocate it as an emancipatory strategy. In this sense, at least, I endorse the first part of Bhaskar's claim: emancipation depends upon explanation. This book, however, is about the second part of Bhaskar's claim: it seeks to demonstrate that in the social world, explanation does indeed depend upon emergence.

2 | *Emergence*

Theories of emergence offer justifications for claims of causal efficacy. This book argues that they can justify the claim that certain sorts of social structures have causal power, and this chapter
describes the version of emergence theory that will be used to justify
that claim.

Recent years have seen a widespread revival of interest in emergence
theories across a broad range of disciplines. They have been employed
by philosophers (e.g. Kim 1999; Searle 1992), physicists (e.g. Gell-
Mann 1995), sociologists (e.g. Archer 1995; Sawyer 2005), biologists
(e.g. Kauffman 1995) and information scientists (e.g. Holland 1998),
amongst others. But not all the scholars who have employed emergence theory have explained and justified their use of it, and those
that have done so have often disagreed about what the concept of
emergence means, let alone how it works. There will not be room in
this chapter to examine those debates in detail, but it *will* explain the
relational version of emergence theory that I propose to apply to the
social world, and give some indication of its relation to these wider
debates.

The chapter begins by explaining the relational conception of
emergence, then more briefly contrasts this with the most influential
alternative: the *strong* conception of emergence that is espoused by
many philosophers of mind. Finally, the chapter addresses the relation
between emergent properties and the causal histories of the entities
possessing them, using the concepts of *morphostasis* and *morphogenesis*. The subsequent chapter continues the argument by connecting
up the relational theory of emergence to a critical realist theory of
cause and showing how the resulting combination addresses the questions of reductionism and downward causation that are often considered problematic for theories of emergence.

Relational emergence

Most contemporary emergentists in the natural sciences and the complexity theory tradition employ a version of what I will call *relational* theories of emergence.[1] Although there are many inconsistencies both within and between the various versions that they use, it is not the purpose of this section to explore these; rather, it will seek to offer a single coherent version of relational emergence theory. Let us begin with a little history.

Origins

The term 'emergent' was coined in 1875 by G. H. Lewes, along with the term 'resultant', in a development of John Stuart Mill's distinction between 'homopathic' and 'heteropathic' laws, which several writers have identified as the root of the modern concept of emergence (Lewes 1874: 9; Lloyd Morgan 1923: 2–3; McLaughlin 1992: 59–65; Mill 1900: 244–5).[2] Despite his use of *laws*, where a contemporary realist would sometimes write *powers*, parts of Mill's brief discussion bear some intriguing resemblances to recent realist accounts of emergence and causation:

the component parts of a vegetable or animal substance do not lose their mechanical and chemical properties as separate agents, when, by a peculiar mode of juxtaposition, they, as an aggregate whole, acquire physiological or vital properties in addition. Those bodies continue, as before, to obey mechanical and chemical laws, in so far as the operation of those laws is not counteracted by the new laws which govern them as organised beings. When, in short, a concurrence of causes takes place which calls into action new laws bearing no analogy to any that we can trace in the separate operation of the causes, the new laws, while they supersede one portion of the previous laws, may co-exist with another portion, and may even compound the effect of those previous laws with their own. (Mill 1900: 245)

[1] By contrast with the *strong* variety, this could be labelled *weak* emergence, but there are several possible varieties of emergence theory to which this label could apply. Mark Bedau, for example, advocates a theory of weak emergence that is quite different from the relational theory of emergence advocated here (Bedau 1997).

[2] There is as yet no definitive history of emergence, but there are several useful sources on which this section draws: Blitz (1992); McLaughlin (1992); Sawyer (2005: ch. 3).

Both Mill and Lewes were influenced by Comte, whose case for the new science of sociology rested on a denial of the reducibility of the social (Sawyer 2005: 38). In a separate development of Comte's thought, Émile Durkheim developed an emergentist approach to sociology, which as Sawyer has argued, has been widely misunderstood (Sawyer 2005: 100). Durkheim clearly thought in emergentist terms:

> Whenever certain elements combine and thereby produce, by the fact of their combination, new phenomena, it is plain that these new phenomena reside not in the original elements but in the totality formed by their union. The living cell contains nothing but mineral particles, as society contains nothing but individuals. Yet it is patently impossible for the phenomena characteristic of life to reside in the atoms of hydrogen, oxygen, carbon and nitrogen. (Durkheim 1964 [1894]: xlvii)

And he clearly applied this logic to the social world: 'We assert not that social facts are material things but that they are things by the same right as material things, although they differ from them in type' (Durkheim 1964 [1894]: xliii). Given that what Durkheim meant by 'social facts' has a great deal in common with what we mean today by 'social structures', this may be the first statement of the core argument of this book.[3]

Since then there have been a number of cycles of revival and neglect of the concept (well documented by Blitz 1992). The most recent cycle can perhaps be traced to work in the 1970s that has directly influenced today's emergentist thinkers (Blitz 1992: ch. 13). Most pertinently to this book, Bhaskar's *A Realist Theory of Science* was founded on an emergentist approach to causal powers, which he drew in part from the work of Rom Harré (Bhaskar 1975; Harré and Madden 1975), while in parallel the relevance of emergence to the mind–body problem started to be investigated in neuroscience and the philosophy of mind (Sperry 1969). More recently, emergence has become an important element in complexity theory, although here the intellectual influences can perhaps be traced back to von Bertalanffy and his general systems theory (Bertalanffy 1971: 53–4). Although there has no doubt been some cross-fertilisation, these three research

---

[3] I tend to the view that social groups *are* material things as well (see Sheehy 2006: 5, ch. 4), though they differ from most material things in some interesting ways that are discussed in chapter 9.

programmes have largely proceeded in parallel with each other, with
the result that there are different (although overlapping) conceptions
of emergence and its foundations in each of them. Broadly speaking,
the philosophers of mind have tended to adopt a strong conception
of emergence, whereas the realist and systems theory traditions have
adopted relational conceptions.

Emergent properties

For thinkers in this relational tradition, emergent properties are defined
as properties or powers of a whole that are not possessed by its parts.[4]

However, a number of clarifications and expansions of this claim
are required. First, we must distinguish between synchronic and temporal conceptions of emergence. As was pointed out in chapter 1, lay
usages of *emergence* generally refer to temporal emergence, which
denotes the first appearance or initial development of some new phenomenon. While this is important, and is certainly complementary to
the synchronic conception, I shall generally *not* use the word *emergence* in this sense. Instead I shall discuss this aspect using the term
morphogenesis and focus on the synchronic sense of emergence,
which is concerned with the relationship between the properties and
powers of a whole and its parts at any single instant in time.

Secondly, we must clarify what is meant by *wholes* and *parts*. Both
wholes and parts in the basic definition above are *entities*, and the
terms *whole* and *part* therefore describe roles played by particular
entities in particular cases (an entity that is a whole in one context
can be a part in another). Entities are objects or things, for example
atoms, molecules, cells, trees, human individuals, business corporations and armies. Any entity (except perhaps the most fundamental
material particles, if there are such things) consists of a set of parts
that is in some way structured, such that the relations between the
parts are more than merely aggregative. There may therefore be collections of parts that do not form entities, such as relatively arbitrary
constructs like 'all the rice in China' (Collier 1989: 193). We may
draw on Aristotle in calling such unstructured collections of parts
'heaps' (Laszlo 1972: 28). Furthermore, an entity must have the quality of persistence, in the sense that it must sustain its existence over a

---

[4] These are sometimes called *collective properties* by philosophers.

significant period or time. To summarise, an entity may be defined as *a persistent whole formed from a set of parts that is structured by the relations between these parts.*

Thirdly, we must clarify what is meant by a *property* or *power*. A property is some intrinsic aspect of an entity that can have a causal impact on the world. I use *intrinsic* in order to exclude purely formal relations with other entities, such as 'larger than *x*', from the definition of properties.[5] *Properties* and *powers* may therefore be regarded as synonyms.[6]

Emergence occurs when a whole possesses one or more *emergent properties*. An emergent property is one that is not possessed by any of the parts individually and that would not be possessed by the full set of parts in the absence of a structuring set of relations between them. Perhaps the commonest illustration of emergence in the literature is the example of water used in chapter 1, which has been used to illustrate this point as far back as John Stuart Mill (Mill 1900: 243). The properties of water are clearly very different from those of its components, oxygen and hydrogen, when these are not combined with each other in the specific form that constitutes water. One cannot, for example, 'put out a fire with oxygen and hydrogen' (Mihata 1997: 31). Hence water has emergent properties.[7] Another illustration is provided by colour: 'The collective structure of bulk matter reflects light at certain preferred wavelengths; those determine the color. Color is an emergent phenomenon; it only makes sense for bulk matter' (Cohen and Stewart 1995: 232). Molecules – the parts of bulk matter – simply do not have the property of colour; hence this property emerges from their structured combination into larger wholes.

Emergent properties may be contrasted with *resultant properties* – these are properties of a whole that *are* possessed by its parts in isolation, or in an unstructured aggregation. The classic example of a resultant property is mass – the mass of a molecule, for example, is the sum of the masses of its constituent atoms.[8] Similarly, heaps (and

[5] See Sayer on 'formal relations' (Sayer 1992: 88).
[6] I am adopting a causal powers approach to causation here, as opposed to a covering law approach. This is a question that will be discussed more explicitly in the next chapter.
[7] Those who advocate strong conceptions of emergence would disagree.
[8] For a particularly thorough account of what it means for a property to be resultant, or aggregative, see Wimsatt (2000).

entities) may have attributes like group size and average height that are not possessed by their component parts, but these are all aggregative or resultant, as opposed to emergent, properties, since they result from the simple addition of the properties of the parts. A property that is resultant at one level may be (and perhaps must be) emergent at a lower level.

As Mill pointed out (though in different terms), it is entirely possible – indeed it is normal – for entities to have a mixture of emergent and resultant properties. In addition to their (emergent) ability to douse flames, for example, bodies of water have the resultant property of mass, which is a simple addition of the masses of their component atoms of hydrogen and oxygen.

This does not mean, however, that entities can be dispensed with in favour of an account in terms of properties or powers alone. Properties are not free-floating phenomena; they always occur as the effects of a particular configuration of lower-level parts.[9] Mass, for example, cannot exist except as a property of a particular thing. Now, admittedly, if a whole is an organised set of parts, and each part is itself an organised set of parts, then unless there is some lowest-level thing that is not *just* organisation, then any entity can ultimately be decomposed into a set of relations between relations. Nevertheless, an entity remains a *real* and persistent set of relations between relations, with causal powers that are irreducible to any of its lower-level decompositions (see the discussion of reduction in chapter 3). This real set of relations is different from the properties that depend upon it, and any attempt to eliminate the entities from this picture obscures the nature of emergence.[10]

Composition and levels

The composition of entities by their parts is central to the conception of emergence advanced in this book, as it has been from the earliest versions of the concept. McLaughlin, for example, tells us that,

[9] Bhaskar clearly takes this view; for example: 'Most things are complex objects, in virtue of which they possess an ensemble of tendencies, liabilities and powers', in Bhaskar (1975: 51).
[10] One of the problems with many discussions of emergence in the philosophy of mind is that they proceed as if properties and the relations between them can be analysed without any consideration of their relationship to entities.

According to [early twentieth-century] British Emergentism, there is a hierarchy of levels of organizational complexity of material particles that includes, in ascending order, the strictly physical, the chemical, the biological, and the psychological level. There are certain kinds of material substances specific to each level. And the kinds of each level are wholly composed of kinds of lower levels, ultimately of kinds of elementary material particles. (McLaughlin 1992: 50)

Most emergentists have continued to take the view, as I do, that the concept of emergence is inherently compositional (see, for example, Buckley 1998: 78). By this I mean that any entity's emergent properties depend upon its being composed of a collection of lower-level entities that are its necessary parts, and on the properties of those parts; but *not* on the presence or properties of other entities that are not its parts.[11] As we shall see in chapter 3, the *realisation* of an entity's causal powers may depend on interactions with other entities, but the *possession* of those powers does not.

One implication is that entities with emergent properties or powers are themselves composed of other such entities, which are in turn so composed, and so on.[12] A plant, for example, consists of cells, the cells consist of molecules, the molecules consist of atoms and so on. Any given entity, then, can be seen as internally stratified into many different levels or layers, each level representing sets of parts that are combined into the entities at the next level up. In considering any individual entity, then, it may be useful to represent its structure as a number of layers, each being a successive decomposition of the whole into its parts (see the discussion of *lamination* in chapter 3).

Once we have recognised that our universe is populated with entities composed of parts, which are themselves in turn composed of parts and so on down to the lowest possible level, we may think of these entities in terms of higher and lower levels, with each level consisting of entities composed from the entities at the next lower level. It is then

[11] Critical realists, such as Bhaskar and Collier, have sometimes adopted a compositional definition of emergence, but at other times have seemed to deny such a view. For fuller discussions of this ambiguity, see Elder-Vass (2005) and Kaidesoja (2009).
[12] It is not clear in the current state of science whether this nesting proceeds indefinitely or whether there is some lowest level of entity that will eventually be reached in this series of progressive decompositions. We can ignore this question for the purposes of the argument presented here.

a common step to identify these levels with the different sciences that study them. In this conception, the universe is populated by a hierarchy of entities and our study of it is divided into distinct sciences that explain the behaviour of the entities in each level or domain of the hierarchy.

However, when we turn from individual entities to consider the whole set of entities that populates our universe, the idea of strata or levels becomes potentially misleading. One problem is that above any given level it is possible that a variety of different classes of higher-level entity may emerge. Each of these classes may behave in a significantly different way. Thus, for example, both meteorology and plate tectonics study entities that emerge from various types of aggregations of molecules – as does biology. It is therefore more accurate to see emergent reality as branching in a tree structure than as layered in homogeneous strata.

A second problem is that some emergentist thinkers consider levels or layers to be emergent in their own right, and indeed see emergence primarily as a relation between levels. Emmeche *et al.*, for example, talk quite specifically of the emergence of primary levels and sub-levels, and seem reluctant to accept that individual classes of entities also emerge (Emmeche *et al.* 1997: 91–2, 106).[13] I argue, by contrast, that emergence is a relation between entities and their properties, not between levels as such. The implication is that emergent domains, whether branches or levels, are merely collections of similar entities, and hence the concept of levels is a secondary one, derivative from the emergence relations between things and their parts.

The role of relations

The relational approach to emergence argues that emergent properties arise *because of* the particular relationships that hold between the parts in a particular kind of whole. In other words, the source of emergence is the organisation of the parts: the maintenance of a stable set of substantial relations between the parts that constitute them into a particular kind of whole. Higher-level entities are not just a simple

---

[13] Occasionally Collier and Bhaskar also seem to imply that it is the emergence of levels that is primary, for example Collier (1989: 102). See Kaidesoja (2009).

aggregation of their component parts. A soup composed of the set of molecules that previously made up a pile of vegetables, for example, is still a soup and not a pile of vegetables. Instead, the composition of higher-level entities is a *structured* one, in which particular characteristic relations must hold between the lower-level entities for the higher-level entity to exist. These particular molecules, for example, must be present in a particular spatial arrangement to constitute carrots, potatoes and the like, and it is this set of *relations* between the components of a higher-level entity that makes them more than the sum of the parts – that constitutes the emergent higher-level entity from the lower-level components.

The critical role of organisation as the source of emergent properties has been identified by authors in all the well-developed literatures on emergence. The neuroscientist Roger Sperry, for example, has argued 'The emergent properties of the entirety and the laws for its causal interactions are determined by the spacing and timing of the parts as well as by the properties of the parts themselves' (Sperry 1986: 266). In linking sociology to complexity theory, Smith has written 'What defines such an emergent phenomenon is that it cannot be understood merely as an aggregative product of the entities or parts of the system but arises through their organization. Interaction often yields structures, forms that cannot be understood through simple linear decomposition of a system into its interacting parts' (Smith 1997: 55). And complexity theorists like Holland have stressed this same point: 'Emergence is above all a produce of coupled, context-dependent interactions. Technically these interactions, and the resulting system, are *nonlinear*' (Cilliers 1998: 43; Holland 1998: 121–2).[14]

---

[14] Some complexity theorists claim that emergence depends upon complexity itself, that is, upon 'self-organization in complex systems' (Goldstein 1999: 49). But water molecules, for example, are not *self-organised complex systems*, as these terms are used amongst complexity theorists, and yet on a relational understanding of emergence they are entities with emergent properties. Hence I would agree with Corning's rejection of 'the claim that emergent effects can only be the result of "self-organization"' (Corning 2002: 62). Different kinds of entities need different kinds of theories to explain the mechanisms that produce their emergent properties, and complexity theory may be useful in helping us to understand some of these mechanisms, but even quite simple objects can have emergent properties and it may be entirely possible to explain *these* properties without the help of complexity theory.

Relational approaches to emergence argue not only that higher-level properties are co-occurrent with particular organisations of parts, but also that these higher-level properties can be *explained* by such organisation. As von Bertalanffy puts it:

The meaning of the somewhat mystical expression 'the whole is more than the sum of the parts' is simply that constitutive characteristics are not explainable from the characteristics of isolated parts. The characteristics of the complex, therefore, compared to those of the elements, appear as 'new' or 'emergent'. If, however, we know the total of parts contained in a system and the relations between them, the behaviour of a system may be derived from the behaviour of the parts. (Bertalanffy 1971: 54)

Although relations are thus crucial to emergence, this is sometimes exaggerated into the view that it is relations and not entities that compose our world – or the social world, at least. Bhaskar, for example, seems to do this when he turns to the social world, citing Marx: 'society does not consist of individuals [or, we might add, groups], but expresses the sum of the relations within which individuals [and groups] stand' (from *Grundrisse*, quoted in Bhaskar 1998 [1979]: 26 – the internal comments are Bhaskar's). Collier writes of 'societies (composed as they are of relations between people, and ramifications of those relations)' (Collier 1994: 145). The claim that societies are composed of relations rather than individuals, however, seems to me to confuse the issue. It is worthwhile in this context to revisit the application of the same principles to natural science. Molecules, for example, are composed of atoms, but not random, unrelated collections of atoms; they exist only as a result of stable and systematically organised inter-relations between the atoms that compose them. Those relations constitute the *structure* of the molecule, while the *parts* of the molecule are the atoms themselves. There is no obvious reason why we should not treat social entities in a parallel way. As Collier himself says, 'The latticework of relations constitutes the structure of "society" ' (Collier 1994: 140). But it is one thing for the latticework of relations to constitute *structure* (i.e. the mode of organisation), and quite another for those relations to be seen as the *parts* of higher-level wholes.

A related confusion is the claim that relations in themselves are causally efficacious. A version of this argument is advanced by Fleetwood, who recognises that 'there is no such thing as a "relation as such", or a relation without relata' (Fleetwood 2008: 257), but nevertheless argues that relations are causal and even 'emergent entities' (Fleetwood 2008: 258) on the grounds that they make a difference to the causal influence of the things that they relate. I certainly accept that relations make a difference to causality, as should be clear from my argument above, but it is equally clear that relations only have a causal impact when combined with the things that they relate. Causal efficacy is a product of the parts and the relations combined, and thus of the whole entity that is produced when this set of parts is combined in this type of relation.

The relational argument for emergence, then, is that it is because a higher-level entity is composed of a *particular stable organisation* or configuration of lower-level entities that it may be able to exert causal influence in its own right. It is the way that a set of parts is related to each other at a given point of time that determines the joint effect they have on the world at that moment. Emergence, then, is a synchronic relation amongst the parts of an entity that gives the entity as a whole the ability to have a particular (diachronic) causal impact. The relation between a whole and its parts is thus a relation of composition, and not of causation.

Mechanisms and reduction

Nevertheless, we can often explain how the relation or interaction between the parts produces the overall effect. This process of interaction between the parts may be called the *mechanism* or *generative mechanism* that produces the emergent property concerned.[15] Returning to the case of water, for example, it is possible to explain why water has the property of being liquid at certain temperatures, why it has the property of being solid (ice) at others and why its solid form is less dense than its liquid form (unlike most other materials), purely as a result of the properties of hydrogen and oxygen atoms and

[15] Bhaskar uses the term *generative mechanism* (Bhaskar 1975: 14) and Bunge the term *mechanism* (Bunge 2003: 20). Bunge's work has spawned a significant literature on mechanisms in the social world. See, for example, the special issue of *Philosophy of the Social Sciences* introduced by Pickel (2004). On occasion, however, this literature seems to lose contact with Bunge's theory of emergence.

the sorts of bonds that form between them (Ball 2000: ch. 6; Gribbin and Gribbin 1999: 84–7).

From the account so far it might seem that the relational theory of emergence is thoroughly reductionist, given its acceptance of the possibility that higher-level properties can be explained in terms of lower-level entities, their properties and the relations between them.[16] Stephan, for example, has described this variant of emergence as *weak emergence* and argued that it is 'compatible with reductionistic approaches without further ado' (Stephan 2002: 79). But, to introduce an argument that will be developed further in the next chapter, we must distinguish here between different varieties of reduction. This explanation provides an *explanatory reduction* – an explanation of how the properties or powers of the higher-level entity result from the properties of its parts and the way they are organised, or in other words, a description of the generative mechanism responsible for the higher-level property. However, this does not entail an *eliminative reduction* in which the causal power of the higher-level entity itself becomes redundant to the explanation (Elder-Vass 2005).[17] As Harré and Madden put it, 'While the power or ability ... is understood by referring to its nature, such reference does not explain away the power' (Harré and Madden 1975: 11). To see why, we need what I call the *redescription principle*.

This is the principle that *if* we explain a causal power in terms of (a) the parts of an entity H; plus (b) the relations between those parts that pertain only when they are organised into the form of an H; *then* because we have explained the power in terms of a combination – the parts and relations – that exists only when an H exists, we have not eliminated H from our explanation. The entities that are H's parts would not have this causal power if they were not organised into an H, hence it is a causal power of H and not of the parts. The *lower-level* account of H's powers merely *redescribes* the whole, which remains implicit in the explanation. In other words, 'upper- and lower-level

---

[16] Reductionism is discussed in more depth in chapter 3.

[17] Searle makes the same distinction, using the term 'eliminative reduction' (Searle 1997: 29–30, 212). Bhaskar uses 'explanatory reduction' in a similar sense (Bhaskar 1975: 181). Excellent arguments for non-eliminative versions of reduction can be found in Gell-Mann (1995: 112) and Campbell (1974). Wimsatt has given a particularly strong account of reductive explanations and their compatibility with emergence (Wimsatt 2006).

accounts refer to the same thing, as a whole and as a set of configured interacting parts' (Wimsatt 2006: 450) and hence a casual explanation that invokes the set of configured interacting parts implicitly invokes the same ontological structure as one that invokes the whole. As Geoff Hodgson has put it, in a discussion of methodological individualism, 'explanations in terms of individuals plus relations between them amounts to the introduction of social structure alongside individuals in the *explanantia*' (Hodgson 2007: 211).[18]

A great deal of the debate on emergence in the philosophy of mind seeks to make just this kind of distinction between the causal contribution of an entity and the causal contribution of that entity's parts, organised as they are when they form that whole – what Kim calls the entity's 'microstructural property' (Kim 1999: 6–7). However, as the last paragraph implies, there is no ontological distinction, but only a descriptive one between a thing and its 'microstructural property'. The causal power of a thing cannot be eliminatively reduced to a causal power of its 'microstructural property' because the microstructural property just *is* the thing.

Still, the whole debate over emergence would be redundant if there were not *some* way to distinguish between the causal power of a whole and the causal powers of its parts. How, then, can we do so? Only, I suggest, counterfactually. We cannot distinguish between the causal power of a whole and that of its full set of parts, organised as they are now into that very whole. But we *can* make a counterfactual distinction between the causal power of a whole and the causal power that its parts *would* have if they were *not* organised into such a type of whole.[19] Such claims are testable (given that other relevant aspects of the context can be reproduced in an appropriately similar way) when it is possible to disassemble a whole and test the powers its parts have after disassembly. Or by finding relevantly similar entities to the parts and seeing how they behave in isolation from each other. Or by looking back to how the parts behaved before they were assembled into this kind of whole. It is only on this basis that we can distinguish between the causal powers of an entity and the causal powers of its

---

[18] Another approach, favoured by Tony Lawson (personal communication), is to dispute that the relations between an entity's parts really belong to the lower level, since a 'lower-level' explanation of the properties of the parts would not include an explanation of the relations between them.

[19] Cf. Parsons' discussion of 'synthesis' in Durkheim (Parsons 1937: 354–5).

full set of parts. It is just this kind of counterfactual analysis that will be used in the chapters on agency and social structure to establish the claim that people and social entities have causal powers in their own right.

This argument implies that, because an emergent entity is nothing more than its parts and their organisation, any explanation that depends upon *both* the properties of its parts *and* upon the characteristic way that they are related within this type of higher-level entity is in effect an explanation in terms of the higher-level entity – it is an explanation that depends upon the existence of just such an entity. Unless the parts existed and were organised into just such an entity, any causal influence that depends on such parts being organised in such a way could not occur. A resultant property *can* be explained without reference to the relations between the parts of the higher-level entity. But emergent properties *depend upon* the existence of particular sets of relations between the parts of the entity possessing the property and so the higher-level entity cannot be eliminated by any reductionist strategy from causal accounts that depend upon the exercise of its powers. Any attempted eliminative reduction of an emergent property will suffer from a loss of relevant structure – it cannot succeed without invoking a particular *configuration* of lower-level entities as the relevant causal factor, but it cannot do so without reintroducing the higher-level entity into the analysis.

Intrastructuration

Once we have grasped the significance of counterfactuality in establishing emergence claims, we may approach what is perhaps the most challenging aspect of the theory of emergence developed here. This is what Bhaskar calls *intrastructuration*. This concept appears in Bhaskar's *Dialectic*, where he argues that emergence 'consists in the formation of one or other of two types of superstructure (only the first of which has generally been noted in the Marxist canon), namely, by the superimposition (Model A) or intraposition (Model B) of the emergent level *on* or *within* the pre-existing one – *superstructuration* or *intrastructuration* respectively' (Bhaskar 1998: 599). Although here he talks in diachronic or temporal terms of the formation of structures and thus in terms of morphogenesis, the argument clearly implies that these structures continue to exist and possess synchronic emergent powers. A similar argument is expressed in directly synchronic terms by Bunge: 'P is an *emergent* property of a thing b if and only if either b is a complex thing (system) no component of which possesses P, or b is an individual that possesses P by virtue of being a component of a system (i.e. b would not possess P if it were independent or isolated)' (Bunge 1996: 20).

The former case would seem to correspond to superstructuration, and the latter to intrastructuration. Bunge's formulation, however, has the merit of making clearer that there is still a compositional basis to intrastructuration: in such cases, the properties of an entity are altered as a consequence of its having become part of a particular type of whole. Here, these new properties of the part are still a consequence of the composition of the whole by its parts; all that is different from the usual case of emergence is that it appears to be the part that is exhibiting a different property, rather than the whole. Bunge argues, for example, that atoms change their form when they become parts of a molecule, rather than simply being held together while retaining their previous form (Bunge 2003: 12). A more significant example for the purpose of this book would be the case of a human being who becomes part of an organisation, and who changes as a result of adopting a role in it.

We need, however, to modify one aspect of Bunge's formulation. What is at issue here is the question of whether a property of an entity that is the consequence of its being part of a larger whole is really a property of the part at all, or whether it is really a property of the whole that happens to be localised in some respect within the part. What is seen in Bunge's account as a property of an atom that has become part of a molecule, for example, might be better represented as being a property of the molecule itself, localised in the atom.

Perhaps this may be seen more clearly if we take the example of a human finger pressing a key on a computer keyboard. The concept of intrastructuration prompts two questions about this event: first, is it the finger or the person of which it is a part that has the causal power to press the key? And secondly, is it the finger or the person that actually does press it?

The causal power question is easily answered by considering the counterfactual question of whether the finger would be able to press the keyboard if it were not part of the whole human. Clearly it would not: the ability to press the key depends upon a larger configuration of bones, muscles and the like, that are not part of the finger, and upon the brain's ability to send signals to the finger through the nervous system. Hence the causal power to press the key is a power of the whole human and not of the finger.

The second question is more open. The most plausible answer, it seems to me, is that *both* the person and the finger press the key. The finger does so very directly and the person does so *through* the finger, which is one of its parts. Thus when the finger presses the key it acts both as a finger and as a part of a larger whole. The finger, I would want to say, is the part of the person that *implements* the person's causal power to press the key. In such cases, the two elements cannot be empirically but only analytically disentangled: there is no event 'finger pressing key' that can be empirically distinguished from the event 'person pressing key' and yet using the counterfactual method we can distinguish between the two corresponding causal claims.

In the chapters that follow I will suggest that this argument can be generalised to people and social structures: that sometimes, when a person acts, they do so both as an individual and as a part of a structure. In such cases the structure acts *through* the person and the person *implements* the structure's causal power. This case is perhaps a step more challenging than the key press case, because it is difficult for us to conceive of the finger as having causal powers of its own, whereas human individuals, I will argue, *both* have causal powers of their own *and* implement causal powers that belong properly to higher social entities.

Strong emergence

There are many different theories of emergence, which vary in many different ways from each other, and it would take us too far from the theme of this book to examine the full range of issues that arise in the debates over all these differences. It does seem necessary, however, to touch briefly on what I take to be the most influential competing approach, the *strong* conception of emergence that has been widely debated in the philosophy of mind, in order to give a sense of some of the issues at stake and some of the distinctive features of the relational approach.

Origins and definition

These philosophers of mind have been strongly influenced by the early twentieth-century British school of emergentists, most notably C. D. Broad, C. Lloyd Morgan and Samuel Alexander. These thinkers turned to emergentism in an attempt to find a middle way between the doctrines of vitalism and mechanism in explaining the existence of life (Broad 1925: ch. 2; Stephan 1992: 25). Vitalism asserted that physical bodies were alive because the physical elements were combined with a non-physical vital spirit, commonly called entelechy, and it was the presence of this mysterious entelechy that accounted for life. Mechanism denied the existence of any such vital spirit, and insisted instead that life was nothing more than a consequence of the set of physical parts that made up a living body – a consequence that would ultimately be explainable completely in terms of lower-level laws. Vitalism, then, was an extreme ontological dualism, whereas mechanism was a species of what we would now call reductionism.

The thinker from this group who has influenced recent philosophers of mind most strongly is C. D. Broad. For Broad,

the emergent theory asserts that there are certain wholes, composed (say) of constituents A, B, and C in a relation R to each other; that all wholes composed of constituents of the same kind as A, B, and C in relations of the same kind as R have certain characteristic properties; that A, B, and C are capable of occurring in other kinds of complex where the relation is not of the same kind as R; and that the characteristic properties of the whole R(A,B,C) cannot, even in theory, be deduced from the most complete knowledge of the properties of A, B, and C in isolation or in other wholes which are not of the form R(A,B,C). The mechanistic theory rejects the last clause of this assertion. (Broad 1925: 61)

For Broad, then, a property of a whole is emergent if it cannot be explained from the properties of lower-level parts *and their substantial relations with each other*.[20] In this sense, a property can *only* be emergent if there is *no* way of providing an explanation of how it

---

[20] I owe the term 'substantial relations' to Sayer (1992: 88); I use it here to exclude comparative relations between the parts – for A to be bigger than B, for example, plays no direct part in constituting them into a particular kind of whole.

comes about as a result of the interaction of lower-level entities and properties. Any property that was emergent in such a sense (if one existed) would not just be autonomous of lower levels; it is of the essence of this concept of emergence that *no* scientific explanation of the property would be possible. As Kim has pointed out, Broad and other early emergentists saw emergent properties as 'not *explainable*, or *reductively explainable*, on the basis of their "basal conditions", the lower-level conditions out of which they emerge' (Kim 1999: 6). Horgan, similarly, writes that 'there is no explanation for why emergent properties come into being, or why they generate the specific non-physical forces they do. These facts are metaphysically and scientifically basic ... they are unexplained explainers' (Horgan 2002: 115–16). This variant may therefore be labelled *strong emergence*, because, unlike the relational variant, it denies any possibility of explaining how any given case of emergence actually works.[21]

Broad illustrated his concept of emergence with examples drawn from chemistry, which he saw as irreducible to physics. Here he makes the point by using the classic example of water:

Oxygen has certain properties and Hydrogen has certain other properties. They combine to form water, and the proportions in which they do this are fixed. Nothing that we know about Oxygen by itself or in its combinations with anything but Hydrogen would give us the least reason to suppose that it would combine with Hydrogen at all. Nothing that we know about Hydrogen by itself or in its combinations with anything but Oxygen would give us the least reason to expect that it would combine with Oxygen at all. And most of the chemical and physical properties of water have no known connexion, either quantitative or qualitative, with those of Oxygen or Hydrogen. Here we have a clear instance of a case where, so far as we can tell, the properties of a whole composed of two constituents could not have been predicted from a knowledge of the properties of these two constituents taken separately, or from this combined with a knowledge of the properties of other wholes which contain these constituents. (Broad 1925: 62–3)

Any supposed example of strong emergence, however, is always vulnerable to the possibility that at some future time a scientific

---

[21] This usage of *strong emergence* is drawn from Bedau (1997) and Stephan (2002).

explanation might be found for it. At such a time, the claim to strong emergence would evaporate. Unfortunately for Broad's argument, this is exactly what happened to his examples from chemistry, only a few years after the publication of the passage quoted here. The emergentist philosophy as a whole lost credibility as a result, and despite occasional attempts at revival, remained rather marginal until the 1980s (McLaughlin 1992: 54–5, 90).

Contemporary strong emergentism

Perhaps the leading figure in the revival of interest in emergence amongst philosophers of mind has been Jaegwon Kim. Kim and the many philosophers who have been influenced by his work continue to define emergence very much in Broad's terms – as strong emergence. However, although he finds strong emergence to be a logically coherent concept, Kim is sceptical of the claim of strong emergence to provide a viable alternative to dualism or reductionism (Kim 1993).

There are two key reasons for this scepticism. First, it seems unlikely that any properties at all genuinely are strongly emergent (Kim 1999: 18). The whole tendency of modern science has been to provide more and more explanations of how higher-level phenomena can be explained in terms of the properties of lower-level parts and the relations between them. Even where such explanations do not currently exist, it tends to be assumed within the scientific worldview that this is owing to gaps in our knowledge, rather than to the inherent unexplainability of the phenomena concerned, and thus that suitable explanations will be found at some point in the future. Kim tentatively suggests one group of properties that may be unexplainable and hence strongly emergent: qualia (Kim 1999: 9, 18).[22] But qualia are highly controversial properties in their own right, and it is not at all clear why they should not be explainable.

The second reason for Kim's scepticism is that, even if some properties were found that *were* strongly emergent, it is not clear that strong emergence constitutes a middle way between dualism and reductionism. Broad himself insisted that strong emergence could be an entirely natural phenomenon, and not one that depended on introducing

---

[22] *Qualia*: 'The subjective qualities of conscious experience ... Examples are the way sugar tastes, the way vermilion looks' (Honderich 1995: 736).

supernatural forces (Broad 1925: 67–8). However, natural or not, the existence of strongly emergent properties would seem to represent an ontological dualism. Strongly emergent properties can only exist when the relevant lower-level parts are present (the A, B, C of Broad's definition) in the relevant relations to each other (the R), but Broad denies that they are explainable by the interaction of the parts and their relations. If this is an epistemological claim, it is inevitably provisional and constantly awaits refutation by the progress of science. But if it is an ontological claim, as seems to be intended, then the assertion that something can exist without being caused in some way by the presence of and relations between its parts seems to imply that there is a realm of nature that is as distinct from its physical base as the Cartesian soul is from its body. Kim therefore suggests that strong emergence must inevitably collapse either into dualism – if there really are strongly emergent properties – or into reductionism – if and when those properties come to be explained (Kim 1999: 5).

Kim himself seems to have ended up in a position that has a great deal in common with the theory of relational emergence advocated here. He argues, for example, that 'Micro-reductively explainable causal powers may be new causal powers, net additions to the causal structure of the world' (Kim 1998: 117, also see 85). Nevertheless, he continues to think of *emergence* as meaning *strong emergence*, and so does not seem to regard these 'new causal powers' as emergent properties (Kim 1998: 117–18).

Some other philosophers of mind have developed emergentist arguments that have much more in common with the relational conception of emergence (for example: Marras 2006; Searle 1992, 1997; Wimsatt 2006). But there are also those, mostly it would seem philosophers of science, who have continued to pursue Broad's version of emergence, and from time to time papers appear claiming that certain types of case are indeed strongly emergent (e.g. Boogerd *et al.* 2005; Newman 1996). There are as yet, however, no well-established examples of strong emergence in the literature. While this does not rule out the possibility that strong emergence exists, it seems at best to be very rare. Hence, unlike relational theories of emergence, the strong version would seem to be incapable of providing a *general* defence against reductionism, and given the absence of established cases, it is questionable whether it provides any defence at all. However attached some philosophers may be to a concept of emergent properties that cannot be explained scientifically, the relational version of the concept seems potentially far more useful. One objective of this book is to *demonstrate* that usefulness by applying that concept to the social world.

Morphogenesis and morphostasis

The last part of this chapter will address one final essential component in the explanation of how emergence works, using the concepts of *morphogenesis* and *morphostasis*. Both important terms were coined by Walter Buckley (Buckley 1967: 58–9), and have been introduced to the realist literature on emergence and further developed by Margaret Archer (Archer 1979, 1982, 1995).

For an entity to have emergent properties, it must first of all exist, and the concepts of morphogenesis and morphostasis are used in explaining how this comes to be. All entities depend for their continued existence on the maintenance of their parts in the particular set of relations that is required to constitute the whole from them: on their *morphostasis*. We can express this by saying that each type of entity has its own characteristic set of *compositional consistency requirements*. For example, for a string of DNA to exist, it must be composed only of certain sorts of molecules, arranged in a certain characteristic pattern. Although there are a huge number of possible variations of the arrangement of these molecules within this characteristic pattern, there are certain limits on the form that this pattern may take, which we may call the *structural range* of DNA. When a string of molecules falls outside these limits, it is not DNA and does not possess the characteristic set of properties of DNA. Every different type of entity has a different set of such compositional consistency requirements and a corresponding structural range.

For a particular entity to exist and to have the properties characteristic of the type of entity concerned, then, it must fall within the structural range of the type concerned. But we cannot take this for granted; if we are to explain the possession of emergent properties we must be able to give, not only a synchronic explanation of how the parts that it has produce the properties concerned, but also a diachronic *causal* explanation of how the entity came to exist in this form.

Now, there is no single causal explanation of any particular state of affairs, since this will inevitably be a consequence, not of a single previous state, but rather of a series of previous states at different points in the past. It is a matter of judgement which previous states of affairs we consider most relevant in any particular case, although it is common to think in terms of the most recent change as the most relevant cause. We might say, for example, that a particular pen exists (or is made of a particular material, or has a particular weight, etc.) because of the manufacturing process that was used to make it. This would be a *morphogenetic* causal explanation of the existence and properties of the pen – Buckley defines *morphogenesis* as 'those processes which tend to elaborate or change a system's given form, structure or state' (Buckley 1967: 58).

Behind this event, of course, lies a series of others, such as the previous design and manufacture of the machines that made the pen, the bringing of the materials to the factory, and so on, which we tend to ignore in most of our causal explanations. What is more important for the current argument, however, is that we also tend to ignore what happens *after* the most recent relevant change. Yet the existence of the pen at this moment is caused not only by its original manufacture, but also by the set of causes that have kept it in the form of a pen ever since. Hence for every entity that continues to exist for more than an instant, there must be some set of causal factors that maintains its stability. These factors provide a *morphostatic* causal explanation of the existence and properties of the entity concerned – Buckley defines *morphostasis* as 'those processes in complex system–environment exchanges that tend to preserve or maintain a system's given form, organization, or state' (Buckley 1967: 58).

As has already been suggested, morphostatic causes need not be purely internal to the entity concerned (i.e. they need not operate purely within and between its parts). Thus, for example, the continuing existence of an animal depends upon the internal activities of the animal, such as the functioning of its nervous, digestive and respiratory systems, but it is equally dependent upon the continuing existence of a suitable environment (such as one with a suitable atmosphere, level of atmospheric pressure and level of gravitational force). A particularly important special case of external causation in morphostasis is the need, implied by the laws of thermodynamics, for complex systems to draw energy from their environments (Laszlo 1972: 37; Prigogine and Stengers 1984).

Now, although it is clearly necessary for there to be a morphogenetic explanation of the coming into existence of any given higher-level entity, there is a sense in which it is the morphostatic explanations of its continuity of structure that provide the critical basis for emergence. Any number of implausible combinations of lower-level entities may be brought about by a vast range of morphogenetic causes over the course of time, but it is only those combinations that have continuity of structure that persist. Furthermore, it is only those combinations that persist that are likely to have constantly repeated causal effects, and hence provide the empirical material that enables us to hypothesise the existence of an underlying causal mechanism. In particular, it is only those entities that persist that are likely to contribute to further levels of morphogenetic causation, which bring about the next higher level of emergence. It is difficult to conceive of a higher-level entity whose components do not themselves have a continuing existence of some sort.

It is an entity's morphostatic causes that ensure it continues to meet its compositional consistency requirements; this is simply another way of saying that they keep the higher-level entity in continuous existence from moment to moment. Now at any time, it is possible that a more powerful morphogenetic cause may overcome these morphostatic causes for any given entity – such as the effect of heat if I throw my pen into a fire and it then melts and deforms. At this point, the emergence of the higher-level entity is dissolved, and any point-in-time consistency requirements for the pen simply lose relevance. It is the contingent ability of morphostatic causes to resist such effects that sustains the existence of higher-level entities and hence any emergent properties they may have. Some such morphostatic causes may be particularly strong: persistent entities are not just accidentally sustained but often arise from combinations of parts that have strong tendencies to cling together in a stable configuration.[23] This makes the entities concerned highly resistant to destruction. Nevertheless, such resistance is always a causal achievement; it cannot be taken for granted as if there were some natural tendency to stability.

Morphostasis, it should be stressed, may be compatible with certain types of change in the entity concerned. Thus, for example, some types of entity have what we may call interchangeable parts: they can

---

[23] My thanks to Andrew Sayer for drawing this to my attention.

survive a change in which a part is replaced by another function-
ally equivalent one. Holland offers the example of 'the standing wave
in front of a rock in a white-water river. The water molecules making up the wave change instant by instant, but the wave persists as
long as the rock is there and the water flows' (Holland 1998: 7). In
the social world this is a familiar phenomenon: organisations may
continue to exist in much the same form for many years despite the
regular replacement of their role incumbents by other human individuals. In such cases, we can reasonably say that morphostasis has
been sustained even when a part has been exchanged for another one
of the same type, and indeed the ability to renew its parts in this way
may make a significant contribution to sustaining the existence of the
higher-level entity as a whole.

    In some cases morphostasis can also be sustained when entities go
through more radical changes – in particular, when they go through
certain sorts of structural alteration. This seems uncontroversial when
such changes are part of the normal processes that occur within the
entity. When an animal walks, for example, or an engine turns, the
spatial relations between their parts alter, but within what we may call
the normal range of operation of the entity. The form of the entity, we
may say, is inherently changeable within a certain structural range, and
changes within this range are consistent with morphostasis. The question becomes a little muddier when changes occur beyond this range.
When an animal grows in size and alters in shape during its normal
process of growth, for example, there is a certain sort of stasis – of the
kind of thing that it is and of its identity as an individual – but also a
degree of change in its properties. Many social institutions and organisations are capable of developing in this kind of way. In such cases,
their continued existence is not simply the product of morphostatic
causes, but the outcome of an ongoing interplay between morphostatic
causes, morphogenetic causes and structural possibilities.

Morphogenesis

As we have seen, morphogenetic causes are those that bring about
or change the form or existence of an entity. I have already touched
on some aspects of morphogenetic cause – such as the difficulty of
identifying a specific cause as *the* morphogenetic cause of an entity
in a causal history that inevitably stretches back over a whole series

of prior events. And I have mentioned the ongoing interplay or even conflict between morphogenetic causes that are tending to alter or destroy an entity and the morphostatic causes that are working to preserve it in its current form. This section will examine this latter interplay in a little more detail.

In general, morphogenesis encompasses processes that (a) contribute to the initial development or creation of any entity; and (b) contribute to the subsequent modification of its form within the structural range of the entity type. There is a continuum between the second of these and those processes that tend to take an entity's form beyond the structural range of its type. These are also processes that alter the form of the entity, and hence may be considered morphogenetic, but their effect is to bring the existence of the entity to an end. This may be entirely destructive, as when an entity is materially reduced to some aggregate of its parts, or it may be simultaneously creative and destructive, as when the entity is transformed into some alternative type of entity at a similar or higher level of organisation.

The structures that concern us in social theory are generally *dynamic structures* that maintain themselves, not in a stable internal relationship, but by constantly striking a balance between internal parts and relations that are in tension with each other. This is how Laszlo characterises social structures, which he says 'adjust and adapt, maintaining themselves in a dynamic steady state rather than in one of inert equilibrium' (Laszlo 1972: 46).[24] Such structures contain within themselves the potential for change; if their normal state is a dynamic one, then a change in their environment may lead them to adapt by moving to a new point of dynamic equilibrium, or indeed by moving without finding such a point at all. This may lead to one of a variety of outcomes: convergence on a variable but constrained pattern, continuing adaptive steps over a period of time or collapse of the structure. In such systems, there is a constant interplay between morphostatic and morphogenetic causes.

As Buckley puts it,

Thus, the complex, adaptive system as a continuing entity is not to be confused with the structure which that system may manifest at any time (a

---

[24] Although not all dynamic structures are social; most biological systems, for example, are also dynamic structures.

persistent error or ambiguity in Parsonian theory). Making this distinction allows us to state a fundamental principle of open, adaptive systems: *persistence or continuity of an adaptive system may require, as a necessary condition, change in its structure.* (Buckley 1998: 86)

Buckley emphasises in particular that in such a system, variation or deviation is not abnormal and disruptive but normal and indeed essential to the continuing survival of the system (Buckley 1998: 71).

The concepts of morphostasis and morphogenesis, then, are capable of elaboration and combination in ways that enable us to start describing complex adaptive systems that are reminiscent of social structures. In particular, such systems demonstrate an intriguing interaction between equilibrating and dis-equilibrating causal factors, which suggests that social theory based on the analysis of such systems may be able to overcome one of the problems typically attributed to Parsonian social systems theory – its focus on social stability to the point of denying mechanisms for social change. This is a benefit that is very clear from Archer's morphogenetic approach to emergent social systems (Archer 1979, 1995, 1996 [1988]).

Conclusion

This chapter has outlined a relational theory of emergent properties. Although some philosophers have argued for a stronger conception of emergence, I have argued that this relational theory of emergence is *strong enough* to justify the claim that entities possessing relationally emergent properties have causal powers in their own right.[25] This is the claim that will be put to work later in this book.

A full understanding of any given case of emergence, however, depends on being able to explain *both* the causal mechanism *and* the morphogenetic and morphostatic processes that create and sustain its existence. In chapter 4, this insight will be formalised into a methodological framework for analysing putative cases of emergence. In this framework, any claim that an entity possesses an emergent property

---

[25] As Bedau has argued, there is no reason for us to accept that emergence concepts must be 'ineliminably and unacceptably mysterious', and indeed avoiding such problems is a strength of 'weak' emergence theories (Bedau 1997).

must be supported by the answers to five questions: (a) what are its parts?; (b) what are the relations between those parts that are characteristic of this particular type of entity?; (c) what set of morphogenetic causes has produced the entity in its current form?; (d) what set of morphostatic causes stabilises the entity and ensures its continued survival?; and (e) through what mechanisms do its parts and relations produce the specific properties of the entity?

The chapter has thus begun the task of providing a general understanding of emergence that we can apply to the analysis of the social world. This task remains incomplete, however, until we have examined the implications for the web of causal relations within which any given entity operates. In other words, we must examine the relationship between emergence and causation in more detail, and thus the question of whether and how emergence enables us to negotiate a viable path between dualism and reductionism. This will be the subject of the next chapter.

3 | Cause

The theory of emergence matters because it provides the essential foundation for understanding how causal forces operate in the world. This chapter is dedicated to explaining the relationship between emergence and cause in general, so that the rest of this book can go on to show how this underpins the ontology of the social world. In particular, the first half of this chapter connects up the relational account of emergence given in chapter 2 to the critical realist model of cause developed in the early work of Roy Bhaskar. The combination of these two, it argues, provides a much stronger understanding of cause than the influential covering law model of cause arising from the work of David Hume and Carl Hempel. The second half of the chapter aims to show how the relational conception of emergence enables us to overcome two common challenges to emergentism. The first is the reductionist claim that the causal impact of emergent higher-level entities can be explained purely in terms of the impacts of their parts. The second is the argument that emergentist theories imply, but cannot explain, the phenomenon of *downward causation* – a causal impact of wholes on their own parts, such as the effects that social structures may have upon the individuals that compose them (to be illustrated in chapters 6 and 7).

Covering law theories of causality

It is of the essence of the concept of cause that any given type of cause influences outcomes in a similar way across all relevantly similar cases. Thus, causality operates to determine individual events, but the causal factors that determine these events are generic in the sense that whenever they are present, they will have an influence that is in some way consistent. Without such consistent regularities, it would be quite impossible for us to disentangle the causal influences that affect our world, and quite pointless for us to speculate about general causal laws or mechanisms.

The 'covering law' model of causality interprets such regularities as exceptionless *laws* that enable us to deduce what will occur whenever the preconditions for the law to operate are present (Honderich 1995: 170). This model has its roots in David Hume's sceptical discussion of cause. Hume argued that when we see what we take to be causality in action, all we actually observe is what he calls a 'constant conjunction of ... events' (Hume 1977 [1748]: 50) – a repeated experience that whenever an event of type A occurs, it is followed by an event of type B. The idea we form that there is a necessary connection between A events and B events – some sort of natural force that A has to produce B – cannot, according to Hume, be justified; all we have good reason to believe is that there is a constant conjunction of A's and B's. Hence, he argues, cause is nothing more than such a constant conjunction.[1]

Hume's approach was developed in the twentieth century by the positivist philosopher Carl Hempel, in his deductive-nomological or covering law model of cause (Hempel 1968). In this model, cause is again nothing more than the law-like (*nomological*) claim that an event of type A is always followed by an event of type B. Given that this is the case, he argues, we can *deduce* that when A occurs, B will follow, and thus predict an event of type B. Cause, once again, is nothing more than a constant conjunction of events, an exceptionless regularity in their sequence. Hempel's argument, unlike Hume's, rests on the assumption that there is some sort of necessity to such regularities – there are, it seems, natural laws at work here. But like Hume he avoids any reliance on the idea that there might be something more behind them: cause remains nothing more than the empirical regularity itself; the law is simply that the regularity will continue.

Many criticisms are possible of these models of causality.[2] This section will focus on three. Consider, first, a conceptual criticism. For a realist, when we have said that A is always followed by B we have not identified a cause at all. Such regularities are not causes or explanations of events, but rather are themselves something that is caused, something that requires an explanation. Consider the following case:

---

[1] There is scope for doubting whether Hume was quite this sceptical about cause – some readers have seen him more as a sceptical realist (Read and Richman 2007).

[2] See, for example, Manicas (2006: ch. 1); Mayes (2005).

in our experience of living on the Earth, night is always followed by day. This is an apparently exceptionless empirical regularity, and the covering law model would seem to imply the following: (a) that night causes day; and (b) that there is nothing more to be said about the causal process at work. But for a realist, the fact that night is always followed by day is not a causal explanation, but a phenomenon that *requires* an explanation, and such explanations are to be developed by identifying the mechanisms behind the regularity concerned. Night, we might say, is followed by day for the following reasons: (a) night is the condition of being on the side of the Earth that is facing away from the Sun; (b) day is the condition of being on the side that faces towards the Sun (and thus the light that it produces); and (c) the alternation between the two is produced by the rotation of the Earth relative to the Sun. It is this mechanism that *causes* the empirical regularity, this interaction between the entities concerned and their properties (including, for example, the causal power of the Sun to produce light, itself the product of a mechanism discussed below).

Consider, secondly, an empirical critique of the covering law model: strictly speaking, there are no exceptionless regularities. Eventually, even the constant succession of night by day will come to a halt when our sun burns out or the Earth collapses into it. And most of the regularities we deal with are far less secure than this one. Apples may usually fall from trees to the ground, for example, but sometimes they are caught in mid-flight by people and eaten. Financial crises may generally be followed by a rise in unemployment, but government intervention might sometimes prevent this. Hempel's model cannot cope with such irregularities.[3] In the natural sciences, scientists can sometimes reproduce certain regularities with a very high degree of reliability, but they do so by creating what Bhaskar calls closed systems in their experiments – by excluding causal influences that might interfere with the mechanism they are studying (Bhaskar 1975: 33). But the regularities they observe here may be disturbed as

---

[3] Hempel was aware of this as a problem in the social sciences and offered an amended version of his model, the inductive-statistical model, in response. However, this model is even less substantial than the D-N model; in effect all it says is that if there has been a high relative frequency of an A producing a B in the past then we can predict that it is likely that a future A will produce a B (Hempel 1998). As flimsy as this seems as an account of cause, it remains the basis of a great deal of positivist quantitative social science.

soon as these systems are opened out again – as soon as we seek to observe them in the open systems of the world beyond the laboratory (Bhaskar 1975: 13).

This brings us to a third critique of the covering law model, outlined by Bhaskar in *A Realist Theory of Science* (1975). Science, he argues, would be unintelligible (and indeed pointless) if the regularities that scientists uncovered in these closed systems were of no relevance to the outside world. But although these regularities may be disrupted in open systems, it is not the empirical regularities themselves that scientists are really studying. What they are seeking to identify is the causal mechanisms that produce them. The intelligibility of science rests on the truth of the belief that these causal mechanisms continue to operate in open systems, even though their effects may sometimes be masked because of the interference of other mechanisms, and even though this means that the mechanisms do *not* produce exceptionless empirical regularities. If this were not so, then scientific experiments would tell us nothing of value about the world at large. This is why the Humean idea of causality as 'constant conjunctions' of empirical experiences is untenable (Bhaskar 1975: 33–5). Causality continues to operate in the absence of such conjunctions.

Realism and causal powers

Bhaskar offers us an alternative way of understanding causality, a *causal powers* theory. This draws on a different, realist, tradition of thinking about cause, one that goes back at least as far as Aristotle, but one that has been less influential than the covering law model in twentieth-century social science. As Groff puts it, 'realists about causality think, *contra* Hume, that causal relations are relations of natural or metaphysical necessity, rather than of contingent sequence' – and that this necessity arises from the nature of the objects involved in those causal relations (Groff 2008: 2–3). The most immediate influence on Bhaskar's theory was the work of Rom Harré, who outlined something very close to an emergentist account of cause in the co-authored book *Causal Powers* (Harré and Madden 1975).[4]

---

[4] Harré has since moved away from emergentism. For a penetrating account of the changes in his thinking, and indeed of some possible inconsistencies in Bhaskar's own view, see Kaidesoja (2007).

In Bhaskar's account of cause, there are two key elements – the concept of *real causal powers* and the combination of the causal powers of different entities to produce *actual causation*. This section will relate each of these in turn to emergence, then discuss Bhaskar's important account of *multiple determination*, and relate it to the complex *laminated* structure of entities with emergent causal powers.

Bhaskar's ontological domains

First, we must distinguish Bhaskar's conceptions of the *real* and the *actual*. In the argument we have already considered from *A Realist Theory of Science*, Bhaskar argues from the intelligibility of experimental activity to the conclusion that 'there is an *ontological* distinction between scientific laws and patterns of events' (Bhaskar 1975: 12). It is only if scientific laws can be distinguished from empirical regularities that they can have any relevance in open systems where those regularities are not produced, and since they do have such relevance, they must be distinct. Such laws, he argues, depend upon the existence of 'natural mechanisms', and 'it is only if we make the assumption of the real independence of such mechanisms from the events they generate that we are justified in assuming that they endure and go on acting in their normal way outside the experimentally closed conditions that enable us to empirically identify them' (Bhaskar 1975: 13). Similarly,

events must occur independently of the experiences in which they are apprehended. Structures and mechanisms then are real and distinct from the patterns of events that they generate; just as events are real and distinct from the experiences in which they are apprehended. Mechanisms, events and experiences thus constitute three overlapping domains of reality, viz. the domains of the *real*, the *actual*, and the *empirical*. (Bhaskar 1975: 56)

The empirical domain includes those events that we actually observe or experience and the actual is the domain of material existence, comprising things and the events they undergo. The real also includes 'structures and mechanisms' that generate those events (see below). The relationship between these domains is summarised in a table, reproduced here as Figure 3.1. Bhaskar clearly intends the domain of the empirical to be a subset of the domain of the actual, which in turn is a subset of the domain of the real (Bhaskar 1975, note to

	Domain of real	Domain of actual	Domain of empirical
Mechanisms	x		
Events	x	x	
Experiences	x	x	x

Figure 3.1 Bhaskar's three domains: populating entities (Bhaskar 1975: 56)

table 1: 56, 1993: 207) (and see Elder-Vass 2007d). This section is concerned with the relation between the real and the actual.

Real causal powers

Bhaskar identifies real causal powers with 'relatively enduring structures and mechanisms' that are 'nothing other than the ways of acting of things' (Bhaskar 1975: 14). In other words, 'the generative mechanisms of nature exist as the causal powers of things' (Bhaskar 1975: 50). These things 'are complex objects, in virtue of which they possess an ensemble of tendencies, liabilities and powers' (Bhaskar 1975: 51). Although this formulation does not directly invoke the concept of emergence, the relationship with emergence is clear: the powers and properties of an object or entity can be ascribed to the organisation of its parts into a particular kind of complex whole.[5] In other words, real causal powers are emergent properties (Mumford 2008: 140). This is why Bhaskar argues that 'explanation depends upon emergence' (Bhaskar 1986: 104). And Collier makes the connection still clearer: 'As against atomism and holism, Bhaskar's emergence theory allows us to conceive of real, irreducible wholes which are both composed of parts that are themselves real irreducible wholes, and are in turn parts of larger wholes, with each level of this hierarchy of composition having its own peculiar mechanisms and emergent powers' (Collier 1994: 117).

What may not be clear from this is why Bhaskar regards causal powers as real but not actual. There is a certain ambiguity in his

---

[5] Kaidesoja has suggested that Bhaskar offers three different and incompatible understandings of emergence, only one of which is consistent with the version of emergentism offered here (Kaidesoja 2009). While I have questioned some details of Bhaskar's position myself (Elder-Vass 2005), I take the view that it is the version that is consistent with my argument that is dominant in his work.

argument that is fruitful to explore. On the one hand, as he says, 'the generative mechanisms of nature exist as the causal powers of things'; and if the actual is the domain of what exists, this would seem to make things, their causal powers and their mechanisms part of the actual. In this view of causality, causal powers can only operate when they are properties of actual things. But on the other hand, there is something about causal powers that is independent of any particular actual entity that possesses them, and it is this that Bhaskar is gesturing towards when he argues that causal powers as such are real but not actual. Consider the power of some types of bird to fly. While the operation of this power depends on the existence of an actual bird with the requisite parts (wings, muscles, feathers, brain, etc.) in the requisite relations to each other, it is true independently of the existence of any such bird that if a creature appeared with the requisite parts in the requisite relations to each other, then that creature would have the power to fly. This is a fact about reality that is true independently of what actually exists in the world, and it is just such facts that science uncovers. These are the mechanisms that are real but not actual; such mechanisms are implicit in the nature of the universe, whether (and before) we seek to actualise them, and it is only if such mechanisms are real that science makes sense.

This is one of the reasons why temporal emergence is less significant than it might seem. It is not the case that new emergent properties are created from nothing the first time that they appear and are then somehow available for further instantiation. On the contrary, the idea that there are *real but not actual* causal powers implies that it was always true that if an entity of a given type appeared it would have the powers that follow from its characteristic parts and structure. Furthermore, in most cases there is no significant sense in which subsequent instances of an entity 'inherit' an emergent property from the first one. There are exceptions to this second point: cases in which further instances of the entity are biologically descended from the first one, or produced by imitation of the first one, or intentionally produced from the same design. But except in cases like these, there is no necessary causal link between the different instances of an entity that transmits properties from one to the next. And even in these cases, the first appearance of an entity of a given type does not *create* the (real but not actual) causal powers of that type but merely instantiates them, just as subsequent appearances do.

Even when they are actualised by being instantiated in actual things, however, mechanisms and powers do not generate exceptionless regularities; rather, they operate as *tendencies* (Fleetwood 2001: 211). In other words, they tend to produce certain effects, but this tendency may be blocked by countervailing powers, and so there is no guarantee or necessity that these tendencies will be realised in any given case. This brings us to the question of actual causation.

Actual causation

Actual events, Bhaskar argues, are not produced by single causes as the covering law model suggests, but by a complex interaction of the causal powers of the entities involved. Outside the closed systems of the laboratory, multiple causal powers constantly interact with each other. Tony Lawson likes to illustrate this with the example of the falling leaf (personal communication). Gravity operates on the leaf and tends to make it fall directly towards the surface of the Earth, but few leaves fall in the straight line this might lead us to expect, since the aerodynamic properties of the leaf and the resistance of the air (magnified enormously when there happens to be a wind blowing) tend to alter the direction of fall. We cannot explain the path taken by the leaf unless we recognise that multiple entities and their multiple causal powers affect that path and examine how these causal powers interact to cause it. In other words, actual events are always the product of an unruly mess of interacting powers that happen to rub up against one another at that particular moment and place.

There may be many different kinds of causal power, depending on many different kinds of mechanism, but all of them fit into this generic model of cause. One significant type is what Harré and Madden call *liabilities* (Harré and Madden 1975: 88–9). When an event takes the form of a change in a thing, this change may depend not only on the ability of an 'affecting' entity to have an impact, but also on a *liability* of the 'affected' entity to be affected in this particular way. Rocks, for example, have a liability to be eroded by wind and rain, whereas oceans do not. Liabilities, however, are simply a variety of emergent causal power – a power to change in certain ways in response to certain kinds of stimulus.

Like other powers, liabilities interact in the process of actual causation. The power of water to put out a fire, for example, cannot be exercised unless there is a fire to put out and depends upon the liability of fire to be affected in certain ways by water. This causal power of water exists unexercised unless and until the conditions for its exercise are met, and the presence of a fire with this liability is such a condition. When we have both fire and water, the putting out of the fire results from the interaction between the causal powers of water and the causal liabilities of the fire. For most purposes, therefore, we can treat liabilities as a sub-class of emergent causal powers.

Given this analysis of real causal powers and actual causation, the work of developing causal explanations may be broken down into two complementary processes. On the one hand, we must identify causal powers. We may need to observe partial empirical regularities – what Lawson calls *demi-regularities* or *demi-regs* (Lawson 1997: 204–9) – in order to be able to hypothesise these. This analysis of demi-regs allows us to theorise the existence of underlying causal mechanisms that are responsible, subject to circumstances, for the observable degree of regularity – a process that critical realists have labelled *retroduction* (Lawson 1997: 24). On the other hand, to explain specific events, we must identify the set of causal powers that interacted to produce them and how they affected each other – a process that critical realists have labelled *retrodiction* (Lawson 1997: 221). These two processes are complementary because the real causal powers identified by retroduction become building blocks in the retrodictive construction of explanations of actual events. While most of this book is concerned with retroduction, with identifying the causal powers of social entities, chapter 8 will look at how we can construct retrodictive explanations of social events by examining how the various social powers of people and social entities may interact in some specific situations.

Multiple determination and level abstraction

Bhaskar himself addresses this question of the contribution of many different causal powers to any given event using the concept of 'multiple determination'. In considering actual natural and social events, he argues, we must accept that different causal mechanisms and the interactions between them account for different aspects of the events concerned, and that no single law 'determines' the whole result:

The question 'how is constraint without determination possible' is equivalent to the question how 'can a thing, event or process be controlled by several different kinds of principle at once?' To completely account for an event would be to describe all the different principles involved in its generation. A complete explanation in this sense is clearly a limit concept. In an historical explanation of an event, for example, we are not normally interested in (or capable of giving an account of) its physical structure. (Bhaskar 1975: 110–11)

Bhaskar's argument, however, does not relate *only* to the interaction of causal powers between entirely distinct entities; he is also concerned with the relations between causal powers at different compositional levels of a given entity. Any such entity, as we saw in chapter 2, is composed of parts that are themselves composed of parts, and at each level of composition new causal powers emerge.

Now, for most purposes, when we discuss any given entity we are in the habit of ignoring the role of its parts. To treat an entity in this way is to take what I propose to call a *level abstracted* view of it – a view that considers the effects of the whole entity in isolation from the existence or effects of its parts. I argue, however, that for some purposes we sometimes need to treat a whole entity quite explicitly as a stratified ensemble of parts at various ontological levels. This is to take what I propose to call a *laminated* view of the entity.[6] These two terms are illustrated in Figure 3.2.

Here, L1 represents the highest level of a whole – for example, a plant. L2 represents the first decomposition of the whole into its parts – in this case, perhaps, the cells of the plant and the relations between them that constitute them into a whole plant. L3 represents the next decomposition – here, the molecules that make up the cells and the relevant relations between them. And the pyramid may continue downwards, until its base is lost in the mists of our limited understanding of sub-quantum science. Of course, a plant is not made up of the whole plant *plus* its cells *plus* its molecules and so on; each

---

[6] The term *laminated* was introduced by Collier and reused by Bhaskar (Bhaskar 1993: 404; Hartwig 2007: 441–2). Collier may not have used it in quite the same sense as I do here, which is strictly compositional, but the metaphor – of multiple layers of material bonded together into a single piece – is irresistibly suggestive. Level abstraction and lamination are discussed in Elder-Vass (2007d), although there I used the term *downwardly inclusive* rather than *laminated*.

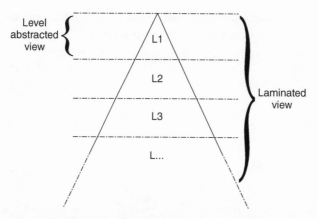

Figure 3.2 Internal stratification

of these levels represents a different decomposition of the same whole; it is only our view of the plant that must sometimes encompass the recognition that the whole plant is simultaneously each of these different decompositions.

Any given higher-level entity, then, can be seen as a pyramid of successively lower-level parts and the causal impact of the higher-level entity as a whole includes the causal impacts of those parts.[7] At each level, the entities formed from the lower-level parts have causal powers in their own right by virtue of how those parts are organised. The total causal impact of a higher-level entity conceived of in these laminated terms, then, includes the impact of all its lower-level parts as well as the causal powers that are emergent at its highest level.

We are also accustomed to thinking of events in level-abstracted terms, but these too may be thought of in laminated or pyramidal terms. Hence, for example, when a pen falls to the floor, there is a series of lower-level events that are inseparably part of this individual event: each of its parts also falls, as do the molecules that compose those parts and so on through the atoms, subatomic particles and so forth. Given that we do not have fully adequate understandings of the lower end of this spectrum, we must accept that only partial descriptions and hence only partial explanations are possible of the lower-level set of events that composes the higher-level event. For most

---

[7] Lloyd Morgan uses the 'pyramid' analogy in a partly similar way (Lloyd Morgan 1923: 14–16).

practical purposes we can and indeed must ignore the lower levels of this hierarchy, but for the purpose of understanding the ontology of events and causation we must recognise their significance.

In decomposing the behaviour of a laminated entity across its ontological levels, it is the organisation that appears at each level, the set of relations between the relevant lower-level entities, that is the 'extra' piece of explanatory information that appears at that level; and this is what makes the 'multiple determination' approach viable. We attribute a portion of the causal influence on a particular event to the level of organisation at the topmost level, a portion to the organisation at the next level down and so on. This allows us to construct causal accounts of multi-levelled single instance causation in which all the levels of the prior situation can have an appropriate influence on the various levels of the outcome.

Consider the case of photosynthesis by a plant. In certain circumstances, many plants 'convert' carbon dioxide from the atmosphere into oxygen. At the highest level of the event (i.e. a case of photosynthesis) we may simply say that it was caused by the power the plant has to photosynthesise. Many useful explanations may indeed rest on this power, and a scientist could investigate, for example, the differential rates at which plants produce oxygen in different contexts without worrying about how photosynthesis worked at the cellular or molecular level.

But there are some parts of the event concerned that would inevitably remain unexplained by such an account. At another level (the molecular), the process of photosynthesis is a chemical reaction, and we could not explain either *how* photosynthesis works or *which* lower-level parts of the entities involved are affected, and in what way, without looking at this process at the molecular level. This would not be an account of a different event, but a different account of the same event – one that is abstracted at a different level from the whole event.

And yet, the lower-level account still gives us only a partial account of the causal process at work here, because any explanation at only the molecular level will miss the key *higher-level* causal factors that are also necessary for the event to occur. Thus, these molecules would not have been brought into an arrangement that made this chemical reaction possible unless they had been organised into the form of the plant in the first place (with organisation into cells as an equally essential middle level). The causal power of photosynthesis thus belongs to the plant and not to the molecules, but to provide a complete causal explanation of what happens when photosynthesis occurs we need a causal account that operates at multiple levels simultaneously, invoking both the causal powers of the plant and the causal powers of its molecules.

In other words, it is impossible to explain fully the causation of the event except as the outcome of a causal interaction between the whole 'pyramids' – between the entities concerned, viewed in laminated terms – and not just the single points at the top – the same entities viewed in level-abstracted terms.

We can see why this is a useful way to look at causation if we consider the problem posed to level-abstracted accounts by multiple realisability: the possibility that a higher-level outcome is consistent with a variety of different lower-level configurations. Such accounts are underdetermined, in that they can provide an account of the change that occurred at a higher-level, but not an account of how the implicit lower-level changes occurred, thus leaving the higher-level change floating unsecured without any confidence in how its components could have been brought to a state consistent with it. Laminated accounts, by contrast, resolve this underdetermination since the whole range of states of all the component entities and sub-entities involved in the multi-levelled event are available to contribute to the causation of the lower-level changes.

It is because (actual) phenomena are inherently laminated that we need to deploy accounts of different (real) causal mechanisms, each of which emerges at a specific level, to explain different aspects of them. Thus explanation at each level, in the 'area of autonomy' left by the incomplete explanations at other levels, requires a 'putatively independent science' of that level (Bhaskar 1975: 114). And it is in combining all these level-specific explanations of the different levels of a particular event that we 'completely account for an event'. Events, in all their multi-levelled glory, are the products of the combination of a variety of causal mechanisms operating on the prior state of the set of entities involved. Although, of course, because we do not have viable sciences of every level, we can only produce incomplete subsets of the 'complete' multi-layered account, which is why such a complete account can be seen only as 'a limit concept' (Bhaskar 1975: 110–11, as quoted above). And in practice, we will not be interested in such complete accounts: we may be perfectly happy to explain an event at a given level while ignoring its lower-level ramifications.

Now all this suggests that the abstracted explanations we commonly employ are massive simplifications of the real, multi-level causal processes. The causation of any individual event operates across the whole pyramid of entities and sub-entities, not at a single level of it. Our ordinary causal explanations are analytical abstractions from this. Causation is never truly 'independent' of what is happening at other levels in the individual instance; it is only analytically independent when generalised. Cause as we generally understand and apply it is therefore an attempt to simplify and extract from the impossible complexity of actual causation.

Bhaskar's theory of causal powers and the relational theory of emergence provide the tools with which we can make sense of this complexity. Because causal powers emerge at a specific level (e.g. the ability to photosynthesise belongs only to the plant as a whole; the molecules or cells of the plant could not photosynthesise if they were not organised into the form of a plant), then it is entirely reasonable to think of them in level-abstracted terms. Nevertheless, they can only lead to actual events when they are combined with a multiplicity of causal mechanisms from other levels of the ontological strata. Thus real causal powers can be described in a level-abstracted form, while actual causation always occurs in the form of multi-levelled events with different causal powers impacting upon different levels of those events. We can often abstract from the lower-level events and causes when they are of limited relevance to the causal question we are seeking to address, but in other circumstances, answering other questions, we may need to recognise that they are significant. Bhaskar's model of actual causation and multiple determination provides a framework for constructing causal explanations that recognise the complementary contributions of emergent properties at a variety of different levels.

With this account of causality at our disposal, we can address the questions of reductionism and downward causation.

Reductionism

To be a reductionist (or, to be more precise, an *eliminative reductionist*) about a causal claim is to argue that the claim is false because the real causal influences emanate not from the claimed source but from some lower-level source. This section will contrast this eliminative conception of reduction with the notion of *explanatory reduction*; in an explanatory reduction, the higher-level claim is explained by showing how it arises from lower-level elements and the relations between them, but this is not taken to entail that the higher-level claim can be eliminated. This section will argue that emergent causal powers cannot be eliminatively reduced, and will explain why, expanding on the redescription principle advanced in chapter 2. It will, however, accept that emergent causal powers can be explained. Such explanations are commonly thought to entail reducibility, but I will argue that in fact they confirm, rather than undermine, the case for the causal effectiveness of emergent properties.

Eliminative reductionism

Eliminative reductions, as described most famously by Ernest Nagel, occur when a higher-level theory is shown to be logically equivalent to a lower-level theory, with the result that the higher-level theory can be dispensed with entirely (Nagel 1998 [1974]). Now, although eliminative reductionism is often, as here, couched in terms that relate to a covering law conception of cause, the argument can be extended to a causal powers approach. In causal powers terms, eliminative reductionism is the claim that the effects of a higher-level mechanism are nothing more than a summation of the effects of lower-level mechanisms, with the consequence that all properties and events at these higher levels can be fully explained by reference to properties of lower-level entities. Thus eliminative reductionists deny both the causal effectiveness of the higher-level entities and their properties and the need for (or value of) any science conducted in terms of these higher-level properties.

Such claims could potentially be applied to any causal power except those of fundamental physical particles, if there are such things. Eliminativists in the philosophy of mind, for example, declare that mental properties are reducible. They argue that all causal value of mental entities or properties arises from their physical components and that explanations in terms of the mental can always in principle be reduced to explanations in terms of the physical, thus making explanations in terms of the mental ultimately redundant (Kim

1993: 210). Analogously to this argument, methodological individualists in the social sciences claim that any causal powers claimed for social structures are reducible, such that all social explanations can in principle be reduced to individual ones.

All versions of this argument implicitly depend on the belief that it is possible to justify the claim for the causal effectiveness of entities at *some* levels of a multi-levelled structure, while rejecting that of entities at other levels. Reductionists, however, often fail to offer any positive argument to justify their belief in the causal effectiveness of the levels they favour. Without such an argument, of course, reductionism is logically incoherent. A coherent reductionism must not only *dismiss* arguments for the causal effectiveness of higher levels, but also *establish* some for the causal effectiveness of lower levels.

Thus, for example, the methodological individualist argument that all causal influence of social structures should really be ascribed to human individuals assumes that those human individuals themselves have causal capabilities. But human individuals themselves are composed of cells, which in turn are composed of molecules, which in turn are composed of atoms and so on. Now, if a generic critique of emergence could be advanced to support the claim that there can be no social causation (which I deny), it would also seem to substantiate similar claims that there could be no human causation, no molecular causation, no atomic causation and so on all the way down (see Humphreys 1997: 3–4 for another version of this argument). Any case that is made against emergence *in general* undermines the ontological basis of lower-level explanations just as much as that of higher-level explanations: these eliminative reductionists are merrily sawing off the branch upon which they sit.[8]

In principle, eliminativist arguments could avoid this reduction *ad absurdum*, since they could advance a theory that implies that emergence beyond a certain level is impossible, while remaining valid below that level. There is some such belief *implicit* in methodological individualism. It may seem, for example, that our personal phenomenal experiences of agency warrant the belief that human individuals *must* be causally effective agents. This belief may be sound, but the

[8] Durkheim made much the same point over a hundred years ago (Durkheim 1974 [1898]: 28–9).

following chapters will argue that our causal capabilities as human individuals derive from our possession of emergent properties in just the same way that the causal capabilities of other entities do. If this is so, then the same type of argument that justifies attributing causal powers to human beings may also justify attributing them to some social structures.

Explanation without elimination

Chapter 2 has already argued that emergent causal powers cannot be eliminatively reduced because explanations of how they work always depend, not only on the properties or powers of the parts of the entity possessing the higher-level power, but also on the relations between those parts. Such explanations therefore depend on something more than the powers of the parts, and therefore do not succeed in explaining the higher-level power entirely in terms of lower-level powers.

For example, the liquidity of water over a certain range of temperatures can be explained as resulting from the way that its molecules try to bond with each other, which in turn is a consequence of their sub-molecular structure and their degree of movement at the energy levels corresponding to those temperatures (Gribbin and Gribbin 1999: 84–6). This is the sort of 'mechanistic' explanation that is incompatible with Broad's conception of strong emergence. It explains a property of a higher-level entity (a body of water) in terms of the properties of its parts (hydrogen and oxygen atoms) and the way that they are related to each other when they take the particular form of water molecules (let us call this relation 'H_2O molecular bonds' for the purpose of this argument). It was because supposedly reductive explanations like this could be made of Broad's candidates for the title of emergent property that his emergentism fell into disrepute.

But this does not constitute an eliminative reduction at all. It would only be an eliminative reduction if the property of the whole could be explained purely in terms of the properties of the parts, ignoring any connective relations between them. Thus, for example, the mass of this same body of water is a simple sum of the mass of the hydrogen and oxygen atoms that compose it, irrespective of whether or not they are organised into water molecules, and we can therefore eliminate the entity 'water' and its distinctive properties from an explanation of this mass.

But when we seek to explain a property of water in terms of 'hydrogen and oxygen atoms and H_2O molecular bonds', we have *not* eliminated the entity 'water' from the explanation of the property, for the simple reason that 'hydrogen and oxygen atoms and H_2O molecular bonds' just *is* water. In such an explanation we have not replaced the higher-level entity in our explanation, we have merely redescribed it. If the higher level is to be explained by the lower-level entities *and* the relations between them, we have covertly reintroduced the higher-level back into the explanation, since it is nothing but the addition of these relations as an ongoing feature that distinguishes the higher-level entity from the mere collection of lower-level parts. This is what chapter 2 called the *redescription principle*.

This argument does not deny that we may be able to explain the relationship between higher and lower levels. It is not the attempt to explain higher-levels that is eliminative reductionism's flaw; it is the belief that such explanations entail elimination. Even though they can in principle be explained, emergent higher-level properties are still causally effective in their own right. As Marras has put it, 'When we say that F causes G, we generally assume that there is an underlying mechanism ... The efficacy of these mechanisms does not *pre-empt* the claim that F causes G, but *explains how F causes $G* ... We need to distinguish the *attribution* of causal powers from the *explication of the mechanisms* by which such causal powers are exercised' (Marras 2006: 567).

Some confusion enters this debate because the term *reduction* is sometimes used to refer to explanations that do not entail elimination – this is what is referred to above as *explanatory reduction*. Holland, for example, despite dismissing simplistic reductions in terms of the parts alone, does nevertheless advocate an approach to emergence based on what he calls 'reduction'. But this is a form of reduction that no longer claims to eliminate the higher level in favour of the lower. What it does seek to do is to explain how the higher level comes about, how it comes to be emergent, by examining its parts and their relations to each other. The use of the term 'reduction' at all in this context is perhaps misleading, given the eliminative connotations it often seems to carry, but so many approaches to reduction take this form that it would seem idiosyncratic to refuse to use the term. The point has been put well by both Fodor and Gell-Mann:[9]

It seems to me (to put the point quite generally) that the classical con-strual of the unity of science has really misconstrued the *goal* of scientific reduction. The point of reduction is *not* primarily to find some natural kind predicate of physics co-extensive with each natural kind predicate of a reduced science. It is, rather, to explicate the physical mechanisms whereby events conform to the laws of the special sciences. (Fodor 1974: 107)

I know of no serious scientist who believes that there are special chemical forces that do not arise from underlying physical forces. Although some chemists might not like to put it this way, the upshot is that chemistry is in principle derivable from elementary particle physics. In that sense, we are all reductionists, at least as far as chemistry and physics are concerned. But the very fact that chemistry is more special than elementary particle physics, applying only under the particular conditions that allow chemical phenomena to occur, means that information about those special condi-tions must be fed into the equations of elementary particle physics in order for the laws of chemistry to be derived, even in principle. Without that caveat, the notion of reduction is incomplete ... At each level there are laws to be discovered, important in their own right. The enterprise of science involves investigating those laws at all levels, while also working, from the top down and from the bottom up, to build staircases between them. (Gell-Mann 1995: 112)

One important consequence of this approach is that rather than elim-inating higher-level theories, explanatory reductions do precisely the opposite: they provide extra justification for them by demonstrating that they are well founded in the theory of the lower level, that they are consistent with other accepted bodies of theory, and indeed that they extend their explanatory power (Kitcher 1998; Meyering 2000: 181). In Gell-Mann's word, they are not eliminated but 'cemented' (Gell-Mann 1995: 112).

Downward causation

A further challenge to emergence theories arises from the question of *downward causation* – the capability of an entity with causal powers

[9] Also see Campbell (1974) for a classic statement of non-eliminative reductionism.

to have a causal impact on its own parts. Significant attention has been devoted to the problem of downward causation in the philo-sophical literature on emergence.[10] Kim has argued that emergentism logically implies downward causation, and by implication the concept of emergence itself stands or falls depending upon whether the argu-ment for downward causation can be sustained (Humphreys 1997: 3; Kim 1992: 121). This is of particular relevance in the discussion of social structure, since this book will be arguing that social structural power is exercised by social groups and may have a causal impact on the members of those groups.

This section argues that downward causation works in just the same way as any other type of causation. In both cases the causal mechan-ism depends ultimately on the presence of the *level of organisation* represented by the 'causing' entity. In both cases, the operation of the higher-level causal effect will depend on the causal effects of the parts, but as we have seen in the account of explanatory reduction, it is only when they are organised in the form of the 'whole' causing entity that they have this effect.

Let us illustrate the principle with an example – the emission of light by a star. To simplify enormously, stars emit light in the form of a stream of (wavelike) particles called photons. Their emission is the result of the extreme conditions of pressure and temperature in the star's core, and these in turn result from compression of the various nuclear particles that form the core by the enormous forces of gravity that are generated by the mass of the star itself (Gribbin and Gribbin 1999: 189, 195). Now the point here is that the emission of light can in a sense be accounted for by the interaction between the particles themselves, but that interaction itself presupposes a certain set of relationships between the entities concerned (proximity, temperature, etc.) and that set of relationships only occurs as a result of the exist-ence of the star. The same particles organised in some other way (e.g. distributed evenly across space) would not emit light; hence its emis-sion can only be accounted for by combining the part played by the particles with the part played by the relationships between them, and the relationships between them are precisely what constitute them

---

[10] The history is discussed in McLaughlin (1992: 51). An important early exposition of the argument for emergent downward causation is Sperry (1969), and a critique is provided by Klee (1984).

into a star. It is only when those particles are arranged in that manner that a star exists, and only when they are arranged in that manner that light is emitted. Thus the emission of light from a set of particles that would not otherwise emit it must be accounted for by the level and form of organisation that constitute them into a star.

The star, then, has a downward causal effect on the particles, causing them to emit light, which is another way of saying that this is the effect the group of particles, *organised as a star,* has on individual members of the group. We can thus offer an explanatory but not an eliminative reduction of this causal mechanism – one which recognises that the role of the higher-level structure cannot be eliminated from the story without doing violence to the causal account. It would be pure ontological prejudice to insist that the real causal work is going on only at the lower level when both levels are necessary to the process concerned.

Some authors, however, perceive an inconsistency between the idea of a higher-level whole having a causal effect on one of its parts while the whole is itself constituted by that part (amongst others). Stephan, for example, criticises Sperry for his claim that 'emergent phenomena ... have a causal impact qua emergent phenomena on the very microstructure that determines the emergent phenomena' (Stephan 1992: 44) and Klee criticises Sperry in similar terms (Klee 1984: 60–1). To Stephan, at least, this seems to suggest a circularity, or an overdetermination, in which different and incompatible states of the lower-level entity may be simultaneously mandated by the various causes working at different levels.

Now I suggest that this apparent problem comes from the neglect of the role of time, and in particular from the neglect of the different time status of cause and composition.[11] In downward causation, a higher-level entity causes a change in one of its parts over a period of time – cause is a diachronic relationship. But the composition relationship is a synchronic relationship – it is a logical statement of the relationships that must exist between a group of parts at a given moment in time (let us call this time t) for them to constitute a whole of a given type. Remember that composition is not in

---

[11] My argument here is similar in some respects to Archer's critique of the role of time in Giddens' approach to social structure (Archer 1982: 466–71, 1998: 358–60).

itself a relationship with any determinative force; it is only binding to the extent that the (diachronic) morphostatic causes that maintain it continue to do so. For the higher-level entity to have a causal impact of any kind, the relevant morphogenetic and morphostatic causes must have led to the satisfaction of the entity's compositional requirements at time t. Hence the state of the system at time $t + 1$ is determined by the combination of these morphostatic causes, if they are still operating, with any other causal mechanisms that happen to be operating, including the downward causal mechanism generated by the state of the higher-level entity at time t. The outcome, logically, may include changes in the parts that are consistent with the continuing existence of the whole, or changes in the parts that destroy the structural integrity of the whole, or indeed changes in the parts that transform the whole from one type of higher-level entity to another. Thus the part played by a downward causal mechanism may even in some actual cases be the critical factor in destroying the entity possessing the mechanism – suicide, for example. None of these outcomes is inconsistent with the compositional consistency requirements that describe the *initial* conditions in which the whole will be formed by the parts, since it is always contingent whether these conditions will be maintained over time, and there is no reason why a causal power of a higher-level entity at time t should not be a factor in affecting whether these conditions continue to exist at time $t + 1$.

This picture of downward causation should enable us to clarify one last challenge that has been raised in the literature on downward causation. Kim argues that downward causation implies that 'these "higher-level" mental events and processes cause lower-level physical laws to be violated' (Kim 1992: 120). There is no such implication. The causal mechanisms arising from higher levels of organisation supplement those arising from lower levels, they do not violate them.[12] In the case of light being emitted from a star, for example, the star has a downward causal effect on the particles that it causes to emit photons as a result of bringing them into a relationship in which they exercise causal mechanisms that they already possessed, but would not have exercised had they not been organised into a star.

---

[12] Bhaskar and Mill also express this view in quotes cited above.

To put the point slightly differently, in this case *both* the lower-level particles and the star taken as a whole have causal powers that contribute to the outcome. The whole laminated event is produced by *all* of the interacting levels of the laminated entity that is the star. The actual outcome depends upon all of these levels being present.

Of course, there may also be other configurations in which a different higher-level causal power combines with the same lower-level causal power to produce an event that is similar to one or another of the sub-parts of this laminated event. Thus, for example, a particle may be induced to emit a photon when it is not part of a star, but for this to occur, some other higher-level configuration must be created that has this effect. For example, a scientist may set up an experiment that induces a particle to emit a photon, but in such a case there is still a higher-level entity exercising a causal power to co-determine the outcome: the experimental apparatus itself.

Thus, the star example nicely illustrates the point that events may be co-determined by the causal powers of higher- and lower-level entities, even where the lower-level entities concerned are parts of the higher-level entity concerned, and even where the events that result are changes in those very same lower-level entities. If this is the case in the natural world, then it may also be the case in social events, and the application of this argument to the concepts of social structure and agency will be at the heart of the remainder of this book.

Conclusion

This chapter has constructed an account of cause in a world of emergent properties and examined some of its implications. Following Bhaskar, it has shown that such an account depends on a careful separation of real causal mechanisms from the actual causation of events, so that we can see the latter as the outcome of an interacting set of mechanisms or powers. These causal mechanisms arise from the extra *organisation* that appears at each level of structure of laminated entities. Therefore, actual laminated events are to be explained as the outcome of an interacting set of level-abstracted real causal powers. Where the higher-level entity has genuinely emergent causal powers, these cannot be successfully eliminated from causal explanations by any reductionist strategy. Nor is there any ontological reason why mechanisms at one level should not affect entities at another, and this argument is unaffected by the question of whether or not the affected entities are parts of the affecting entity, and so relational emergence is capable of sustaining downward causation.

This conception of cause applies not only to the 'natural' world, but equally to human social behaviour, and this is a theme we will return to as we move on now from the general theory of emergence to the application of the resulting ontology to the social world.

4 | *Social ontology and social structure*

One of the objectives of this book is to address what I take to be one of the central problems of the social sciences: a radical absence of ontological rigour. Concepts are frequently pressed into service in these disciplines without even the most cursory attempt to establish what their real referents are. In the natural sciences it would be unthinkable to employ a concept like *molecule* or *black hole* or *chimpanzee*, for example, without attempting to understand what range of entities the concept refers to, what they are made of, how their parts must be structured to make such an entity, what properties and powers flow from that structure, how these entities come into existence and how their existence is maintained. But social scientists often seem happy to employ concepts like, for example, *discourse, the state, institutions, values, value, money* and *agents*, while ignoring some or all these questions. There is frequently a presumption that we can usefully analyse the social role of such concepts while utterly disregarding their ontological basis. Occasionally, this is even justified explicitly, for example by Winch: 'To discover the motives of a puzzling action *is* to increase our understanding of that action; that is what "understanding" means as applied to human behaviour. But this is something we in fact discover without any significant knowledge about people's physiological states; therefore our accounts of their motives can have nothing to do with their physiological states' (Winch 1958: 78). The ontological underpinnings of whatever it is that a concept refers to, then, are often taken for granted, or their explanatory significance is explicitly denied, and in the extreme case, concepts may be taken to refer to nothing more than themselves, thus denying the very possibility of their referents *having* ontological underpinnings. Yet these concepts are then treated as if whatever they stand for has the capability to affect the social world.

This book, by contrast, and critical realism more generally, offers a general ontological framework that identifies such capabilities as the

64

real causal powers of things or *entities*. In principle, this framework should be equally applicable to the natural and the social worlds. Hence realists in the social sciences proceed on the assumption that social theories must identify causal powers or emergent properties in the social world. There is a danger, however, of mirroring the onto-logical failures of non-realist approaches. This fault arises if and when we find factors we believe to be causally effective and then simply label them as *causal powers* or *emergent properties* without justify-ing the claims that are implicit in these labels. Such a practice would provide a realist veneer to just the sort of ontological superficiality that realism ought to combat.

If we are to provide a genuinely realist basis for a more ontologic-ally rigorous approach to the social sciences, we need to bridge the gap between the general emergentist ontology outlined so far in this book and the practice of social theorising. Given the argument of chapters 2 and 3 that causation is produced by the interaction of emergent causal powers, and given that the theory of emergence describes the types of structural relations that underpin such powers, we can develop a specifically *social* ontology by seeking to identify these structural relations in the social domain. This chapter outlines a method for doing so, and examines the issues involved in applying it. The method is specified rather more abstractly than most methods for *empirical* research, and like all methods it is incomplete, specifying only part of what anyone adopting it would need to do. Nor does it purport to be a complete methodology for the social sciences – as a minimum, it must be complemented with other methods for empirical research, and no doubt many other issues are ignored here. Nevertheless, it does pro-vide a means of putting into practice an ontological approach to the social world that has been lacking in the social sciences.

In providing such a method, the chapter also provides a bridge between the theory of emergence outlined in the previous two chapters and the application of that theory to the questions of structure and agency in the remainder of this book. The chapter itself is divided into two parts: the first outlines the approach to social ontology that has been applied in developing the argument of this book and the second briefly relates this approach to the diverse usages of 'social structure' in the existing literature. These offer a prime example of the lack of ontological rigour noted above. It is one of the primary purposes of this book to resolve this problem, and this chapter introduces the key ontological principle behind my proposed resolution: that in so far as it describes something that is causally effective in the social world, the concept of *social structure* refers to *the causal powers of specific social groups*.

The elements of emergence

Chapters 2 and 3 have argued that events are produced by interacting causal powers, and they have outlined an explanation of how this happens in terms of certain *structural elements* and how they interact. These structural elements are common to all causal situations and thus we can see them as the most general or abstract components of an emergentist ontology – an emergentist account of what sorts of things there are in the world. We can summarise the argument so far, and provide the raw materials for the approach to social ontology developed in this chapter, by listing and describing these structural elements.

The first significant element of this emergentist ontology is the *entity*. Entities are wholes – to put it crudely, things – composed of other entities, which are their *parts*. Examples would include biological organisms, composed of cells, or molecules, composed of atoms. Because the parts of entities are entities themselves, which also have parts and so on down to some lowest level that is currently beyond the understanding of our science, each entity is a kind of laminated hierarchy of the smaller entities of which it is composed.

Entities may possess *real causal powers*, which may also be called *emergent properties* of the entity. Although these two terms are used somewhat differently, and largely in different literatures, they essentially refer to the same structural element. As I understand emergence, a causal power or emergent property is a capability of an entity to have a certain sort of causal effect on the world in its own right – an effect that is something more than the effects that would be produced by the entity's parts if they were not organised into this sort of whole.

Emergent properties are the product of *causal mechanisms*.[1] Causal mechanisms are processes that depend upon interactions between the

---

[1] This is the claim that distinguishes relational from *strong* theories of emergence; in the latter, it is denied that emergent properties can be explained in terms of lower-level entities or properties and the relations between them.

parts, interactions that only occur when those parts are organised in the particular *relations* that constitutes them into wholes that possess this emergent property (see, for example, Buckley 1967: 42; Bunge 1999: ch. 2). Although emergent properties, and thus real causal powers, can therefore be explained, they cannot be explained away. They exist only when the relevant type of whole exists, hence they are causal powers of this type of whole and not of its parts. This means that emergentist ontologies can resolve the problem of reductionism: they allow higher-level properties to be explained scientifically (an *explanatory reduction*), but they do not allow them to be replaced with properties of the parts in causal explanations (an *eliminative* or *ontological reduction*).

The variety of emergence that I have been discussing so far may be termed *relational emergence*. Relational emergence is a synchronic relationship that requires a counterfactual explanation. It describes a particular sort of relation between a whole and its parts at a given moment in time: the relation of being composed by those parts but also possessing properties that the parts would not possess if they were not organised into such a whole. Relational emergence is to be distinguished from temporal conceptions of emergence, exemplified by lay uses of the term, in which it refers to nothing more than the first appearance of some phenomenon. Relational emergence entails prior or simultaneous temporal emergence, but temporal emergence does not entail relational emergence, since there can be 'heaps' – collections of entities that do not possess emergent properties as a whole. These emerge temporally but not relationally.

Temporal emergence is nevertheless important in the explanation of relational emergence, since an entity and hence its emergent properties cannot come into existence at all without a causal history. The existence of an entity at any given point in time is always contingent; it depends on a causal history in which *morphogenetic* and *morphostatic* causal factors operate. Morphogenetic factors are those that contribute to bringing about the existence of the entity in its current form and morphostatic factors are those that contribute to sustaining that existence over time (Buckley 1967: 58). At any time, causal factors tending to end the existence of the entity may overcome the morphostatic causes tending to sustain it, hence the contingency of the entity's existence. Similarly, morphogenetic factors may *alter* the form of an entity more subtly. In some cases such changes may be consistent with the continuation of the entity's causal powers; in others, the entity may be so changed that some of its causal powers are eliminated, or indeed enhanced or replaced with different ones. Hence synchronic emergence is fully consistent with the possibility of change.

Events, finally, are caused by interactions between the causal powers of the entities involved. Thus they are not usually determined by a single causal power or a single *law* as in Hempel's nomological-deductive model of causation, but rather they are *multiply determined* or co-determined by a variety of interacting powers, which may be possessed by entities at a variety of levels of the hierarchy of composition (Bhaskar 1975: 110–11).

To summarise, an emergentist ontology identifies a number of *structural elements* that we would expect to find in any object of scientific enquiry: *entities*, made up of *parts* (which are themselves entities), organised by particular *relations* between the parts and possessing *emergent properties* in virtue of these relations. In order to explain these entities, relations and properties, we need to identify the *mechanisms* by which the parts and relations produce the properties, the *morphogenetic causes* that bring this set of parts into this set of relations in the first place and the *morphostatic causes* that keep them so. And once we are equipped with these elements, we can go on to explain *events*, and sometimes event *regularities* or partial regularities, by showing how the emergent properties or causal powers of the entities concerned interact to co-determine these events.

A method for social ontology

So far this book has been developing an abstract, generalised or *metaphysical* ontology. By applying such an ontology to the needs of particular disciplines or groups of disciplines in combination with the specific empirical knowledge of those disciplines, we can generate domain-specific ontologies. Such domain-specific ontologies, which identify the sorts of elements that populate the domain, have been called *regional ontologies* by Benton and Craib and *scientific ontologies* by Bhaskar (Benton and Craib 2001: 5; Bhaskar 1986: 36). This chapter describes a method for creating such regional ontologies. To some extent the method could be applied in creating *any* regional ontology, but it has been developed from an engagement with the specific question of constructing a *social ontology*: a regional ontology for the social sciences.

The argument that the social world cannot be theorised or explained successfully without paying explicit attention to its ontological foundations is one of the most characteristic claims of critical realism (see, for example, Archer 1995; Bhaskar 1998 [1979]; Lawson 1997). As we shall see, however, once we start to examine *how* to develop a social ontology, we also learn that this relationship works both ways: we cannot construct a regional ontology successfully without paying explicit attention to the *theory* of the discipline(s) concerned. Social ontology and social theory are inextricably interwoven.

The core of the proposed method is very simple. I have already identified the structural elements of a general emergentist ontology; to develop a regional ontology, we must *map the concepts of the discipline concerned onto this structural vocabulary*. Thus, we must identify the following:

• the particular types of *entities* that constitute the objects of the discipline;
• the *parts* of each type of entity and the sets of *relations* between them that are required to constitute them into this type of entity;
• the *emergent properties* or *causal powers* of each type of entity;
• the *mechanisms* through which their parts and the characteristic relations between them produce the emergent properties of the wholes;
• the *morphogenetic causes* that bring each type of entity into existence;[2]
• the *morphostatic causes* that sustain their existence;
• and the ways that these sorts of entities, with these properties, *interact to cause the events* we seek to explain in the discipline.

In a well-developed science, this might seem straightforward. In each theory within the discipline, it would be clear what the entities were, what properties they possessed, what mechanisms were responsible and how these interacted in causal histories. We could read the

---

[2] The identification of the morphogenetic and morphostatic causes that contribute to an entity's development corresponds to Archer's methodological recommendation that we develop 'analytical histories of emergence' (Archer 1995: 324–8).

textbooks and pop the concepts into the relevant ontological boxes. At times parts of the natural sciences have appeared to be well developed in this sense, with sets of theories that entailed plausible and locally consistent scientific ontologies. Even in the natural sciences, however, scientific revolutions – such as the discoveries of quantum theory and relativity – have shaken our understandings of the corresponding scientific ontologies and reminded us that all such ontologies are inherently fallible.

Yet the social sciences are at least one step further removed from the status of 'well-developed science' – they consistently lack plausible, well-defined and locally consistent scientific ontologies. One of the pitfalls of the social sciences is that we may assume that they *do* have such ontologies and accept unthinkingly the sorts of ontological categorisations that appear implicit in social theories, or even in our everyday language about the social world.

For an example of the latter, consider *money*. The word is constantly used in everyday life, and frequently in the social sciences, as if money were a thing; in our terms, a type of entity. But as soon as we start to examine the ontology of money, it becomes clear that this cannot be so. For money to be a type of entity, it would have to have a characteristic type of parts, organised in a characteristic set of relations. But coins can be money, cheques can be money and electronic transfers generated by swiping credit cards can also be money. One response to this diversity of realisers of money might be to suggest it represents a family of types of entity, which include coins, cheques and credit card balances amongst others. A more plausible one, perhaps, is that being money is a *property* possessed by a variety of different types of entity, by virtue not only of their internal structure (although this does matter), but also of their relationship to certain social institutions. This would require a refinement of the portrayal of mechanisms in the previous section, since it now appears that mechanisms may rely not only on an entity's parts and their relations to each other, but also on the relation of the whole to other entities (considering this option would be an example of what I call the metatheory test below). Alternatively, we might resolve this by concluding that money is not a property of material things like coins but rather a property of the social institution itself. I do not mean to suggest that one or the other of these paths actually does offer a viable solution to the challenging problem of the ontological status of money; the point of the example is only to illustrate the need for real work to answer such questions.

For the social sciences, then, the task of determining what type of structural element any given concept might represent is often far from trivial. On the one hand, it can be immensely difficult. The complex inter-relations between human beings, non-human physical objects, social structures and cultural or conceptual systems in the social world make it extremely challenging to disentangle the entities and properties involved, and there are many competing schools of thought on many of these questions. On the other, resolving these questions is fundamental to resolving the ontological confusion in which these disciplines find themselves.

Applying the method

When it comes to applying this method in practice, there is a common theme to the techniques required, which can be summed up in a single word: iterate! This section will discuss five types of iteration that are potentially useful, each of them characterised by submitting our proposed ontology to a particular type of test.

In general, the need for iteration arises from the combination of two factors: uncertainty and interdependence. The ways in which we formulate our views about the entities involved in the social world, for example, are inextricably intertwined with our conceptualisations of their parts, relations, properties and mechanisms. This brings us to the first type of iteration, which I shall call the *local complementarity* test. We will generally begin a regional ontology with the initial hypothesis that some concept of interest represents a particular kind of structural element – perhaps an entity or an emergent property. We then validate this initial hypothesis partly by working out the implications of this belief for the complementary set of structural elements. If we find that it is impossible to come up with a viable characterisation of a postulated entity's parts, for example, as in the case of money in the example above, we may have to revise our ontological classification of it, and this in turn will imply a new set of understandings of its complementary structural elements. Similarly, if we postulate that some concept represents a property, we will need to identify what entity it is that possesses the property, and in virtue of what relations between its parts. Regional ontologies are not made up of isolated entities, properties and the like; they are complementary networks of mutually consistent structural elements. Only when we have a plausible complementary *set* of such classifications, can we move on from this point.

A second type of iteration follows from the hierarchical or laminated nature of emergence.[3] It is all very well to postulate that a certain entity, composed of certain parts, has certain emergent properties. But those parts themselves are also entities, according to the emergentist ontology, and so we must be able to justify this implicit claim for *their* ontological status as well. This is simple enough if the parts themselves are theorised uncontroversially as entities in some neighbouring discipline. Thus we can claim that human individuals are composed of cells and take as given the status of those cells as entities because they are clearly and uncontroversially theorised as such in the biological sciences. Ideally, all postulated entities should be traceable in this way to a base composed of entities theorised by the natural sciences. Let me call this the *downward recursion* test. It is common in the social sciences, however, to ignore this requirement. Signs, for example, are decomposed in structuralist semiotics into signifiers and signifieds; but it is often assumed that signifiers and signifieds are valid entity types, without any attempt to show that they in turn can be decomposed into entities that are their parts. Any ontology of cultural or conceptual systems that rests on the view that these are composed of signs or symbols is ultimately incoherent unless the parts of signs themselves can be identified as entities, with their own parts, relations between them and properties explained by mechanisms.

The third type of iteration is between regional ontology and regional *theory*. Realist regional theory is concerned with identifying the causal mechanisms underlying emergent properties (retroduction), and with explaining how these interact to produce events of interest (retrodiction) (Lawson 1997: 24, 221). But it is impossible to identify mechanisms without identifying the property to be explained, the entity possessing it, and the characteristic set of parts and relations

---

[3] There is no necessity to the sequence in which these different styles of iteration are presented – they may be performed in any order, and indeed it may be necessary to iterate the iterations, going through any given type of iteration more than once.

that underpin the mechanism. In other words, retroduction depends on filling out part of the related regional ontology. Equally, as we shall see when we come to the next type of iteration, if we want to justify the claim that properties – and thus causal powers – belong to particular entities, then we need to describe the mechanism that makes them so. The consequence is that regional ontology is also dependent upon retroductive theory. Hence I call this the *retroduction* test.

Retroduction requires the use of established methods for empirical research, amongst which there are a great many different ways of retroducing mechanisms, including both quantitative and qualitative (particularly comparative) techniques – including, for example, the identification and analysis of empirical demi-regularities (Lawson 1997: 204–21). Hence the method for social *ontology* advocated here is potentially consistent with many alternative methods for doing explanatory social *theory* (and indeed methods that pursue different cognitive interests, such as interpretation or political critique).

When we have postulated a mechanism to explain a property, a fourth variety of iteration beckons, which I shall call the *emergence level* test. This variety of iteration is implicit in the twin problems of reduction and reification. Let me illustrate this with an example: the causal power of an organisation to dismiss an employee. Now a methodological individualist might argue that organisations are nothing more than groups of individuals and hence that this causal power is really a power of the individual manager who makes or communicates the decision. Such an individualist would argue that to attribute this causal power to the organisation instead would constitute an untenable reification; whereas I would argue that the individualist's attribution of this power to the individual manager constitutes an untenable eliminative reduction.

Any attribution of causal power to a particular level of the ontological hierarchy is open to *both* these challenges, and hence to validate our own claims regarding emergent properties and the mechanisms responsible for them, we must develop and apply criteria for identifying the levels at which properties emerge. In fact a single criterion allows us to avoid both untenable reductions and untenable reifications, and this criterion is already implicit in the general theory of emergence: a property is emergent at the level where the parts of the entity possessing it would not themselves have the property if they were not organised into this sort of whole.

Hence, for example, if we attributed the power to dismiss an employee to an individual human being (the one who happens to occupy this managerial role), this would be an untenable eliminative reduction. A manager could not dismiss an employee unless both were parts of an organisation of a certain kind, thus the causal power is a power of the organisation, exercised on its behalf by the manager, and not a power of the manager as an individual. We could perhaps say that this is a power of the role and not of the individual occupying it, as long as we recognise that in speaking of the role here, we imply the existence of the whole organisation (see chapter 7). For an example of the opposite case, consider that managers have the power to speak to employees. If we attributed this power to the organisation rather than the manager, this would be an untenable reification: a person need not hold any particular role in an organisation, or be part of an organisation at all, in order to have this capability, and this is not altered by attaching a different description ('manager') to the person. Hence it is a power of human individuals, not of organisations or roles in them. These two examples also illustrate another significant point: that an individual can act as *both* an individual and on behalf of the organisation, exercising causal powers belonging to both levels, in one and the same action – for example when dismissing an employee using a speech act.

If any hypothesised property fails this test, then we must revise our proposed ontology to relocate the property appropriately, which will in turn have implications for our understandings of the mechanisms involved.

The fifth type of iteration arises from the fallibility of these methodological proposals themselves, and indeed from the fallibility of the ontology that underpins them. From time to time we may find that the method does not work; that the ontological structures that seem most consistent with the actual social world simply do not fit the general ontology outlined here. In such cases we must always keep open two possibilities: either we have failed to apply the method and the general ontology of emergentism correctly, or that method or ontology is flawed in some way. In other words, we must be prepared to iterate the method itself, whether by making small local adjustments, or much more radical changes. Let me call this the *metatheory* test. Thus, for example, the problem with the ontology of signs mentioned earlier in this chapter may be resolvable in one of two different ways. In one potential solution, signs may be connected up to the ontology of the natural world, for example by identifying signifiers and signifieds as mental properties of human individuals and thus seeing signs themselves as composite properties rather than as entities. But if there is no viable way of connecting signs back to natural systems, we may have to abandon the suggestion that all entities can ultimately be connected back to the natural world in this way. This would force us to allow for the possibility of conceptual systems that have a different kind of ontological structure, thus requiring a revision or extension of the emergentist ontology itself.

In practice, such iteration of the metatheory – the general ontology and methodology – is unlikely to take place within the confines of an applied research project. It is more likely that difficulties in a series of projects will lead to dissatisfaction that must eventually be resolved by iterating the metatheory; but the principle remains that the relationship between metatheory and theory is a two-way one. We validate *theory* by working out its implications for the actual world in the form of hypotheses that can be tested against empirical evidence, and then revise the theory if it proves inadequate to the case. In a meta-methodological parallel, we can validate *metatheory* by working out its implications for the development of theory in the form of methodological inferences that can then be tested in the process of theorising. Just as we should be prepared to revise theory that proves inadequate, we should be prepared to revise metatheory if *it* proves inadequate. The formulation of a methodology is a key moment in this cycle of validation, just as the formulation of a hypothesis is a key moment in the cycle of validating a theory.

The methodological techniques outlined in this section, then, involve the pursuit of consistency between the inter-related elements of a regional ontology, and between our ontological categorisations and our understanding of the empirical world. We pursue these by iterating our analysis in up to five different, but inter-related, dimensions:

1. *the local complementarity test* – make a hypothesis as to the type of structural element a concept of interest represents, then validate this by working out the complementary structural elements implicit in this hypothesis; if any of the latter are empirically untenable, revise your initial hypothesis and try again;
2. *the downward recursion test* – when your hypothesis claims that a concept represents a type of entity, identify the parts of this entity

and ensure that these in turn are plausibly defined as entities, following the hierarchy of composition all the way down to a level
that has a well-substantiated entity status;

3. *the retroduction test* – when your hypothesis claims that a concept represents a type of property, identify the mechanism responsible for the property and the parts and relations on which the
   mechanism depends; having done so, return to the first iteration
   technique;

4. *the emergence level test* – in addition, when your hypothesis suggests a property, validate the level at which the property emerges, by
   applying the criterion that a property is emergent at the level where
   the parts of the entity possessing it would not themselves have the
   property if they were not organised into this sort of whole; and

5. *the metatheory test* – when this method seems to lead to untenable
   conclusions, consider revising the method and perhaps the underlying general ontology.

Social structure

This book is the outcome of applying this method to the social
world and in particular to the ontology of structure and agency.
The iterative nature of the process may often not be apparent, since
in common with most writers I seek to present the end product as a
coherent set of arguments, rather than providing a narrative of the
process and the iterations whose products were discarded along the
way. However, there is one set of prior iterations that does require
some attention: those concepts of social structure that are already
familiar to us as a result of being embodied in the existing literature
of the social sciences. The remainder of this chapter seeks to put
these existing concepts of social structure into ontological perspective. In doing so, it will bring out some of the differences between
my proposed analysis of social structure and the existing literature and also suggest some ways in which the approach to social
ontology outlined above might lead us to question those existing
approaches. Neither of these, however, will be pursued in any depth
in this chapter, which merely seeks to position my perspective with
regard to the literature, in preparation for a more thorough examination of both my own and the competing approaches in subsequent chapters.

Despite its widespread use, *social structure* is a term whose meaning is 'strikingly nebulous and diverse' (Lopez and Scott 2000: 1). As Lopez and Scott point out, 'there is little consensus over what the word means, and it is all too easy for sociologists to be talking at cross purposes because they rely on different, and generally implicit, conceptions of social structure' (Lopez and Scott 2000: 1). Indeed, I would argue that the usages of the term in the literature not only differ, but differ in several dimensions.[4]

Perhaps the most obvious sense in which usages differ is that thinkers often seem to have sociologically different kinds of social structure in mind as they formulate their theories. The term *social structure* may be used, for example, to refer to normative institutions, organisations, class, gender, the capitalist system or demographic distributions. It may be that some of the differences between theorists arise simply from this: someone who is theorising normative institutions may quite reasonably come up with a different way of understanding *social structure* from someone who is theorising the capitalist system. Both may develop radically different theories of structure and both may be right, even though their theories appear incompatible, simply because they are theorising different *kinds* of structure.

Although I suspect that such misunderstandings are more common than is generally recognised, I want to focus here on three other ways of understanding the differences between competing conceptions of social structure. The following section will consider Lopez and Scott's typology, which distinguishes between *institutional*, *relational* and *embodied* structure. The next will relate understandings of social structure to the structural elements discussed earlier in this chapter. And the last will relate these arguments to Porpora's classification of theories of structure.

Three facets of social structure

Lopez and Scott argue as follows:

the history of sociology shows the long-term coexistence of two different conceptions of social structure. On the one hand, there is that which we

---

[4] For another survey of the many ways in which the term is used, see Crothers (1996).

identify as the idea of *institutional structure*. Here, social structure is seen as comprising those cultural or normative patterns that define the expectations that agents hold about each other's behaviour and that organize their enduring relations with each other. On the other hand, there is the idea of what we call *relational structure*. Here, social structure is seen as comprising the social relations themselves, understood as patterns of causal interconnection and interdependence among agents and their actions, as well as the positions that they occupy. (Lopez and Scott 2000: 3)

They attribute the roots of both these conceptions of structure to the work of Durkheim. On one hand, they see the idea of *institutional structure* as deriving from Durkheim's *collective representations* – from systems of shared norms, values and ideas that shape social behaviour. As Parsons puts it, institutions 'are complexes of normative rules and principles which, either through law or other mechanisms of social control, serve to regulate social action and relationships' (Parsons 1976: 97). Institutional structure was most characteristically advocated by Parsons and the structural functionalists, and examples include both large-scale institutions like marriage, patriarchy, property and contract, and also 'the micro-institutions of day-to-day existence, such as those concerned with queuing, turn taking in conversations, dinner party entertaining and gift giving' (Lopez and Scott 2000: 23).

On the other hand, they argue that *relational structure* is based in Durkheim's *collective relationships*. Relational structure was most characteristically advocated by Radcliffe-Brown and structural anthropology, for whom social structure is 'the sum total of all the social relationships of all individuals at a given moment in time' (Radcliffe-Brown, quoted in Lopez and Scott 2000: 46). There are, however, some significant divergences between thinkers within this tradition, to the extent that we might even consider this as two traditions, as Crothers does. He identifies one variety (the 'Social Organization' tradition) concerned with structure as 'the concrete relations amongst concrete individuals and concrete groups, e.g. networks', and one (the 'Social Background Characteristics' tradition) concerned with structure as the relations between people and systems of social differentiation or stratification (Crothers 2002: 4). These two approaches can, for example, be found more recently in the work of Emirbayer and Blau respectively (Blau 1976; Emirbayer 1997).

Each of these schools of thought largely ignores the concept of structure implicit in the other, although there have also been thinkers who seek to *link* institutional and relational structure, such as Mauss and Levi-Strauss. With the work of Giddens, Foucault and Bourdieu, though, there appears what Lopez and Scott see as a third conception of social structure (Lopez and Scott 2000: 17–18, 90):

According to this point of view, patterns of institutions and relations result from the actions of individuals who are endowed with the cap-acities or competencies that enable them to produce them by acting in organised ways. These capacities are behavioural dispositions, and so social structure has to be seen as an *embodied structure*. Embodied structures are found in the habits and skills that are inscribed in human bodies and minds and that allow them to produce, reproduce, and trans-form institutional structures and relational structures. (Lopez and Scott 2000: 4)

For Lopez and Scott, despite the past disagreements between advo-cates of these different conceptions, they represent not mutually exclusive approaches, but rather potentially complementary facets of social structure. By implication, this argument rests on the belief that embodied structure provides a linkage between institutional struc-ture, relational structure and individual agency. 'For both Foucault and Bourdieu', for example, 'bodies are seen as the carriers of rela-tional and institutional structures' (Lopez and Scott 2000: 98), though Lopez and Scott themselves remain cautious about the poten-tial of embodied structure to fully integrate the earlier models (Lopez and Scott 2000: 4–5, 106).[5]

It is striking, however, that neither the institutional nor the rela-tional traditions attend to the sorts of questions posed in the first half of this chapter. What are the entities that have these powers and how can they have them? The embodied tradition at least identifies bearers of structural powers, in the form of embodied human individuals, but at the cost of obscuring the role of any larger social wholes.

---

[5] I have discussed their argument in more depth in Elder-Vass (2008b), which argues that to make sense of the relationship between these three facets of structure we must understand the relationship of each of them to the collectivities that possess social powers.

What kind of structural element is social structure?

This brings us to what is perhaps the most important dimension of difference between existing accounts of structure, at least from the perspective of trying to make ontological sense of them. This is the problematic question of what kind of structural element writers have in mind in their conceptions of social structure.

As Raymond Williams has shown, there are at least two senses in which the word *structure* is used in lay discourse, and he argues that there has been a 'persistent ambiguity' (Williams 1976: 253) over which of these senses is to be ascribed to the *structure* in social structure.[6] As Williams explains, the word originally referred to the process of building, but

> The word was notably developed in C17, in two main directions: (i) towards the whole product of building, as still in 'a wooden structure'; (ii) towards the manner of construction, not only in buildings but in extended and figurative applications. Most modern developments follow from (ii), but there is a persistent ambiguity in the relations between these and what are really extended and figurative applications of (i). (Williams 1976: 253)

> It is clear from the history of structure and structural that the words can be used with either emphasis: to include the actual construction with special reference to its mode of construction; or to isolate the mode of construction in such a way as to exclude both ends of the process – the producers ... and the product, in its substantive sense. (Williams 1976: 257)

In other words, the label *structure* can be used legitimately to refer to different structural elements. It can, for example, refer to a whole entity that is structured by the relations between its parts ((i) in Williams), which I shall call *structure-as-whole*, or it can refer to the way that a group of things (generally the parts of a whole) is related to each other ((ii) in Williams), which I shall call *structure-as-relations*.[7]

---

[6] Charles Crothers has also related Williams' argument to the debates on social structure (Crothers 2002: 7).

[7] Elsewhere in this book I rely generally on the context to make clear which usage is implied in each case. This seems more accessible than Collier's more rigorous suggestion that we use 'structuratum' as a synonym of what I call *structure-as-whole*, and 'structure' to mean only *structure-as-relations* (Collier 1989: 85).

Many accounts of *social* structure refer to *structure* as if it means structure-as-relations. Thus, for example, we have already seen Lopez and Scott describing *relational structure* as 'the social relations themselves, understood as patterns of causal interconnection and interdependence among agents and their actions' (Lopez and Scott 2000: 3). This is a perfectly legitimate use of *structure*, although the ambiguity described by Williams means that even this usage can cause confusion. For example, it may be implied that social structure-as-relations can be causally effective. Yet relations alone cannot have causal powers; indeed a relation cannot exist at all in the absence of the things related. It is only when specific entities (and thus specific causal powers) enter into a relationship that causal consequences can follow. As was shown in chapters 2 and 3, when we claim that a set of lower-level entities and the stable substantial relations between them have a causal effect, this is synonymous with claiming that there is a higher-level entity formed from these parts and relations that is the causally effective element. Ultimately, then, the idea that structures have causal powers is incoherent if structure is taken to mean structures-as-relations and not structures-as-wholes. Those accounts of social structure that simultaneously treat structures as relations and also claim that structures are causally effective, I suggest, rely systematically on the persistent ambiguity identified by Williams to retain the appearance of coherence – they talk of structure-as-relations, while in fact the causal part of the argument relies on *structure* meaning structure-as-wholes.

But there are also still more confusing (and confused) readings of structure at large in the sociological literature. Sometimes *social structure* is used to refer to *neither* structure-as-relations *nor* structure-as-whole. At times, *social structure* seems to refer to what we might call *structure-as-empirical-regularity* and at others, to refer to *structure-as-properties*. The more these different senses of structure are mixed up, the harder it becomes to make sense of claims that social structure can be causally effective.

Perhaps the most neglected sense of structure in the sociological literature is structure-as-whole. There are some theorists who have used structure in this sense, such as Nadel and Tönnies (Lopez and Scott 2000: 47, 52). But it is more common to deny the existence or causal value of social wholes, or to assume that it is of little importance to the study of social structure. In the extreme case (which Lopez and Scott reject), some accounts of social structure 'hold that there is no whole or totality separate from the *structuring* activities and practices that are engaged in by individual actors' (Lopez and Scott 2000: 5). Here structure-as-relations is held to exist without its structuring any concrete whole at all.

This book argues that we can only make sense of social structure by reinstating this sense of structure-as-whole and identifying the social *entities* that can possess causal powers. These are the entities that are *structured by* structure-as-relations, that *possess* the properties sometimes misleadingly identified as structures themselves and that *cause* those (partial) empirical regularities sometimes misidentified as structures.

But what exactly are these social entities? In so far as they consider this question at all, the commonest response amongst sociological theorists is that to be found in the *Blackwell Dictionary of Modern Social Thought*: 'In social structure the parts are relationships among persons and the organized body of the parts may be considered to be coincident with the society as a whole' (Heer 2003). *Society*, however, is an amorphous, poorly bounded and unclearly defined agglomeration that is more analogous to portfolio terms like *nature* or *humanity* than to any causally effective natural entity. The coherence of any bounded concept of society is extremely problematic. Those who use the concept often seem to assume that a society is co-terminous with the territory controlled by a particular state. States themselves may well control territory with well-defined spatial boundaries, at least in some respects. But they do not map neatly onto *societies*; there are many potentially cross-cutting social systems that follow different boundaries, or none at all (Walby 2005). One consequence of globalisation, for example, is that fewer and fewer social entities are co-terminous with states. But many – for example multinational corporations, religions and families – have never structured themselves on this basis. Given the lack of coherence of the concept of society, it is hard to see how such a poorly defined entity could have real causal powers.

Instead, I suggest, most of the powers that have usually been attributed to societies belong to somewhat smaller and more clearly definable social entities: structures at an intermediate level between individual and society that can have more specific effects. The neglect of these intermediate levels is a common problem in treatments of social structure. Mouzelis points out, for example, that 'Parsons, following Durkheim, operates within a society–individual scheme that systematically ignores the complex hierarchy of actors that provides the bridge between individual role players on the micro-level, and systematic incompatibilities on the macro-level' (Mouzelis 1991: 18–19). Chapters 6 and 7 will develop this argument by examining the ontology of two specific types of social structure: normative institutions and organisations.

Four concepts of social structure

Porpora provides a typology of approaches to social structure that focuses on a different dimension of methodological controversy from Lopez and Scott, and he emphasises not the compatibility of the different positions in the existing debate on social structure but their incompatibility. He lists four different concepts of social structure: 'patterns of aggregate behaviour that are stable over time'; 'law-like regularities that govern the behaviour of social facts'; 'systems of human relationships among social positions'; and 'collective rules and resources that structure behaviour' (Porpora 1998: 339). Each of these corresponds to a particular position in the perennial debate between methodological individualism and methodological collectivism (or sociological holism, as Porpora calls it), which was summarised in chapter 1, that is, the debate over the relationship between structure and agency.

The first concept, 'structure as enduring patterns of behaviour' (Porpora 2002: 44), is a variety of what I have called structure-as-empirical-regularity, and is characteristic of methodological individualism, which Porpora illustrates with the work of Collins. In this perspective, social structure is ontologically epiphenomenal – a by-product of individual behaviour that has no causal efficacy in its own right – although methodologically it may be a useful concept for describing properties that really belong to aggregations of individuals. As Collins argues, 'strictly speaking, there is no such thing as a "state", an "economy", a "culture", a "social class". There are only collections of individual people acting in particular kinds of microsituations – collections which are characterised thus by a kind of shorthand' (Collins 1981: 987–8). Methodological individualism is a species of eliminative reductionism that, at least implicitly and sometimes explicitly, denies that social entities can have emergent properties and hence causal influence in their own right. As such, it suffers from all the faults of eliminative reductionism in general, as discussed in chapter 3. But it cannot be dismissed as reductionist on purely *a priori* grounds; any denial of a level-specific reductionism rests upon a demonstration that the proposed reduction would suppress genuinely emergent properties. In other words, it must be subjected to the *emergence level test* outlined in this chapter. The outcomes of this test may well differ for different types of structural claim; chapters 6 and 7 will argue, for example, that we can refute reductionist critiques of claims for the structural power of organisations and normative institutions. On the other hand, I have argued elsewhere that demographic distributions are resultant rather than emergent properties and therefore reducible (Elder-Vass 2007a).

Porpora's second concept of social structure – 'structure as law-like relations among social facts' (Porpora 2002: 44) – is characteristic of methodological collectivism or sociological holism – traditionally associated, for example, with the methodological work of Durkheim, the later work of Parsons and Althusser's structuralist Marxism. As Porpora argues, 'Because this conception of social structure rigidly divorces sociology from psychology, it represents social structure as something entirely devoid of the influence of human agency. On this sociologically holist view, social structure operates mechanically and naturalistically over the heads of individual actors' (Porpora 1998: 342). This is the mirror image of reductionism – a denial of the causal influence of the lower level (human individuals) from which social entities emerge – and it is equally untenable as an ontological position. The rejection of this position is almost universal amongst contemporary sociologists, but it is sometimes extended inappropriately. The rejection of ontological holism does *not* entail the automatic rejection of all theories that posit a causal relationship between higher-level social entities. What it *does* entail is that any such relationship should ultimately be grounded in an explanation of how the interaction of human individuals underpins it. In other words, such claims must be subjected to the *retroduction test*.

Porpora's third concept – 'structure as a system of social relations among social positions' (Porpora 2002: 44) – is, he suggests, 'most characteristically associated with the Marxian tradition', but in more recent years has been adopted by a number of other groups, including symbolic interactionists, network theorists and sociological realists (including Porpora himself) (Porpora 1998: 343). In this view,

> social structure is a nexus of connections among [human actors], causally affecting their actions and in turn causally affected by them. The causal effects of the structure on individuals are manifested in certain structured interests, resources, powers, constraints and predicaments that are built into each position by the web of relationships. These comprise the material circumstances in which people must act and which motivate them to act in certain ways. (Porpora 1998: 344)

This third approach, like that developed in this book, allows for both human individuals and social structure to have causal efficacy in their own right, with the two interacting continuously. Porpora's description of structure, however, falls within what Lopez and Scott call the *relational structure* tradition and corresponds to a concept of social structure as *structure-as-relations* (Elder-Vass 2007e). In counterposing to this a concept of social structure as the causal power of social wholes, therefore, this book not only advances a realist account of structure but also seeks to clarify and improve the account of structure *within* the realist tradition.

Finally, Porpora's fourth version of the concept – 'structure as rules and resources' (Porpora 2002: 44) – describes the approach taken in Giddens' *structuration theory*, and arguably corresponds to *embodied structure* as described by Lopez and Scott. For Giddens, as for the advocates of the third version, both social structure and individual agency are necessary elements in sociological explanation. But for Giddens, structure has no existence other than as the subjective conceptions of rules held by individuals and their perceptions of the resources to which they have access (Giddens 1984: 17). As Archer has argued, this represents a denial of any real distinct influence to structure, through the conflation of structure and agency (Archer 1982). In the terms of this chapter, Giddens' ontology fails the *local complementarity test* by failing to show how structural influence is produced by a mutually consistent hierarchy of entities and their powers (see chapter 6).

However we classify the existing accounts of social structure, then, few if any of them conform to the model advocated in this book, of structure as the causal powers of specific social groups. In the chapters to come I aim to show that such a model enables us to make sense of claims of the causal significance of social structure in a way that these existing accounts cannot.

Conclusion

This chapter provides a bridge between the general theory of emergence and cause developed in the previous two chapters and the analysis of social structure that is the primary focus of the book. That bridge takes the form of a methodological framework for identifying emergent causal powers and their foundation in specific entities and mechanisms. To put it more precisely: to develop a social ontology we must identify the inter-related structural elements of the social world. We must identify the entities that possess emergent causal powers, the mechanisms responsible for those powers and the parts and the relations between those parts that are characteristic of the type of entity concerned and necessary to the mechanisms underlying its powers. This is a process that is likely to require multiple iterations and the chapter has described several varieties of iterative tests that can help us arrive at a consistent and coherent ontology.

This method provides us with the tools required to make sense of the concept of social structure. The existing accounts of social structure are remarkably diverse and by examining several different typologies of these accounts this chapter has introduced the claim that they are riddled with failures of ontological clarity. It is one of the objectives of the book to resolve these failures, and this chapter has identified the basic principle that will motivate its proposed solution: to the extent that it refers to something genuinely causally effective, the concept of *social structure* refers to *the causal powers of specific social groups*.

Later chapters will justify that principle by identifying some of these social groups and their powers. In each case, I will argue, the essential parts of those social groups are human individuals, and so, in accordance with the *downward recursion* principle, the ontology of social structure also depends upon the ontology of human individuals and their causal powers. The next chapter, therefore, will consider the question of human agency, as an essential prerequisite to understanding the ontology of social structure.

5 | *Agency*

As human beings, we are inclined to believe that the conscious exercise of our own capacities makes us the source of what happens in society. But is this just an anthropocentric illusion? Can human beings really be regarded as agents with a causal impact on our social world, and if so, how can we justify such a claim? What is it about human beings that gives us the power to act, and how does our sense that we are making decisions relate to how our actions are really determined?

This chapter will argue that we human individuals do indeed have causal powers of our own, and that those causal powers are emergent properties. Thus, in explaining the powers of human individuals – their capability for exercising agency – we must consider the questions identified in chapter 4: what are the parts, and how are they related, that make up human individuals? How does this sort of structure lead to the powers that they possess? And how is this sort of structure brought about and sustained? We cannot give an ontologically coherent response to these questions without recognising the biological nature of human beings. As a work of social theory this book will neglect most of the physiological details, but we cannot ignore the biological basis of human capacities entirely if we are to construct an adequate understanding of human social functioning. Nor, however, can we neglect the fact that human behaviour is causally influenced by external factors. Although it is often suggested that human agency entails the freedom of human action from the external constraint of social structure (Jary and Jary 2000: 9; Loyal and Barnes 2001: 507), this chapter will argue that agency is entirely consistent with social impacts on our behaviour. Human action may be affected by social causes without being *fully determined* by them. The critical realist account of the co-determination of actual events by a multiplicity of causes, potentially from a variety of levels in the hierarchy of emergence, provides the framework needed to reconcile the claim for agency with the recognition of the causal impact of external factors on human action (both natural and social).

There are a number of different definitions of agency and we must distinguish at the outset between two groups of these – the concepts of *political agency* and *individual agency*. Political agency is the possession of 'the power to bring about effective change in collective life' (Coole 2005). Political agency, however, may potentially be exercised by things other than individual human beings – in Archer's account, for example, it is exercised by groups (Archer 1995: 257–8). This chapter is concerned, however, with the specific powers of human individuals and therefore with agency in its second sense: individual agency.

The first two parts of the chapter will address the questions: how do the causal powers of humans emerge and how are these causal powers combined with external causal influences in the determination of human behaviour? They offer a theory of agency – of human action – based on the emergent properties of human individuals, as part of a hierarchy of entities with emergent powers, including both the biological parts of human beings and the social entities composed (at least in part) of human beings.

The remainder of the chapter will relate this emergentist theory of action to two important existing approaches. Pierre Bourdieu and Margaret Archer have advanced what seem at first sight to be incompatible theories of human agency. While Archer stresses our reflexive deliberations and the consequent choices of identity and projects that individuals make, Bourdieu stresses the possibility of acting without such deliberations, and his concept of *habitus* gives a central role to social conditioning in determining our behaviour. Despite this, I argue that central elements of these two approaches, with some modification, can be synthesised to form part of the emergentist theory of human action sketched out in this chapter.[1] This is not to suggest that Archer and Bourdieu can be reconciled; their divergences are multi-layered and the resolution of the theoretical conflict depends in particular on rejecting the apparent conflationism of Bourdieu's ontology.

---

[1] An early call for hybridising reflexivity and the habitus was made by Mouzelis, and a number of attempts to do so have been surveyed by Adams (Adams 2006; Mouzelis 1995: 113–14).

The emergence of the mental

Human individuals, I argue, have emergent causal powers. For the purpose of explaining how societies work, the most important of these powers is our generic power to act, including our power to act communicatively. The next two sections will therefore be concerned with the emergent roots of our power to act and with an analysis of the sorts of factors that affect how we can and do realise that power.

The current section will consider the ontological status of mental phenomena and in particular the question of their relation to the networks of neurons that make up our brains, although it will engage only very briefly with the underlying neuroscience.[2] This section, then, constitutes an analysis of what parts of human individuals, and what organisation of those parts, underpin the emergence of our power to make decisions. The following section will consider the relationship between such decision making and the causation of human behaviour; a relationship, I will argue, that is less obvious and straightforward than is generally assumed. It will then go on to fit this into a wider account of how the causal powers of a variety of different entities can co-determine human action. Taken together, these two sections offer an explanatory reduction of human action in terms that allow appropriate roles to both mental phenomena and the 'hardware' of our brains, while leaving open paths for social structures to influence us that will be discussed in the second half of this chapter and the next one.

We must begin by asking what mental phenomena are. While there is some agreement on what sorts of things this term refers to – sensations, beliefs, desires, intentions, concepts, reasons and decisions, for example – the criteria that circumscribe the mental are more controversial. I shall accept Searle's approach, which implies that mental phenomena are thoughts of any type of which we can be conscious. Thus, for something to be mental, we must be able to think it. This does not mean, of course, that we are conscious of it or thinking it all the time; we always hold a great many concepts and beliefs that we are not conscious of at that particular moment (Searle 1992: 172).

---

[2] Nor will it attempt to explain or explore the nature of our *experience* of the mental, which is emphasised in phenomenological approaches, or in philosophical analyses of *qualia*.

This immediately leads us on, however, to another question: how can mental phenomena exist? What is it that connects them to our bodies? This is the mind/body question that has preoccupied philosophers of mind since Descartes, but it is increasingly being recognised that the newly developing sciences of the brain will help us to answer it. Indeed these neurosciences are starting to provide answers already, although they are still highly incomplete.[3] What they do seem to show is that mental phenomena, both when we are conscious of them and when we are not, are somehow produced by the networks of neurons that make up a large part of our brains.

John Searle, for example, argues that consciousness itself must have neurophysiological causes: 'the *mental* state of consciousness is just an ordinary biological, that is, *physical*, feature of the brain' (Searle 1992: 13). Searle sees this as an emergence relation: 'The brain causes certain "mental" phenomena, such as conscious mental states, and these conscious states are simply higher-level features of the brain. Consciousness is a higher-level or emergent property of the brain in the utterly harmless sense of "higher-level" or "emergent" in which solidity is a higher-level emergent property of H_2O molecules when they are in a lattice structure (ice)' (Searle 1992: 14).

Although much of the underlying neuroscience is as yet undeveloped, there are features of the mechanism that seem reasonably well established. In particular, the networks of neurons and synaptic connections between them that make up much of our brains are conditioned or configured by our experience. The mechanisms by which such networks can be conditioned to store knowledge, beliefs and the like are relatively well understood at one level as a result of computer simulations of neural networks (Holland 1998: ch. 5). Our mental states, such as beliefs, seem to be underpinned at the neuronal level by connections of varying strengths (frequencies) between neurons and groups of neurons. These connections tend to be strengthened when we have experiences that appear to confirm the mental state, and weakened when we have experiences that appear to undermine it. Hence these neural connections do not represent individual

---

[3] The term 'neurosciences' encompasses a range of disciplines and subdisciplines, which have mushroomed in recent years, each seeking to explain different aspects of the functioning of the brain, although the different pieces of the jigsaw are still far from being pieced together (Rose 2006: 2–5).

experiences, one at a time, but a kind of weighted summary of them. Our experiences, then, are a morphogenetic cause of the particular configurations of neurons and synapses that are the primary emergence base of our mental states. We should also recognise that at least some mental states also depend on other elements of the body – emotional states, for example, may also depend on hormone production and sense perception depends on the sense organs concerned and the portions of the nervous system that transmit signals from these organs to the brain itself. It may therefore be more appropriate to see mental states as depending on the whole body and not just the brain. These mental states, I argue, are emergent properties of the human individual concerned and they have causal effects – in particular, effects on our behaviour – that the various body parts underpinning those states could not have if they were not organised as parts of a whole human being with the mental state concerned.[4]

It is the effects on our neural networks, and therefore on our beliefs, of our experiences that 'condition' us to possess certain mental states. Such conditioning need not be conscious – if we experience a particular pattern of stimuli repeatedly then our brain will learn from it without any necessary conscious intervention, as for example in the phenomenon of subliminal learning (Freeman 2000: 191). On other occasions, our conscious thinking may itself provide inputs to the learning process. This conditioning mechanism provides the route by which 'socialisation' or analogous processes may play a significant role in establishing our beliefs and dispositions.

On the basis of this account, we can loosely describe the structural elements responsible for the emergence of mental properties: (a) the parts are cells of the human body, primarily neurons; (b) these neurons are related by synaptic connections that connect some pairs of neurons and not others, and in which the synaptic connections can have various strengths (firing frequencies); (c) this network can

---

[4] There is a great deal of debate amongst philosophers on whether mental properties are emergent. Jaegwon Kim, in particular, has expressed a careful scepticism for many years (see, e.g., Kim 1992, 1993, 1997, 1999). This scepticism, however, is addressed to strong theories of mental emergence; and there is a hint more recently of more relational theories of mental emergence (like Searle's) gaining ground. This remains very much a live issue, with new papers appearing constantly, including, for example, a special issue of *Synthese* on reduction and emergence in 2006.

produce a meaningful mental state because the varying strengths of these connections underpin our ability to think of concepts as having certain types of relationships with other concepts; (d) the network connections underpinning a given mental state are created as a result of our experiences and may be modified, weakened or strengthened by further experiences; (e) the network representing a given concept is sustained over time by physiological processes that need not concern us here, except to say that such networks may fade over time and be forgotten or partially forgotten, but repeated exposure to or exercise of particular mental states will tend to lead to renewal of their strength.

This picture of mental phenomena and their emergence base is incomplete and highly simplified. However, I believe it is sufficiently accurate to serve its purpose here: to make clear that a full account of human action must recognise and seek to theorise the biological basis of that action and its relationship to the higher-level influences on that action, and to show that this relationship can potentially be theorised as an emergence relation of mental phenomena from our physical brains and bodies.

This does not, of course, commit us to any form of biological reductionism: the claim that human behaviour can be explained *entirely* in terms of the properties of our biological parts. Biological reductionism exists in a number of varieties, depending upon which sorts of biological entities are assigned causal effectiveness, but all varieties of it tend to deny that we as human individuals have any causal powers or decision-making capability in our own right and also that our behaviour may be given sociological explanations. One variety, implicit in sociobiology and evolutionary psychology, seeks to explain human behaviour entirely or at least primarily in terms of our genes (see, e.g., Tooby and Cosmides 1992; see also the critical responses in Dupre 2001; Edwards 2003; Rose and Rose 2001). More relevant here, though, is neurophysiological reductionism, which seeks to explain human behaviour entirely in terms of our neurons. But neurons are not enough to produce our human causal powers, unless they are combined in the particular set of structural relations that makes them into a human being. The person we are, the character we have, the sorts of projects we want to pursue, flow from the combination of all our parts into a single biological and social human individual with a body and a brain. That person will have been shaped over time by both genetic and neurological effects, but ultimately they possess powers that can only exist when all the various parts of the human being are brought together into a unique whole with emergent properties of its own. One merit of the emergentist approach is therefore that it enables us to connect the human individual back up to the whole person, including the non-mental aspects of the body – its emotions, physical needs, health and disease, and the use and constraint of that body in time and space.[5]

The argument of chapter 3, in other words, applies to human beings: we can explain the powers of human individuals without explaining them away. Thus we can accept that some day we may be able to explain the neurological underpinnings of human behaviour without this entailing neurological reductionism. It is as whole human beings that we have the capacity to decide, to act and to affect the social world.

An emergentist theory of action

With this picture of mental properties and their emergence base, we can now turn to the question of how they contribute to the determination of human action. Davidson has famously argued that mental properties, specifically *reasons*, can be causes of our actions (Davidson 2001).[6] How could this be the case?

We must begin by asking what is meant by *reason* in this context. There are at least three alternatives. The first is an after-the-event description of what we now believe our motivation was for the action in question. We could call this a *post-event reason*, a rationalisation or a justification. But the verbalisation of such after-the-event descriptions is a separate action from the one we are attempting to explain. Such verbalisations may misrepresent our thinking at the time of the action, and since they occur after the event to be explained, they cannot be its causes. At best, they are useful but fallible evidence about our motivations at the time of the original action. The second version of the concept is a *conscious reason*. Conscious reasons would be

[5] See, for example, Sayer's discussion of the role of emotions in the judgements that affect our dispositions (Sayer 2005a: 950), and the *corporeal realism* developed by Shilling (Shilling 2005: ch. 1).
[6] Various objections have been raised to Davidson's argument – for useful replies to many of these see Bhaskar (1998 [1979]: 80–97).

causes if a process of conscious consideration of the reason in question contributed causally to a decision. The third alternative we may call an *unconscious reason*. This would count as a cause of an action if there were beliefs, desires and hence reasons implicit in our neural networks at the moment immediately preceding the action – as mental entities that we were not conscious of at the time – and these combined to generate our action without our being conscious of the fact. Davidson appears to intend the second of these alternatives, but I will argue below that to construct a viable version of the argument requires that we explain human behaviour in terms that combine explanations of both the second and the third type.

The argument is most easily approached by considering how decisions and behaviour are related to each other over time. Experimenters have shown that to take a conscious decision and implement it takes a minimum of a quarter of a second; yet top tennis players, for example, can react to a serve in a tenth of a second (Dennett 2003: 238).[7] How can this be? Dennett argues that 'the tennis player commits to a simple plan and then lets "reflexes" execute her intentional act' (Dennett 2003: 238). The 'simple plan' here consists of a set of consciously chosen strategies, the precise strategy to be adopted being conditional on what type of serve is received, and the 'reflexes' consist of the ability of our brain and body not only to execute predetermined strategies but also, when they have already been suitably trained by previous experience, to determine *how* to execute them (e.g. just how high and how wide to swing the racquet head) independently of any further conscious decision making. Thus, the conscious decision takes place at one time and the execution of that decision is done non-consciously at a later moment.[8] There is a decision *before* the other player serves, but there is no decision *between* the serve and the return, only an implementation of that previous decision. Furthermore, the conscious decision only partially defines the behaviour to be undertaken, leaving other details to be 'filled in' non-consciously.

---

[7] Although Dennett and Searle have clashed repeatedly over the nature of consciousness, the arguments from their work employed here would appear to be compatible with each other.

[8] I follow Searle here in using *non-conscious* to refer to brain entities and events of a type which we can never be conscious of, and *unconscious* to refer to those that we are not conscious of at the time but could be conscious of at some other time (i.e. *mental* states of which we are not currently conscious) (Searle 1992: 155).

Yet it is also true that our brains at least sometimes offer us the opportunity to consciously review and alter our behaviour when we are on the point of implementing it, as suggested by Freeman: 'Brain activity preceding the initiation of an intentional act starts before the onset of awareness of an intent to engage in that action. The subjects also report that, after becoming aware that they are about to act, they can abort the action' (Freeman 2000: 170). In cases such as this, it seems that the brain activity preceding the initiation of the action represents the beginning of an action implementation process, which may be driven to some extent by past decisions, but which is potentially modifiable by a 'last-minute' conscious review.

I suggest that *all* decision making works as follows: that we do make conscious decisions but these decisions are only the *indirect* and *partial* causes of our behaviour, in that (a) they occur a variable length of time before the action concerned; and (b) they are always incomplete regarding the details of the action to be taken.

Let us imagine, for example, the case in which I decide 'I'll have lunch when I've finished writing this paragraph'. Clearly I could represent this as a decision based on a conscious reasoned balancing of a number of beliefs and desires, and argue that these reasons caused my subsequent action of ceasing to write, getting up from my chair, walking into the kitchen and preparing my lunch. However, it is clear that this is an incomplete account of the causation of this behaviour. First, some explanation is required of how my decision at one point in time becomes activated at another, say ten minutes later, when I come to finish the paragraph. Note that this is far from an automatic process. I may, for example, become engrossed in what I am writing and go on for several more paragraphs before I remember my intention. Or I may find the current paragraph impossibly difficult and decide to give up and have lunch before I finish it. Or I may finish the paragraph, start getting up for lunch, but alter my decision at the last minute because something else now seems more important. Yet, if I do have lunch at the end of the paragraph, my earlier decision to do so surely contributed causally to that outcome.

Second, this decision is incomplete as a determination of my action because it says nothing about *how* I will implement that decision. It is quite likely, for example, that when I get up out of my chair, I shall walk through to the kitchen without paying the slightest conscious attention to how I move my legs in order to achieve this – there is no conscious decision at all involved in this part of my behaviour. As Freeman says, 'we perform most daily activities that are clearly intentional and meaningful without being explicitly aware of them' (Freeman 2000: 23). Thus, some parts of the behaviour I have decided upon are not themselves decided upon. Other parts may be decided upon, but as a result of some other decision at some other time. Take the question of how I sit when I eat – another part of implementing this decision to have lunch. I may have decided years ago to sit up straight at the table when eating and go on to do so without re-making this decision.

Decisions, then, may have variable size or scope, in the sense that, say, a decision to drive to work has greater scope than the decision to turn left at a particular junction on the way. This in turn has greater scope than the decision to turn the steering wheel a bit further to get round this corner successfully (although, of course, experienced drivers often do not make conscious decisions about how far to turn the steering wheel; they delegate this to a non-conscious skill established by previous training). Thus any single case of human behaviour may represent the (full or partial) realisation of a series of nested decisions of various sizes or scope.

Hence our decisions, and with them the conscious reasons that motivate them, are merely inputs, amongst others, into the determination of our behaviour. Furthermore they are inputs with variable degrees of effect. As Barnes and Loyal have suggested, 'Might it not be that all actions are chosen but that there is a range of chosen actions from those readily modified to those carried out with implacable will and determination?' (Loyal and Barnes 2001: 523). Decisions, then, do not seem to produce behaviour directly, but rather produce dispositions to behave in a given way in the future in certain circumstances. Indeed, we may define a *decision* as an event in which an episode of conscious reflection (a process) leads to changes in our dispositions (our tendencies to behave in particular ways). These dispositions then seem to be held with varying degrees of commitment, through being implemented in the brain as neural networks, in an analogous way to beliefs that we hold with varying degrees of confidence.

This suggests a model of the determination of human behaviour that fits well with the Bhaskarian conception of actual causation as the outcome of the interplay of a variety of causal powers. Let me represent this analytically as a series of steps:

1. *experience*: as a result of our experience we develop beliefs and also sometimes unconsciously acquire dispositions to act in certain ways, which are implemented at the neural level as neural networks;
2. *decision making*: we possess the power to think consciously about our plans, beliefs and dispositions, and make decisions, which are co-determined causally by our thinking powers and the network of beliefs that they work upon;
3. *decision storage*: having made decisions, these are stored in our neural networks as new or modified dispositions (note that there may be multiple loops back to step 2 before an action actually occurs, including the 'last-minute' conscious review of some of our decisions); and
4. *action implementation*: our actions are determined directly and immediately by non-conscious brain processes that use our beliefs, previous decisions and skills as inputs.

This same story can be told in two apparently contradictory ways. We can tell it with our conscious thinking 'in charge', on the grounds that we do consciously make decisions about what we are going to do – thus emphasising reflexivity. Or we can tell it with our non-conscious behaviour determination processes 'in charge', on the grounds that those decisions are merely inputs to the real determination of our actions, that they can be overridden and that they only ever relate to part of the determination of what we do in any single action – thus emphasising dispositions. While each of these stories may have its merits for the purpose of answering different questions, the most balanced story is one in which our conscious decision-making and our non-conscious behaviour determination appear as complementary and mutually necessary components in the causation of our actions.

This approach falls into the category of *dual-process* theories of human cognition, which have recently become popular amongst social psychologists (Chaiken and Trope 1999). Vaisey goes as far as to say that 'The idea that human cognition is based on two basic processes – one fast, automatic, and largely unconscious, and one slow, deliberate, and largely conscious – is now uncontroversial' (Vaisey 2009: 1683).

Where does this leave Davidson's account of reasons as causes? Whether we read it in the second or the third of the senses I suggested earlier, as a conscious or a non-conscious account of the role of reasons, my account suggests that reasons *can* be causes of our actions, but they are only ever partial and contingent causes. Reasons are emergent mental properties (and thus causal powers of the individual concerned) that co-determine our *decisions* and decisions are stored in our brains as neural configurations – dispositions – which in turn co-determine our actions. But other factors are also involved and these other factors can lead to some of our decisions not being realised. There are therefore good reasons why there is no exceptionless empirical regularity connecting reasons and actions: like any other causal power, the causal powers of reasons to motivate actions are contingent on the operation or non-operation of other causal powers with the capacity to co-determine our decisions and our subsequent behaviour.

Reasons, then, can indeed be causes, and one important consequence of this is that the social sciences must seek to understand those reasons, as advocates of interpretive sociology and hermeneutics have argued since the time of Dilthey and Weber.[9] However, they are only co-determining causes and always operate in conjunction with a complex of other factors in determining our actual behaviour. Despite our intuition that our actions are determined immediately and directly by our conscious decisions, the process by which our behaviour is determined (including the 'filling in' of details beyond our conscious decisions) is at least partially non-conscious.

Thus, the theory of action briefly outlined here shows how it might be possible that our actions are directly and non-consciously determined by our current dispositions, while allowing that those dispositions are themselves the outcome of a series of past events. Those events include the following: (a) very recent reflections that we tend to see as directly causally effective 'decisions'; (b) older reflections that shaped our dispositions consciously at the time, but which we may now have forgotten; and (c) experiences that affected our dispositions (e.g. in the subliminal acquisition of a habit or skill) without our ever consciously deciding how. It is these non-conscious influences on our behaviour that Bourdieu has theorised with his influential concept of the *habitus*.

[9] But I reject the argument that interpretation is inconsistent with causal explanation and should *replace* it in the social sciences, as Winch has argued (Winch 1958).

Bourdieu's habitus

Habitus, for Bourdieu, is the set of dispositions inculcated in each of us by the conditioning that follows from our social environment.

> The conditionings associated with a particular class of conditions of exist-ence produce *habitus*, systems of durable, transposable dispositions, struc-tured structures predisposed to function as structuring structures, that is, as principles which generate and organize practices and representations that can be objectively adapted to their outcomes without presupposing a conscious aiming at ends or an express mastery of the operations necessary in order to attain them. (Bourdieu 1990b: 53)

The conditioning that follows automatically from the opportunities and necessities inherent in our social position, he argues, tends to 'generate dispositions objectively compatible with these conditions and in a sense pre-adapted to their demands' (Bourdieu 1990b: 54). This is an effect that is particularly powerful in early life, generating a durable attitude to the world that motivates us to see the world in the terms dictated to us by our early social position and to behave in the ways more or less mandated to us by that position (Bourdieu 1990b: 53). Since all those who share a given social position are exposed to the same opportunities and necessities, they tend, accord-ing to Bourdieu, to develop a similar habitus. Hence their social prac-tices tend 'to be objectively harmonized without any calculation or conscious reference to a norm and mutually adjusted in the absence of any direct interaction or, *a fortiori*, explicit co-ordination' (Bourdieu 1990b: 58–9).

Thus, the habitus, produced by social conditioning, tends to encour-age us to behave in ways that reproduce the existing practices and hence the existing structure of society. This conditioning is so effective that the dispositions it generates are below consciousness and in some cases embedded in the most physical ways in which we use our bodies, becoming 'embodied history, internalized as a second nature and so forgotten as history' (Bourdieu 1990b: 56). Thompson illustrates the point with Bourdieu's explanation of accents: the disposition to form our mouths into certain shapes, and thus produce a certain accent, when we speak is one that is generally neither consciously learned nor consciously considered when we speak, yet it tends to reflect our social

origins (Thompson 1992: 17). This is an example of what the neuroscientist Walter J. Freeman calls 'classical conditioning of behaviour,
by which we can learn without being aware of the process and the outcome or being able to recall them' (Freeman 2000: 191).

The dispositions that make up the habitus do not operate in a rule-
like fashion, mandating particular specific actions; rather, each disposition provides a 'generative capacity' (Bourdieu 1990a: 13; Bourdieu
1990b: 55), a transposable potential to react in a certain style, which
may be realised in a range of different behaviours depending upon
the situation (Bourdieu 2000: 149). Thus, what the habitus produces
is not automatically determined actions, but a '"creative", active,
inventive capacity' (Bourdieu 1990a: 13): a capacity to improvise
(Postone *et al.* 1993: 4). This, however, is not a creativity that necessarily involves conscious deliberation of our action. The habitus,
Bourdieu tells us, provides 'a spontaneity without consciousness or
will' (Bourdieu 1990b: 56), and this is typical of his way of presenting
the habitus – he frequently neglects the role of conscious thought in
both the *development* and the *operation* of the habitus.

The omission of conscious thought from the *development* of our
dispositions is clearly untenable as a general claim, but perhaps the
less serious problem for Bourdieu's argument. Many (though certainly
not all) of our dispositions seem to be *learned* quite consciously via
explicit verbal instruction, rather than being absorbed and embodied
unconsciously. Sayer illustrates the point nicely with the example of
learning to stop at red traffic lights: this may become a habit that we
reproduce unthinkingly once we have acquired it, but it is a habit we
consciously develop because we understand the consequences of not
doing so (Sayer 2005b: 26–8). Bourdieu, however, could presumably
accept this modification of the argument while still maintaining that
such learning subsequently becomes embodied, internalised and forgotten – as happens when we learn a new sport, for example. This
would still leave us with a habitus of dispositions derived largely from
the opportunities and necessities inherent in our social position and
able to operate unconsciously on our subsequent behaviour.

A similar, but more serious, objection can be made to the suggestion
that the *operation* of habitus is unconscious. A number of authors have
criticised Bourdieu for his apparent denial of conscious or deliberative
or strategic decision making in the determination of human behaviour,
in marked contrast to most theorists of agency. In their view, habitus

becomes nothing more than a conveyor belt for the determination of human behaviour by social forces. King lists no fewer than eight authors who have interpreted Bourdieu in this way (King 2000: 418) and Wacquant lists another three (Wacquant 1993: 238). However, as Wacquant points out, there are many authors who see another side to habitus (Wacquant 1993: 238). Brubaker and Bouveresse both suggest that Bourdieu positions habitus as the explanation for a certain class of actions, rather than as the single principle of all actions, and thus as operating alongside other principles, such as rational calculation or conscious norm-observance, which explain other classes of actions (Bouveresse 1999: 49; Brubaker 1993: 214).[10]

One reason for the divergence between these two interpretations of Bourdieu may be that he deliberately positions habitus as part of a critique of rational choice theory. In presenting the theory of habitus as resolutely opposed to 'philosophies of consciousness that situate the mainspring of action in the voluntaristic choices of individuals' (Bourdieu and Wacquant 1992: 25), Bourdieu perhaps overstates the case against conscious deliberation. While he does not deny that agents sometimes make decisions, his critique of rational action theory tends to be dismissive of conscious decision making in a way that may generate the impression that he sees such decision making as entirely marginal and unimportant.

Bourdieu, however, does recognise that reflective choices may be made at times of crisis, or critical moments (Bourdieu 2000: 162; Bourdieu and Wacquant 1992: 131). 'Blips' in the operation of the habitus – occasions when it leads to actions that do not have the expected or desired effect – indicate a mismatch between the habitus and its objective environment. Crises, of a variety of types, are possible causes of such mismatches. The individual may be thrown into a radically new situation by external factors – redundancy or war, for example – or they may face a similarly unfamiliar situation as a result of moving voluntarily into a new field – becoming an academic, say, or moving out of the family home into the housing market. Such mismatches, gaps between expectation and experience, tend to generate not only a need for conscious deliberation but also a need for modifications to the habitus itself (Bourdieu 2000: 149).

---

[10] These issues are discussed in a little more depth in Elder-Vass (2007c: 328–9).

So Bourdieu does recognise at least some role for consciousness in the determination of action. But this still leaves us with another reason for the divergence of interpretations: 'it is not clear *how* dispositions produce practices' (Jenkins 2002: 79) and thus 'it is difficult to know where to place conscious deliberation and awareness in Bourdieu's scheme of things' (Jenkins 2002: 77). In the absence of a clear explanation of how dispositions produce practices, it is understandable that there is confusion about the apparent conflict between Bourdieu's stress on the unconscious operation of habitus and his insistence that it operates through active, creative, invention and improvisation.

Archer versus Bourdieu

Bourdieu, then, does accept that conscious deliberation has a role in determining our practices, but it is a role that is always presented as secondary to the practical logic of the habitus.[11] By contrast, Archer's account of human *social* action places conscious reflexive deliberation at its heart (although not her account of actions in the *natural* and *practical* orders).[12]

For Archer, reflexivity is a power that human beings possess: it is the ability to monitor ourselves in relation to our circumstances (Archer 2003: 9, 14). It is exercised through a process of conscious *reflexive deliberations*, during which we conduct internal conversations with ourselves about ourselves (Archer 2003: 25) – our situation, our behaviour, our values, our aspirations. The inner conversation 'is a ceaseless discussion about the satisfaction of our ultimate concerns and a monitoring of the self and its commitments' (Archer 2000a: 195).

Such reflexivity, she argues, is a precursor to the development of a *personal identity* and a *social identity*. These senses of our identity – of who we are – depend upon us delineating what we care about (thus defining our personal identity) and then relating this to our social context to develop projects based upon our ultimate concerns; projects that we use to guide the conduct of our lives (thus defining our social identity) (Archer 2000a: 9–10, 219). And for Archer

---

[11] Bourdieu also uses the concept of reflexivity, but in a rather different way from Archer (Elder-Vass 2007c: 330–1).

[12] Archer's recent work on reflexivity is summarised clearly and placed in the context of her earlier work in Vandenberghe (2005).

reflexivity is specifically a *causal* power (Archer 2003: 9). Thus in our reflexive deliberations we come to conclusions that affect our behaviour in the social world.

There is a strongly humanistic element to Archer's stress on the conscious nature of our reflexive deliberations and the opportunity that they present us to make decisions for ourselves about how we will conduct our lives. This is not, however, at the expense of social influences on human behaviour; as she says, 'we do not make our personal identities under the circumstances of our own choosing. Our placement in society rebounds upon us, affecting the persons we become, but also and more forcefully influencing the social identities which we can achieve' (Archer 2000a: 10). And indeed Archer has devoted two volumes to showing that social structures and cultural systems have causal powers in their own right (Archer 1995; Archer 1996 [1988]). At the same time, she rejects the implication that one's social position fully determines one's subjectivity or behaviour, pointing out (contra Bourdieu) that these develop in very diverse ways amongst people with the same social background (Archer 2003: 348).

What is critical for Archer in these relationships is that we continue to recognise that human beings, social structures and cultural entities each have their own distinct existences and influences on social outcomes. None of these types of entity can be eliminated from the explanation of social events, nor conflated with each other in such explanations. In accordance with this ontology, Archer rejects views of human action that deny causal power to individual humans and their reflexivity. Thus she criticises those who argue that human action can be explained without recognition of the causal powers of human beings as such – whether because they substitute the powers of our biological parts for the powers of the whole human being (e.g. neurological reductionists) or because they substitute social forces for them (e.g. accounts of human action as socially determined discourse) (Archer 2003: 10–14). She is particularly critical of 'social hydraulics' – the view that 'no recourse need be made to any aspect of human subjectivity in order to explain social action' (Archer 2007: 6). And she criticises the view that human agency and social structure can be conflated, which she perceives most clearly in Giddens' structuration theory (Archer 1982) but also in the work of Bourdieu himself (Archer 2003: 11–12).

Archer and Bourdieu are therefore opposed at two distinct levels: in terms of both their theoretical and their ontological views of human agency. At the theoretical level, the conflict turns on the extent to which human beings influence their own destiny. While Archer rejects 'contemporary social theory that seeks to diminish human properties and powers' (Archer 2000a: back cover), Bourdieu sees human action as driven by a socially derived habitus that provides 'a spontaneity without consciousness or will' (Bourdieu 1990b: 56). At the onto-logical level, the question turns on whether social structure can be seen as distinct from human beings or whether the two are mutually constitutive.

Archer discusses the ontological differences using the example of how Bourdieu might see one of her research subjects ('Graham') – perhaps making some conscious choices, but, 'largely unaware that his horizons have been socially reduced' as a consequence of social conditioning (Archer 2003: 11). For Archer, the problem with this position is that

there never comes a point at which it is possible to disentangle Graham's personal caution (a subjective property of a person) from the characteris-tics of his context (objective properties of society) ... All that is certain is that he does not have the last word about himself, his intentions or actions. Therefore, it becomes impossible that Graham can deliberate upon his circumstances as subject to object, because these are now inseparable for 'Graham'. (Archer 2003: 12)

This is an example of the more general ontological error of confla-tionism, which 'rests upon conceptualising "structures" and "agents" as ontologically inseparable because each enters into the other's con-stitution' (Archer 2003: 1).

Thus Archer sees the divergence between Bourdieu and herself as primarily ontological, mirroring precisely her critique of Giddens' structuration theory (see chapter 6 below and Archer 1982, 1995: ch. 4). By comparison with both Archer and Giddens, however, Bourdieu is rather vague about the ontological relationship between structure and agency. Like both, he clearly rejects both methodological indi-vidualism (in the form of Sartre's subjectivism) and methodological collectivism (in the structuralism of Levi-Strauss and Althusser) and seeks to find a middle way that can accommodate some features of both (Bourdieu 1990a: 9–13). But does he take the conflationist or the emergentist route between these two? Strong support for the accusation of conflationism can be found in Bourdieu's description of habitus as 'systems of durable, transposable dispositions, structured structures predisposed to function as structuring structures, that is, as principles which generate and organize practices and representations' (Bourdieu 1990b: 53). Dispositions are features of human individuals, so here he seems to be equating structure with internal human properties in much the same way that Giddens equates structure with rules (Giddens 1984: 17–25).

This seems to fit Archer's characterisation of conflationism, with agency and structures each entering into the constitution of the other. On the one hand, agents and their knowledge are constitutive of structures (e.g. Bourdieu 1984: 467). And on the other, structures are also constitutive of agents:

Overriding the spurious opposition between the forces inscribed in an earlier state of the system, outside the body, and internal forces arising instantaneously as motivations springing from free will, the internal dispositions – the internalization of externality – enable the external forces to exert themselves, but in accordance with the specific logic of the organisms in which they are incorporated. (Bourdieu 1990b: 54–5)

If both of these claims are maintained, then it is difficult to see how agents can be distinguished from structure and vice versa. However, I suggest, Bourdieu's position can be made compatible with an emergentist ontology with some relatively subtle changes that leave his *theoretical* agenda intact. We need not alter the claim that agents are constitutive of structures: it is perfectly compatible with an emergentist ontology to argue that structures are made up of agents, thereby inherently including in the structure the knowledge that agents have of the structure by virtue of including the agents as its parts and thus their knowledge as properties of these parts. As we shall see in the next chapter, this knowledge plays a central role in the interplay of structure and agency that implements, reproduces and transforms social structures.

The second claim, however, brings us to the heart of the ontological disagreement, with the phrase 'the internalization of externality'. On a metaphorical reading of *internalisation*, this claim is entirely compatible with an emergentist ontology; but on a literal reading, it is entirely incompatible. Let me begin with the metaphorical reading. In this sense, when we 'internalise' some thing, our beliefs about the world are affected by our experience in such a way that we accept a belief about that thing as a fact. Thus, for example, we may intern-alise a sense of inferiority as a result of being persistently treated as though we were inferior by people around us. Metaphorically, we may say that we have internalised our inferiority, but literally, what we mean is that we have acquired the *belief* that we are inferior. Now in this sense of *internalisation*, Bourdieu's passage above means that our beliefs about the world, or our dispositions towards acting in it, are affected by our experiences of social structures and as a conse-quence those social structures have an effect on our behaviour. These beliefs and dispositions are not to be equated with social structure, nor to substitute for the notion of a distinct social structure, but to be seen as features of the human beings who are parts of the structure. This does indeed overcome a 'spurious opposition' between exter-nal and internal forces since it helps to make clear the mechanism through which the external forces causally affect the internal ones. Here, the 'external forces' do not disappear into the body but their effectiveness derives in part from a process that depends upon their effects on the body.

Unfortunately, the literal sense of *internalisation* leads to a very dif-ferent interpretation of Bourdieu's argument, and it is this sense that is encouraged by the description of habitus as 'structured structures predisposed to function as structuring structures'. In this sense, when we *internalise* something it becomes literally part of us. In this sense, habitus is not merely a set of dispositions that has been causally influ-enced by our experiences of social structure. Instead habitus literally *is* structure, internalised into our bodies – a view that closely reflects Giddens' conception of structure. And on this reading, Bourdieu is not simply rejecting a spurious opposition between external and internal forces, but also denying the real distinction between exter-nal and internal forces. Now, beliefs and dispositions are no longer properties of human beings who are distinct from social structures; rather they represent an ontological penetration of the individual by the social structure. On this reading, structures really *are* parts of people. If this is what Bourdieu intends, then his position is indeed conflationist. Such a view, however, is not only incompatible with an emergentist ontology; it is also a clear ontological error, in that it fails to distinguish between a thing and its causal consequences. To be more specific, it fails to distinguish between a social structure and the consequences it has for our mental states. This is the same species of error as the claim that a child leaving a zoo has animals in their head, rather than thoughts or beliefs *about* the animals they have seen.

Distinguishing which of these readings Bourdieu really intends is not easy. He does not seem to have considered emergence at all and he pays little attention to the ontological niceties required to distinguish an emergentist from a conflationist perspective, and so his account is open to a variety of ontological interpretations. At the ontological level, then, I suggest there is scope for synthesising the work of Archer and Bourdieu through an emergentist reading of Bourdieu's ontology.[13] And as I argue elsewhere in this book, the conflationist alternative is untenable. Hence Bourdieu's ontology is only viable if we give it an emergentist interpretation, whatever his own intentions were.

Ontology, however, is not entirely independent of theory; this strategy will therefore only work if Bourdieu's *theoretical* position is compatible with such a reading. And of course we must still consider the second conflict between Archer and Bourdieu: their differing perspectives on the theoretical relationship of human causal powers to human social action. The theory of action outlined earlier in this chapter provides the basis for resolving both of these questions.

Before examining the proposed resolution, we must briefly consider the most obvious way of resolving the theoretical conflict – the argument that some actions are reflexively determined and others are determined by the habitus, so that both Archer's and Bourdieu's theories are right, but about different actions. Thus, for example, I might exercise my reflexivity in deciding how to vote, but be driven by my habitus in the degree of deference I display towards the officials in the polling station. In a sense, both authors allow space for just such a reading of their argument. We have already seen that Bourdieu allows for 'blips' when conscious decision making is required (also see Bohman 1999: 132–3; Bouveresse 1999: 49). And Archer suggests

---

[13] Bourdieu also endorsed a variety of realism: 'So it is the simple observation of a scientific world in which the defence of reason is entrusted to a collective labour of critical confrontation placed under the control of the facts that forces one to adhere to a critical and reflexive realism which rejects both epistemic absolutism and irrationalist relativism' (Bourdieu 2000: 111).

that we possess embodied knowledge and practical knowledge – non-linguistic ways of 'knowing how' to do things in the natural and practical orders – that we can perhaps acquire and act upon without conscious reflexive deliberation (Archer 2000a: 160–2, 166). On this reading Bourdieu's insistence on the role of the habitus and Archer's insistence on the role of reflexivity could be seen as logically compatible, with their different emphases reflecting either a desire to stress the importance of their own theoretical perspective; or an implicit argument about what proportion of our actions fits into each category. But any such reconciliation would require a certain amount of distortion of their arguments. Archer's practical and embodied knowledge, for example, is not ascribed to the influence of social context, but rather to the very physical interactions we have with the material world and, to a lesser extent, our reflections on them (Archer 2000a: 163–5, 169–71). And when it comes to our interactions with the social order, Archer continues to insist on the central place of reflexivity (Archer forthcoming). There is little room in this picture for the mechanisms of the *habitus* at all.[14]

I suggest, however, that there is a stronger way to synthesise these two theoretical perspectives. The heart of the argument is that many and perhaps most of our actions are co-determined by *both* our habitus and our reflexive deliberations; and that despite the apparently conflicting implications of these two perspectives for our sense of our ability to choose our actions, they in fact represent two complementary moments of one and the same process – the process that was described in the first half of this chapter.

Synthesising Archer and Bourdieu

This chapter, I argue, and the emergence relation it describes between the mental and the neural, provides a viable route to synthesising the contributions of Archer and Bourdieu in a unified theory of action, subject to some reasonable modifications to their theoretical perspectives. On the one hand, my argument that our actions are caused by the dispositions stored in our neural networks as a result of past decisions and experiences maps closely onto Bourdieu's claim that

[14] And indeed Archer is strongly resistant to any attempt to reconcile her work with Bourdieu's (Archer forthcoming).

our practices are caused non-consciously by our habitus. Although Bourdieu tends to present this claim in somatic rather than specifically neural terms, he did identify dispositions with beliefs and even with 'the reinforcement or weakening of synaptic connections' in his later work (Bourdieu 2000: 136, 177). On the other, the role I allow to decision-making in amending this set of dispositions provides the mechanism by which the reflexive deliberation emphasised by Archer can enter into the same process of action determination as the habitus. Reflexive deliberation does not appear directly in the action-implementation phase, but indirectly, in the decision-taking phase of the process, which can be invoked up to the very last moment, most obviously when the set of existing dispositions does not provide decisive guidance to the brain on how to implement a given action. This process of interaction between an emergent mental layer invoked in the process of decision making and the underlying neural layer that translates our dispositions into actual behaviour explains how dispositions can indeed produce practices, while leaving space for conscious decision making within the very same process.

Just as importantly, this account shows how it is possible that some parts of our actions can be determined more or less unconsciously while others are determined as a consequence of conscious, and perhaps sometimes rational, decision making. Where the translation into behaviour of a disposition that has been embedded in our neural network is unproblematic – such as the usual way in which we shape our mouth to speak and thus the accent that we produce – then the process of action implementation can proceed with no reference to the conscious level. But where this translation *is* problematic – for example, when we need to decide which way to turn *en route* to a place we have never visited before – then our consciousness must be invoked to provide a conscious decision that will complete the set of dispositions required to determine the action to be implemented.

Thus it is not only in moments of crisis that our habitus does not provide a fully worked-out response to our situation. Such situations are radically more frequent than Bourdieu seems to believe and thus we are constantly presented with opportunities for a reflexive review of our beliefs and intentions. As Crossley puts it, 'We cannot ... make choice an exception in the way he seems to want to do. Choices, albeit rooted in a feel for the game, routinely enter everyday life' (Crossley 2001: 97).

Nevertheless, some aspects of our behaviour may be attributed more directly to habitus and others to conscious reflection. It is, however, typically different aspects of the same behaviour that need to be explained in these two different ways, as opposed to entirely distinct actions. Say, for example, I need to reply to a difficult question. In doing so, I may reproduce an accent by shaping my mouth in ways that I implement entirely without conscious thought, but in the very same speech act I may express an idea that I must carefully think through in a conscious decision-making process. Even the implementation of a conscious decision into the form of a socially competent performance is thus achieved as a matter of routine. We can relate this back to the voting example introduced earlier: it is not that the act of voting is consciously reflexive while the act of speaking to the polling official is driven by habitus. Rather, some aspects of *both* actions are driven by conscious decisions taken in the very recent past, whereas other aspects of the same actions are driven unconsciously from our accumulated set of dispositions – our habitus.

Although this account of action is therefore consistent with many aspects of Bourdieu's habitus, it provides an explicit role for conscious input to our dispositions that Bourdieu largely neglects. Of course, that decision-making itself is always heavily influenced by our existing set of dispositions (Bourdieu 2000: 161; Thompson 1992: 16–17). But it does provide a mechanism for the amendment of our dispositions, most obviously in response to new situations that are not congruent with our previous experience. For example, when we adopt a new role, we may have to think carefully about *how* to perform it and this may be guided not only by the dispositions arising from our previous social positions, but also by consciously absorbed new information, such as instruction from a supervisor, or information from a rule book or manual.

In practice this means that when we act, some aspects of our actions may be determined with little or no conscious input – such as the way our mouth movements form our accent when we speak – while others are strongly influenced by recent reflection. The extent to which reflection affects our actions is, however, left open by this theory. It seems likely that this extent is highly variable, across a number of dimensions. Let us consider four of these.

First, the same individual may be highly reflexive with regard to some aspects of their behaviour, but strongly driven by their social conditioning with regard to others. Consider, for example, the radical male political activist who is highly reflexive in his response to globalisation, war or capitalism, yet uncritically reproduces the attitudes and behaviours towards women acquired from the culture of his upbringing. Secondly, different individuals from the same social group may have very different degrees or styles of reflexivity – a possibility that tends to contradict Bourdieu's argument, but one that Archer provides strong empirical evidence for in her work on different modes of reflexivity (Archer 2003: part II; Archer 2007). Thirdly, individuals from different backgrounds may display a different balance of reflexive and unreflexive action – which is, of course, a key part of Bourdieu's argument – such that on average individuals from an intellectual background, for example, may be more questioning of their dispositions than those from a working class background. And fourthly, different societies in different historical periods may show marked differences in the degree of reflexivity demonstrated by their members; thus, for example, feudal societies usually seem to have discouraged any sort of challenging of the habitus, whereas contemporary post-industrial societies positively demand it, with their constantly changing environments constantly disrupting the assumptions of the habitus and with education systems that must increasingly prepare children to be flexible in later life (cf. Bourdieu 1990a: 73–4).

If these speculations are valid, the contribution of reflexivity to the causation of human action varies by individual, by social class and by historical context. Hence we need to theorise the ways in which reflexivity develops and operates, as well as theorising the less reflexive aspects of the development and operation of the habitus. We need a theory of reflexivity to complement Bourdieu's theory of the habitus and Archer's recent books on agency and reflexivity offer a substantial contribution to just such a theory (Archer 2000a, 2003, 2007).

Once again, however, some reinterpretation of the argument will be required. Archer's analysis of the acquisition of personal and social identity is a compelling story about the development of reflexivity, but it is a story that neglects the role of the habitus. Archer certainly argues that social structure does affect human action, but she does not see its effects being channelled through our dispositions. As we have seen, for example, she argues that 'we do not make our personal identities under the circumstances of our own choosing. Our placement in society rebounds upon us, affecting the persons we become, but also and more forcefully influencing the social identities which we can achieve' (Archer 2000a: 10). Thus both our choices of primary concerns and our choices of roles and projects through which we can pursue them are constrained by our social context. However, Archer tends to stress the externality of social forces, as when she says that the individual is right to believe

> that he lives in a social world that has different properties and powers from his own – ones which constrain (and enable) his actions. These are *temporally prior* to his conceiving of a course of action, *relatively autonomous* from how he takes them to be, but can *causally influence* the achievement of his plans by frustrating them or advancing them. (Archer 2003: 14; see also 134–5)

Structures are thus seen as having an influence on the outcomes of our plans – and on our knowledge of the structural situation and its likely effect on those outcomes – rather than on our subjectivity itself. The reason appears to be her desire to retain human individuals as independent actors in their own right (Archer 2003: 38–9). Like Archer, I strongly believe that we cannot eliminate the first-person perspective, nor the causal powers of human individuals, from the explanation of human action. But I believe we can retain these without denying the impact of the social world on human subjectivity. To say that our social background and experiences influence our dispositions is not to cede all causal power to the social level at the expense of the individual. Our dispositions may sometimes be heavily and unconsciously affected by social factors, but none of us is ever completely at the mercy of our habitus. Nor is our habitus the unmediated product of social structures, but rather the result of a lifetime of critical reflection upon our experiences, including our experiences of those structures.[15] Reflexivity thus becomes a critical attitude towards the dispositions we have acquired from our past, as well as towards the contemporary social situation that we face.

With these reinterpretations, then, Archer's account of reflexivity can be integrated with the theory of action outlined in this chapter and thus with a similarly reinterpreted version of Bourdieu's account

---

[15] For another response to Archer that seeks to retain both reflexivity and the habitus, see Sayer (2009).

of the habitus. The resulting synthesis, I argue, provides us with a powerful and coherent account of human action.

Conclusion

This chapter has reinterpreted Bourdieu's habitus and sought to integrate it alongside Archer's reflexivity within an emergentist social ontology; it has also placed both within a specific theory of action and thus stepped beyond the realm of social ontology and into that of social theory. As we saw in chapter 4, this is entirely consistent with the ontological thrust of this book. The emergentist framework and the level-specific theory play complementary roles and it is impossible to show how the emergentist framework can apply to particular levels without developing at least the skeleton of some level-specific theory. Thus the development – and/or appropriation – of a certain amount of level-specific theory is inescapable if this book is to achieve its objective of showing how emergence applies to social structure and agency.

From Archer, this theory takes both her ontological insistence on the distinct existence of uniquely human causal powers and her theoretical insistence on the need to take account of conscious reflexive deliberation in the explanation of human action. It is thus able to draw on her account of the development of personal and social identity to expand and consolidate its account of reflexivity. But her account must also be modified, most particularly to allow for the role of acquired dispositions in the causation of our behaviour and the effect of social context on those dispositions.

From Bourdieu, the theory takes his penetrating examination of the construction and operation of the habitus and his recognition that our socially influenced beliefs contribute to our reproduction of social structure. But his account too must be revised. Ontologically, in an application of the complementarity test described in chapter 4, it must be clarified by recognising that social structures are not literally internalised by individuals, but only metaphorically, through the influence they have on our subjectivity. Theoretically, it must be modified to show how we, as reflexive beings, are sometimes able to evaluate critically and thus modify our dispositions in the light of our experience, our reasoning capacities and our value commitments.

The consequence of placing Archer's and Bourdieu's theories within the emergentist framework developed here is a coherent view of human action as 'a permanent dialectic between an organizing consciousness and automatic behaviours' (Bourdieu 1990b: 80). While this chapter has only been able to present a brief sketch of the resulting theory of action, I suggest that this synthesis overcomes the imbalances and tensions in these earlier accounts. This arises, I believe, from the adoption of an emergentist perspective in which social structures, cultural systems, human individuals and indeed our biological parts are all recognised as possessing relevant causal powers and examining how those causal powers interact in practice, rather than seeking to deny the causal influence of any of these, or to conflate multiple levels into one.

In the case of agency, the emergentist approach enables us to recognise that human individuals are entities with causal powers of their own as a consequence of the inter-relations between their biological parts. By applying the emergence level test we can see that those powers depend upon the structure and properties of our brains (and indeed our bodies as a whole), but (as chapter 3 showed), this does not mean that we can perform an eliminative reduction to the neurological level. Neurons cannot take decisions. It is only when our neurons are organised into the complex networks that constitute our brains that they can provide the foundation for mental properties such as beliefs and desires that enable whole human beings to make decisions.

But we must also balance this claim for the autonomy of the human individual with a full recognition of the interplay of biology and society with our causal powers in the determination of human action. The theory of action developed here, and its assimilation of Bourdieu's habitus, shows how the interplay of our social context with our biological powers to form and store dispositions and to translate them into behaviour plays a fundamental role in the causation of our behaviour. Our reasons, our dispositions and our beliefs are all emergent properties of the human being as a whole, but they are emergent from a biological base, and social causes play a central part in their morphogenetic and morphostatic histories. It is time, then, to turn to those social causes and how they can have a causal impact on our beliefs, dispositions and behaviour.

6 | *Normative institutions*

This chapter develops and justifies one of the central arguments of this book: that social structure is best understood as the causal powers of social groups.[1] It does so by focusing on one of the many possible types of social structure, one that has played a central role in sociological debates: normative social institutions. The chapter examines in some detail how such institutions are produced by the interactions between members of a specific type of social group, a type of group I shall call *norm circles*. Normative social institutions, it will argue, are an emergent causal power of norm circles.

This chapter is concerned with identifying the mechanism responsible for normative social institutions and thus with *retroduction*. It therefore abstracts from the many complex ways in which this mechanism interacts with others in the social world, including, for example, the important role played by various forms of social power in the workings of many normative institutions. Nor does it cover the ways in which institutions are implicated in the mechanisms of other types of social structure, nor say much about the morphogenetic histories of institutions. The analysis of institutions developed here, then, is not intended as a complete account of how they work, which would certainly need to address all of these further issues. Rather, it is intended as an ontological building block that may then be combined with others to construct a fuller explanation of actual institutions and social events. The following chapter will show, for example, how institutions are implicated in the more complex ontological structure of organisations and chapter 8 will examine how their causal powers interact with others in the determination of actual events.

---

[1] Hodgson has made a similar point: 'Social structures are essentially groups of interacting social individuals, possibly including social positions, and with emergent properties resulting from this interaction' (Hodgson 2007: 221).

Conventional sociological accounts of normative institutions, discussed briefly in the first part of the chapter, have tended to assume that normativity is produced by *society*, but they have rarely been precise in defining the concept of *society*. It is just this sort of ontological vagueness that the method described in chapter 4 is designed to problematise and this chapter is the outcome of applying that method to the question of normativity. It thus seeks to identify the precise social entities responsible for the causal influence of normative institutions and the mechanisms by which they acquire these powers, connecting the argument up to an understanding of the lower-level parts that combine in these mechanisms – in other words, to the account of agency offered in the previous chapter.

These mechanisms are examined in detail in the central sections of the chapter, which introduce the concept of norm circles, examine different but complementary ways of understanding their boundaries and consider the implications of one of their most significant characteristics: their potential for intersectionality. Normative intersectionality arises when an individual is part of multiple distinct norm circles that have different boundaries. This appears to be increasingly common in contemporary societies and is an important factor in explaining normative change, which is examined in the penultimate section.

The final section of the chapter uses the account of normativity developed in these central sections to ground a critique of the ontology implicit in the work of Anthony Giddens on social structure. While this critique complements that made by Margaret Archer and other realists, it also recognises that at the level of theory, as opposed to ontology, structuration theory may be compatible with a realist understanding of structure.

Theories of social institutions

The Durkheimian sociological tradition invokes the concept of social structure – or 'social facts' – to explain normative social practices. By *normative social practices* I mean regularised practices encouraged by dispositions or beliefs about appropriate ways of behaving that are shared by a group of people. There is a vast range of such practices, including those sanctioned by legal systems (e.g. 'you must drive on the right-hand side of the road'), religious belief (e.g. 'you must not eat pork'), rule systems (e.g. 'you may only move the king one square at a time, in any direction') or cultures (e.g. 'on meeting someone, you should shake their right hand'). These various types of rules (or their tacit equivalent, in which the practice is not understood or transmitted in explicitly verbal terms) may be called *norms*.

The social structures that are responsible for normative social practices are generally referred to in the sociological literature as *social institutions*.[2] The concept of *social institution*, however, is almost as diverse in its referents as the concept of *social structure* (discussed in chapter 4). The *Collins Dictionary of Sociology*, for example, begins its definition: 'an established order comprising rule-bound and standardized behaviour patterns. The term is widely acknowledged to be used in a variety of ways, and hence often ambiguously. *Social institution* refers to arrangements involving large numbers of people whose behaviour is guided by *norms* and *roles*' (Jary and Jary 2000: 302).

Despite its acknowledgement of conceptual diversity, this definition leans towards the idea that social institutions are to be identified with patterns of behaviour, and thus represents an example of what was called in chapter 4 structure-as-empirical-regularity. Empirical regularities in themselves, however, are not causes but effects and so, if social institutions are to play a causal role, they must be something more than such regularities.

The commonest strategy in the literature is to ascribe the causal role to norms themselves. There are two varieties of this strategy, both of which can be traced back to Durkheim: one that sees norms as individual representations and one that sees them as collective representations. Both accounts assume that individuals enact particular practices because of the particular normative beliefs they hold

---

[2] In accepting that these *are* social structures, I diverge from some other realists. Fleetwood, for example, has suggested that we should exclude institutions from our definition of social structures (Fleetwood 2008), and Archer sees institutions as culture rather than structure (personal communication). Fleetwood's argument seems to me to obscure the important commonality that institutions have with other forms of social structure: they arise from interactions within groups of people and are causal powers of such groups. I do agree that institutions are cultural, and indeed that *culture* and *normative institutions* are more or less synonymous terms, but for the same reason again I see culture as a type of social structure. We can nevertheless continue to distinguish between institutions and other forms of structure, as we can indeed between different institutions, and thus my argument does not constitute a *conflation* of structure and culture. I have discussed the ontology of culture in more depth in Elder-Vass (2010a).

and that the standardisation of these practices arises at least in part from the fact that the corresponding normative beliefs are shared by members of the cultural community concerned. However, there are two distinct ways of theorising this causal role. The first argues that these normative beliefs are only causally effective as items of knowledge or belief held by individual human agents. The second, however, argues that it is not individual normative beliefs but collective ones that are causally effective here: that individual-level normative beliefs, related to each other in the sense of being shared over a certain community, form the parts of a *collective representation*, to use Durkheim's phrase, and that it is this collective representation that is causally effective. One could argue, for example, that the *commonality* of social practices cannot be explained by the causal effects of individual norms and values, but only by the commonality of those norms and values across the community, and hence that it is the collective norm or value that produces *standardised* behaviour and not the individual one.

Anthony Giddens' structuration theory seems ambivalent with regard to this question. He claims not only that structure 'makes it possible for discernibly similar social practices to exist' but also that it 'exists, as time-space presence, only in its instantiations in such practices and as memory traces' (Giddens 1984: 17). Thus, on the one hand, he claims that structure makes possible the commonality of practices, which would appear to require a quasi-Durkheimian notion of structure as something that is wider than the beliefs of individual human beings. This is the view that also seems implicit when he defines structure as 'rules and resources, organized as properties of *social* systems' (Giddens 1979: 66, emphasis added). Yet on the other hand he insists that structure exists only as instantiations in the practices and minds of individual human beings, and thus denies the existence of collective representations as such (Giddens 1984: 25–6).

Reading Giddens' structuration theory as an account of the structure of institutions seems to leave us with a contradiction. He wants norms and values simultaneously to be more widely binding than their individual instantiations because of their collective character, but also nothing more than their individual instantiations in ontological terms. The former depends upon accepting the claim that 'collective representations' have a causal effect in their own right, while the latter depends upon denying it. And each of these claims seems to depend upon a different way of understanding what a 'collective representation' really is: in the first case, there seems to be an implication that collectives as such can *have* representations, whereas in the second, collective representations are nothing more than a group of individual representations that happen to be similar.

Yet Giddens' ambivalence is perhaps understandable, as neither of these understandings seems satisfactory. On the one hand, it seems necessary to have a mind or at least a brain to form a representation and collectives as such do not have them, only individuals do.[3] On the other, the second option does not seem to provide an explanation of the commonality of practices at all. Some sort of collective pressure is required if we are to provide an explanation of the similarity between the social practices of different people. But this leads to a further challenge: what is the collective that exerts this pressure?

From the beginning, Durkheim linked social facts to the concept of *society* (e.g. Durkheim 1964 [1894]: 13). And by the time of *The Elementary Forms of Religious Life*, he clearly ascribes the causal capacity to exert normative influence to society as a whole:

Society requires us to become its servants, forgetting our own interests ... Thus we are constantly forced to submit to rules of thought and behaviour that we have neither devised nor desired ... Society speaks through the mouth of those who affirm them in our presence: when we hear them, we hear society speak, and the collective voice has a resonance that a single voice cannot have. (Durkheim 2001 [1912]: 154–6)

Although it sometimes seems that for Durkheim the society that influences us is a monolithic one, this is only true of his account of *mechanical solidarity* in pre-modern societies, which he sees as normatively homogeneous, with a large collective element in each individual's moral consciousness. In modern societies, characterised by *organic solidarity*, this collective element declines with the growth of occupation-specific normative collectivities, each with its own set of norms (Durkheim 1984 [1893]). And at times, Durkheim equates the concept of *society* with lower-level social groupings such as religious communities and families (Durkheim 1952 [1897]: 170–1).

---

[3] Durkheim's emergentism has often been criticised on the grounds that it seems to attribute subjectivity to groups (e.g. Catlin 1964: xiv) (and see Lopez and Scott 2000: 108–9, n. 2).

Nevertheless, conceptions of social structure as the power of whole societies remain influential. In the *Blackwell Dictionary of Modern Social Thought*, for example, we read: 'In social structure the parts are relationships among persons and the organized body of the parts may be considered to be coincident with the society as a whole' (Heer 2003). But such statements demand some clarity about what a *society* actually is; and it is often suggested that in this tradition societies are assumed to map onto nation-states (e.g. Sayer 2000: 108). States themselves usually have well-defined boundaries and memberships, but the belief that these boundaries are congruent with those of *societies* is coming to seem increasingly untenable. Alongside states there are many potentially cross-cutting social systems or collectivities that follow different boundaries, or none at all (Walby 2005) and one consequence of globalisation is that fewer and fewer collectivities are coterminous with states. But many, such as multinational corporations, religions and families, have never been so, and many of these surely play important roles in the maintenance of normative institutions.

One response amongst theorists of social structure has been to eliminate or at least attenuate the link from structure to society. Giddens, for example, continues to work with the concept of society, but defines it in much more tentative terms, as clusterings of institutions (Giddens 1984: 164). But this clustering does not entail that all institutions are congruent with particular societies: 'I take it to be one of the main features of structuration theory that the extension and "closure" of societies across space and time is regarded as problematic' (Giddens 1984: 165). In his structuration theory, 'structure exists, as time-space presence, only in its instantiations in such practices and as memory traces orienting the conduct of knowledgeable human agents' (Giddens 1984: 17). There is little sense here of society or indeed any other social collectivity as an external force. As Rob Stones puts it, the 'external structural moment' is 'badly underdeveloped' in Giddens' ontology (Stones 2005: 58). In his own defence, Giddens argues that 'In structuration theory, the concept of "structure" presumes that of "system": it is only social systems or collectivities which have structural properties' (Giddens 1993, Introduction to 2nd edn: 7), but he is characteristically vague about attributing causal power to collectivities.

Giddens, then, seeks to break the connection between structure and society, while recognising that social collectivities are significant, but remains remarkably vague about what those collectivities might be or what sort of causal role they play. He can hardly be said to have successfully replaced Durkheim's notion of 'society' as the power behind normative social institutions. Yet that notion is plainly untenable. This situation invites two varieties of response. The first is to reject the entire Durkheimian tradition of thinking about structure. As Lopez and Scott point out, this has been the response of many postmodernists and post-structuralists who 'hold that there is no whole or totality separate from the *structuring* activities and practices that are engaged in by individual actors' (Lopez and Scott 2000: 5). But there are also critics of structural sociology who do not fall into the postmodernist camp.

John Urry, for example, argues that national societies are the central concept in traditional theories of structure and agency, which he calls a 'sociology of the social as society'; and wants to replace such theories with a 'sociology of mobilities' (Urry 2000: 4). He sees contemporary mobilities as undermining not only the idea of societies as congruent with nation-states, but as undermining any conception of social structure. And Bruno Latour is opposed to what he also calls a 'sociology of the social' – a sociology, for Latour, that takes 'the social' for granted, and a sociology that he specifically associates with the Durkheimian tradition. Latour aligns himself instead with Durkheim's opponent Gabriel Tarde and his advocacy of taking 'the social as a circulating fluid that should be followed by new methods and not a specific type of organism' (Latour 2005: 13). Latour wants to replace the 'sociology of the social' with a 'sociology of associations' (Latour 2005: 9), in which 'there is no society, no social realm, and no social ties, *but there exist translations between mediators that may generate traceable associations*' (Latour 2005: 108–9).[4]

This chapter argues, however, that a second sort of response is preferable: a response that retains the conception of social structure, but breaks the link to 'society' by identifying a different kind of social collectivity as the bearer of structural powers. In particular, it will be concerned with identifying the generic mechanism that is responsible for normative social institutions. In doing so, I will be following Latour's advice to trace the associations at work, but instead of

[4] Latour's alternative to structural sociology is examined in more depth in Elder-Vass (2008c).

tracing these associations with a view to *substituting* them for a social structure, I will be tracing them with a view to *explaining* how that social structure works.

Norm circles

I argue that normative social institutions are emergent properties – causal powers – of *normative circles*.[5] I have drawn the term *circle* from the work of Georg Simmel because he uses it to denote overlapping or *cross-cutting* social groups. Indeed, Simmel named a chapter of his *Sociology* 'Crosscutting social circles' (Simmel 1955).[6] Simmel applies the concept of intersecting social circles more often to questions of identity and solidarity than to questions of normativity, but his discussion of the codes of honour of some circles touches occasionally on the normative impact of intersecting social circles on their members (Simmel 1955: 163–6). This chapter goes beyond Simmel in seeing a specific kind of social circles – those concerned with specifically normative questions – as having emergent causal powers to influence their members, by virtue of the ways in which those members interact in them.

Let us consider, then, the case of a single social institution, in which a single norm tends to produce a single social practice. Part of the mechanism by which the practice is produced is that each member of the group that enacts this practice, which I shall call the *norm circle*, holds a normative belief or disposition endorsing the practice.[7] This does not necessarily entail that each member of the group is morally committed to the norm as representing a just standard of

---

[5] Some earlier papers referred to normative circles as *normative communities* (Elder-Vass 2007b, 2008b). The concept of *community*, however, carries some of the same problematic connotations as *society*. My thanks are due to Margaret Archer and John Scott for pointing this out.

[6] 'Die Kreuzung sozialer Kreise'. Although Bendix titled his translation 'The web of group affiliations', this decision has been criticised by Blau and Schwartz, and also by Frisby (Blau and Schwartz 1984: 1; Frisby 2002: 119; Simmel 1955: 125).

[7] This is not in dispute between theorists of normative behaviour. It corresponds, for example, to Giddens' understanding of *rules* (Giddens 1984: 17–25). Nor is it necessary that these beliefs are held consciously or discursively by the individuals concerned; hence a similar role is played by Bourdieu's conception of the *habitus* (Bourdieu 1990b: 52–65; Elder-Vass 2007c).

behaviour; it entails only that they are aware at some level that they are expected to observe it and will face positive consequences when they do so, or negative ones when they do not. The example abstracts from a variety of possible complexities by assuming a rather simple sort of social institution: one in which every member of the norm circle both endorses the norm and is expected to observe it. This enables us to ignore, for the purpose of clarifying the mechanism, features that would be important in a fuller account of normative institutions, most particularly the question of differences of social power between members of the circle and therefore the possibility that they could be used to enforce social practices that advantaged some at the expense of others.

The entity to which I am ascribing normative power in this argument is the norm circle and we can understand the *social institution* concerned as the causal power that this circle has to tend to produce the corresponding practice through the influence it exerts on its members. Like all causal powers in the critical realist model, normative institutions do not *determine* behaviour but only *contribute* causally to its determination, alongside other causal powers with which they interact, and hence they only *tend* to produce a given outcome (see chapter 3). The parts of the circle, I suggest, are the individuals who are its members. But what is the mechanism by which the circle (as opposed to simply the individuals) generates this causal power?

Although institutions depend on the members of the norm circle sharing a similar understanding of the norm concerned, emergent or collective properties cannot be produced by such formal similarities, as we have seen in chapter 2. It is the commitment that they have to *endorse and enforce* the practice with each other that makes a norm circle more effective than the sum of its members would be if they were not part of it. The members of a norm circle are aware that its other members share that commitment, they may feel an obligation to them to endorse and enforce the norm concerned and they have an expectation that the others will support them when they do so. In other words, the members of a norm circle share a *collective intention* to support the norm, and as a result they each tend to support it more actively than they would if they did not share that collective intention.[8]

---

[8] For a very clear introduction to the concept of collective intentionality, see Gilbert (1990).

They may support the norm by advocating the practice, by praising or rewarding those who enact it, by criticising or punishing those who fail to enact it, or even just by ostentatiously enacting it themselves. The consequence of such endorsement and enforcement is that the members of the circle know that they face a systematic incentive to enact the practice. Not only will other individual members of the circle take an incentivising stance, but when they do so they will be taken to be acting on behalf of the circle as a whole and will be supported by other members of it. It is this commitment to endorse and enforce the norm that is the characteristic *relation* between members of a norm circle.

As a consequence of being members of a norm circle, then, these individuals act differently than they would do otherwise. Even if they held the same normative belief, they would not necessarily act in the same ways regarding it (either endorsing it so strongly or enacting it so frequently) if they were not part of a circle that shares a commitment to endorse and observe the norm. These relations, then, when combined with these sorts of parts, provide a generative mechanism that gives the norm circle an emergent property or causal power: the tendency to increase conformity by its members to the norm. The property is the institution and the causal power is the capability that the group has to affect the behaviour of individuals. That causal power is implemented *through* the members of the group, although it is a power *of* the group, and when its members act in support of the norm, it is the group (as well as the member concerned) that acts.[9]

Now, this is not to deny any significance to the normative beliefs of the individuals concerned. Indeed, it is one of the strengths of the emergentist perspective that it accepts that entities at many levels of a laminated whole can simultaneously have causal powers and that these powers may interact to produce actual events. On this view, it is not only true that individual beliefs themselves are causally effective but also that they are a crucial part of the mechanism underpinning the causal power of the larger group. At the level of the individual, social institutions work because the individual knows both what the expected behaviour is and the pattern of incentives their behaviour is likely to confront. These beliefs tend to encourage the enactment of the practice concerned; but they take the form they do at least in part

[9] See the discussion of *intrastructuration* in chapter 2.

because of the emergent causal effect of the norm circle. Individual beliefs, then, mediate between social institution and individual behaviour. Norm circles have a causal effect on beliefs (and indeed on unconscious dispositions, as stressed in Bourdieu's account of the *habitus*), and these in turn have a causal effect on individual behaviour – reflecting the account of agency given in the previous chapter.

This, then, is a case of downward causation. But it is a significantly different form of downward causation from that discussed in chapter 3. In that model, a whole with emergent powers (e.g. a living animal, with its emergent power to pump blood around its system) had a direct physical effect on its parts (e.g. moving its blood cells). But in social institutions the power of the norm circle to influence an individual member's behaviour is not a direct physical effect. Normative compliance is not physically forced compliance but voluntary compliance; and hence it is *directly* caused, not by the *existence* in the present of normative pressures from the community, but by the individual's *internalisation* of past pressures in the form of beliefs or dispositions. The effect of social institutions on behaviour is therefore a two-stage causal process – in the first stage the norm circle has a (downward) causal impact on the individual's motivations and in the second these motivations affect their behaviour.

The temporal gap between experience of the normative environment and the execution of a norm-compliant act is bridged by the retention of beliefs and dispositions shaped by this experience, and thus corresponds to the account of human agency given in chapter 5. Institutions work, in other words, by changing individuals – by changing their beliefs or dispositions so that the individuals will be inclined to behave in a different way. Their causal effect is on our motivations, not directly on our actions, but by affecting our motivations at one point in time they are able to affect our actions later – an argument that echoes Archer's point 'that structure and agency operate over different time periods' (Archer 1995: 76).

None of this implies, however, that normative institutions necessarily rest on evaluative *consensus*. The argument does entail that members of the norm group share a similar understanding of the norms they are expected to observe and the array of likely responses to their observation or non-observation of them. But there is no necessity that those affected by any given institution agree with the norm concerned in the sense of being *privately* committed to it as a just standard of behaviour. This therefore leaves open two important possibilities: (a) that conformance with norms may sometimes be a consequence of prudential behaviour in the face of unequal power relations rather than consensus over the value of the norm; and (b) that members of the norm group who disagree with its standards (even if they do actually conform with them) may take action directed towards changing those standards, thus initiating the morphogenetic cycle of structural (and indeed cultural) change analysed by Archer (Archer 1995: e.g. ch. 3, 192–4) – an issue that I will return to later in the chapter.

Nor does my argument entail that these institutional influences *necessarily* produce norm compliance. An individual's recognition of the social institution may produce a tendency to comply with the relevant norm, but because their behaviour like all actual events is multiply determined, other causal factors – such as other conflicting normative motivations, the belief that a norm could be transgressed without being detected, or strong emotional drives – interact with this tendency and may lead to it not being realised in any given target act. A parent may steal a loaf to feed his or her hungry children, for example, despite recognising the risk of being punished for doing so and even despite believing it is wrong to steal as a result of experiencing previous advocacy of this norm.

Furthermore, the existence of a social institution does not entail that all members of the normative circle concerned will actually endorse or enforce the norm on every relevant occasion: this sort of behaviour is also the outcome of many interacting factors, of which commitment to the norm is only one. Thus, for example, a member of the circle may fail to support a norm because they consider that there is another more important norm that needs to be supported in the particular circumstances, or because they are showing personal favouritism to an offender, or because they will obtain some personal benefit from a transgression of the norm by someone else.

The existence of a social institution, then, may not lead to enforcement of the corresponding norm on every occasion, but it does imply that there will be a *tendency* for members of the community concerned to endorse/enforce the norm. The institution produces a conditional tendency: *if* an individual transgresses against the norm, they are *likely* to encounter negative sanctions as a result.

This account of social institutions shares a great deal with Durkheim as well as with Simmel. As we have seen, he argued that 'Society speaks through the mouth of those who affirm [its rules] in our presence: when we hear them, we hear society speak, and the collective voice has a resonance that a single voice cannot have'. He also tells us that 'social pressure exerts its influence mentally', and that such influences 'emanate from society' (Durkheim 2001 [1912]: 155–6). We need simply substitute 'norm circle' for 'society' and this would read as a summary of my own argument. Given Durkheim's own emergentist leanings, well documented by Keith Sawyer (Sawyer 2005: ch. 6), this is not entirely surprising.

But this does not mean that *norm circle* is just a euphemism for *society*. This is not an unacceptable return to the 'sociology of the social', for at least two reasons. First, because there may be many norm circles in any social space, which can and frequently do intersect diversely with each other, and the consequence is that we can no longer take for granted any correspondence between a norm circle and any given social totality. Secondly, because now we have an explanation of the *mechanism* by which the interactions between people *produce* the power of the whole.

Norm circle boundaries

One of the strengths of the norm circle concept is that it has no necessary congruence with conventional concepts of 'society'. Once we reject the claim, implicit in some accounts of social institutions, that norm circles are co-terminous with 'societies', then it becomes both possible and necessary to ask a new question: what *are* the boundaries of any given norm circle and how might we identify them empirically? There are at least three different approaches we might take.

First, we might say that for any given normative disposition or belief held by any given individual, the norm circle is the set of actual individuals who have influenced that disposition. This is what I propose to call the *proximal* norm circle. Each person has a proximal norm circle for each of their normative beliefs or dispositions – the set of people who influenced its formation. These proximal norm circles may be different for each distinct norm held by a given individual and will generally be different for each individual holding any given norm. In the extreme case, the proximal norm circle may be a single person from whom the individual has learned the norm – perhaps a parent or a teacher. In many such cases, however, this single person is taken to represent a wider group, which brings us to the second version of the norm circle concept.

This second version depends on the individual's beliefs (conscious or otherwise) about the extent of the norm circle. I shall call this the *imagined* norm circle. Here I am adapting the concept of an *imagined community* that was introduced by Benedict Anderson to help explain the birth of modern nationalism (Anderson 1991). For Anderson, the national community is imagined because the individual member never sees the faces of most of its other members (Anderson 1991: 6). It is important to recognise, however, that *imagined* communities are not *imaginary*. What is imagined is not the *existence* of the community, but its extent: its size and its boundaries. The individual experiencing the attentions of a proximal norm circle learns that they represent a wider group, but the extent of that group may remain obscure.[10] Again, each individual has (at least implicitly) an imagined norm circle for each distinct normative belief or disposition.[11] There may, however, be a tendency for individuals to assume that their normative beliefs and dispositions all arise from congruent norm circles, or at least from a limited number of clusters of congruent norm circles. This suggests the concept of *norm-set circles*, which will be discussed in the next section.

Thirdly, we might seek to establish the network of interlinked individuals who actually do endorse and enforce the norm concerned, irrespective of whether the individual has had any contact with them, as long as the individuals in his or her proximal norm circle are part of that wider network. I shall call this the *actual* norm circle. It comprises all those interlinked individuals who would in fact tend to endorse and enforce the norm concerned if they were to interact with the individual. This group may be either larger or smaller than the *imagined* norm circle for any individual holding the norm. Unlike proximal and imagined norm circles, however, the actual norm circle for any given

---

[10] Berger and Luckmann have described the process involved, but assume, following Mead, that it automatically leads to a recognition that *everybody* is committed to the norm (Berger and Luckmann 1971 [1966]: 152–3).

[11] The imagined norm circle may be unconscious, particularly when the norm itself is unconscious. The individual may unconsciously follow the norm in some contexts and not others, implying a non-universal unconscious imagined norm circle. Or they may follow it in all contexts, implying a universal one.

norm is the same for all individuals within it. Nevertheless, there may be different actual norm circles for different norms.

Although these three versions of the concept of a norm circle are radically different, they are not in competition with each other: each of the three is causally significant and they play complementary roles in a single integrated process. It is the individual's interactions with the *proximal* norm circle, for example, that directly produce his or her disposition to act in conformance with the norm. Each of the members of this circle, however, has their own proximal norm circle, which may extend further into the actual norm circle, and we would expect all such proximal circles for a given norm to intersect to produce a patchwork that covers the whole of the actual norm circle. Each proximal norm circle, in effect, acts causally, but does so on behalf of the whole actual norm circle.

The *imagined* norm circle is causally significant because the presence (or consideration) of members of the imagined circle will tend to produce the individual's conformity with the norm. To the extent that the individual's acceptance of the norm is instrumental rather than internalised as a value, their adherence to it will depend upon the presence of members of the imagined circle. If someone believes, for example, that a particular norm is endorsed and enforced only by a religious community of which he or she is a member, they may be tempted to ignore it when no one present belongs to that community.

And the *actual* norm circle is causally significant because it determines whether and when the individual will be subjected to the endorsement and enforcement of the norm, irrespective of the expectations about such endorsement that arise from their sense of the imagined norm circle. If it turns out in the previous example, for instance, that those endorsing the norm concerned extend beyond the individual's religious community, they may find themselves facing sanctions for their behaviour even though none of the members of their imagined norm circle is present. The extent of the actual norm circle, it should be clear, is independent of the beliefs about it held by any given individual. The two are ontologically distinct. One important corollary of this ontological separation is that the individual can be wrong about the normative environment that they face. Indeed, our empirical knowledge that people can indeed be wrong about their normative environment is further evidence for the ontological distinction between imagined and actual norm circles.

Exposure to unexpected sanctioning behaviour will, of course, tend to produce convergence of the individual's imagined norm circle towards the actual norm circle. In contemporary societies, however, we are only ever likely to encounter small portions of any given actual norm circle and individuals must develop working 'rules', based on their experience, to give them a sense of the true extent of the actual circle. As a result, the mapping of our imagined norm circle onto the actual norm circle will always be approximate and imperfect. The degree of accuracy of this convergence will depend, *inter alia*, on the range of the individual's experiences and normative education and on the quality of their ability to generalise from it.

Irrespective of the degree of convergence, however, I take it that the causal influence of the imagined norm circle is best understood as part of the way in which the actual norm circle acts upon each individual member of it. At the level of the individual's consciousness, the influence of the actual norm circle is mediated through two different forms. In the process of learning the norm, the individual is exposed to the influence of the actual norm circle through the mechanism of the proximal norm circle; and in the process of choosing whether and when to observe the norm, the individual is exposed to the influence of the actual norm circle through the mental image that they have of it: the imagined norm circle. Ultimately, normative social institutions are causal powers of actual norm circles, mediated through the forms of proximal and imagined norm circles.

The analytical distinction between imagined and actual norm circles does not in itself entail that they will be different in extent. It is possible, for example, that an individual may imagine the norm circles for all her norms to be congruent with each other and that the actual norm circles for all her norms actually are congruent. In such cases, there would be a single normative community responsible for all the normative influences on the individual, and indeed, at least at the level of actual norm circles, for all the normative influences on the whole of the community concerned. Perhaps in some pre-modern societies, such as those considered by Durkheim in *The Elementary Forms of Religious Life* (Durkheim 2001 [1912]), this was sometimes the case. But once we recognise that the boundaries of norm circles are contingent and that they may differ for different norms, it becomes possible to conceive of a very different situation, which is surely characteristic of all but the most isolated of contemporary social spaces: normative intersectionality.

Intersectionality between normative circles

As I use the term, *intersectionality* is the property that a group has when it intersects with one or more other groups by virtue of having one or more (but not all) members in common, or the property that a set of groups has when they intersect with each other. This is manifested at the individual level in the shape of people who are members of multiple groups simultaneously. As we have seen, this is a concept that has roots in the work of Simmel and variations of it have been used by a variety of sociological theorists. The most explicit use was perhaps that by Blau and Schwartz, in their book *Crosscutting Social Circles* (Blau and Schwartz 1984), but intersectionality is also, for example, a feature of Merton's account of reference groups (Merton 1968: e.g. 287) and Kadushin's work on elite power (e.g. Kadushin 1968). The concept has also long been a feature of feminist thinking and the term has recently become prominent in feminist discussions of individuals who experience multiple forms of oppression or marginalisation as a result of intersectional identities (see, e.g., Collins 1998; Crenshaw 1991; McCall 2005; Phoenix and Pattynama 2006; Walby 2007; Yuval-Davis 2006: 201). Most of these applications have focused on intersectionality between what we might call identity groups and between common interest groups.[12] This chapter applies the concept to normative groups, but it could equally well be applied to groups of other kinds, such as linguistic communities (Elder-Vass 2008a), for example, and indeed Saussure touches on intersectionality in this context (Saussure 1986 [1916]: 200–1). As I use it, however, intersectionality goes beyond at least some of these other usages, in that it refers not just to intersections between nominal categories, but to individuals as being parts of multiple distinct social entities with real causal powers.

Intersectionality between actual norm circles is possible because individuals hold multiple normative beliefs and dispositions, and there is no necessity that the actual norm circle that endorses and enforces any given norm should map onto (i.e. be congruent with) those for other norms that are held by the same individual. Any given person, in respect of *each* distinct belief or disposition they hold, is influenced by a given norm circle. It may, however, often be the case

---

[12] It may be useful to think of identity groups as *imagined* interest groups.

that these individual-disposition-specific norm circles are congruent for particular sets of linked dispositions for any one individual. Thus, for example, a member of a religious community may hold a cluster of normative beliefs that are endorsed and enforced only by that community. In such cases, I call the group that endorses and enforces this cluster of norms a *norm-set circle*. More generally, I shall use the term *normative circle* to refer to both *norm circles* for single norms and also *norm-set circles*.

Norm-set circles may be thought of in proximal, imagined or actual terms, although once again I consider the actual variety to be the ultimate source of the other two. In proximal terms, particular groups of individuals (e.g. the family, or school friends, or teachers, or work colleagues) will often be the source, not just of single norms but of clusters of norms for any given individual. The individual is then likely to see each of these clusters as being endorsed by a particular imagined norm-set circle. Those endorsed by his or her family might be seen as belonging to whichever identity group the individual most strongly associates with their home environment – with a particular class or ethnic group, for example. Those (different) norms endorsed by teachers might be seen as belonging to the national community and those endorsed by work colleagues as belonging to the organisation in which they work.[13] Alternatively, where these different clusters seem broadly consistent with each other, the individual might imagine them all as part of one large cluster, endorsed by society as a whole. Over the course of time, however, it is the actual rather than the imagined associations of norm circles into norm-set circles that will determine the responses the individual receives to their actions and so we would expect the individual's imaginings of normative clusterings to tend to converge (rather imperfectly) with the actual clusterings.

It is an empirical question, in any given case, whether (and which) groups of norms can be attributed to a norm-set circle, though we might expect such clusters to be common in the contemporary world, given that many of us are socialised through institutions (such as families, schools and religions) that have wide normative ranges. To the

[13] The argument does not rest on any assumption about *which* circles individuals belong to. Those who live outside families, with no formal schooling and no formal work, for example, may still belong to less conventional norm circles – composed, for example, of street gangs, or organised around institutional care environments.

extent that norm-set circles (and indeed any unclustered norm circles) are cross-cutting rather than congruent with each other, individuals become sites of normative intersectionality and *society* becomes a patchwork of overlapping or intersecting normative circles.

Once we recognise that individuals are members of a variety of cross-cutting normative circles, each of which tends to influence their behaviour in certain directions, it becomes apparent that these influences may not always be consistent with each other. My family, for example, may expect one thing of me and my class or workmates something quite different. A theory that simply argues that institutional pressures *determine* individual action is no longer tenable when institutional pressures may counteract each other; at best we can only argue that such pressures *tend* to influence action in certain directions. And once we recognise that multiple such pressures may conflict with each other, then we must recognise the need for individuals in ambivalent normative positions to make *decisions* about which norms to observe in difficult situations. Hence the importance of an understanding of human action that leaves room both for social influence and individual decision making, or, to put it in other terms, that reconciles the roles of both *habitus* and reflexivity (see chapter 5).

In contexts of complex normative intersectionality, skilled social performances depend upon the possession by the individual of a sophisticated practical consciousness of the diversity, applicability and extent of the normative circles in which they are embedded, and indeed of others to which they are exposed, even though they may not be parts of them. Whether or not they are able to articulate this consciousness discursively, members of such societies depend upon it whenever they act.

Change in social institutions

We cannot make sense of social institutions without considering how they work over a short period of time and over such periods it is typically possible to abstract from the process of normative change. To put it more formally, in retroducing mechanisms we can abstract from morphogenesis. Normative change, however, is increasingly common and any adequate general theory of normativity must be able to accommodate *both* stability and change. It is beyond the scope of this book to theorise such change comprehensively, but some brief considerations will help to illustrate the emergentist understanding of institutions and its dependence on a morphogenetic analysis – what Archer calls an 'analytical history' (Archer 1995: 327) – that complements the synchronic analysis developed above.

Archer and Bhaskar have provided complementary abstract frameworks for understanding changes in social structure: Archer's morphogenetic cycle and Bhaskar's Transformational Model of Social Activity (TMSA) (Archer 1995: 154–61). In both, the dynamic of structural reproduction and/or transformation is represented as a cycle with two critical moments. In the structural moment individuals are causally affected by pre-existing social structures and in the agential moment they themselves act, and as a consequence reproduce or transform the social structure concerned. This model maps straightforwardly onto this chapter's account of stable social institutions: in the structural moment, the individual's experience of norm-supporting behaviour by members of the normative community causally influences his or her motivations and in the agential moment he or she tends to act in compliance with the norm (and perhaps even to endorse or enforce it), thus reproducing the normative environment in which such behaviour is seen as desirable.

The same model, however, is capable of illuminating the process of institutional change, because this cycle is not a closed loop. At each point, subsequent actions are only influenced, and not completely determined, by the previous step in the cycle. Like all events, such actions are multiply determined – there are always other factors that interact causally with those modelled in the cycle of structural reproduction. Institutional reproduction does not require that at every turn of the cycle the agential moment produces behaviour supporting the existing institution, only that such behaviour tends to predominate to the extent required to sustain the normative beliefs of the members of the norm circle.

Now, these beliefs themselves depend not upon absolute consistency of our normative experiences, but upon the balance of confirming and dis-confirming experiences that we have. Consider the example of a tenant farmer renting land under an informal traditional tenancy agreement. If the tenant occasionally sees (or hears about) a former tenant begging in the streets and learns that he has been prevented from growing food for his family because he failed to meet his obligations under such an agreement, this will tend rather strongly to confirm the tenant's belief that he'd better meet his own obligations. But if he meets his fellow tenants and hears them bragging about how they have short-changed their landlords and got away with it, he might start to develop a different belief about the incentives he faces and what is appropriate behaviour in the light of them. The net state of his belief about the need to observe the relevant norm will depend on the balance of such norm-supporting and norm-undermining experiences, which have accumulated over time and how he currently evaluates them.

Because there are always reasons why *some* norm transgressions do not meet with norm-enforcing reactions (some examples of which were listed earlier), there is always a degree of uncertainty about the current normative environment, though with stable institutions the balance of support for the prevailing norms will tend to be clear enough for all competent members of the group to understand them. However, because it is possible for other factors to intervene causally in the agential moment, it is possible that the cycle reproducing any given institution may be subverted often enough for the norm to start to weaken, to fade away or to be transformed. This can occur, for example, when the individuals concerned change their beliefs and/ or behaviours for reasons that are external to the institution. There are many reasons why this could occur. For example, they might be exposed to normative beliefs from other circles and find them appealing, or their material circumstances might change in a way that means certain norms now seem unnecessary or counterproductive, or individuals may find that different norms endorsed by the same community lead to incompatible recommendations and find reasons for changing the order of precedence between them. Whatever the reason – and there may be several interacting reasons here too – once significant numbers of members of a normative circle change their behaviours with respect to a previously well-established norm, the normative environment is changed.

When this occurs, other individuals will find that their own beliefs about the normative environment have become outdated: the structure of normative incentives that they actually face is different from the structure they believe they face. One case of unexpected normative behaviour, of course, is unlikely to change these beliefs, since as we have seen such cases are routine even when the environment has not

changed at all. Just as it may take a series of experiences to persuade
someone that a norm exists, it may take a series of experiences – or a
particularly clear negative endorsement by an authoritative source –
to persuade them that a norm they previously believed to apply to
them has altered or ceased to apply. It is also possible, of course, for
individuals to resist normative change, for example by strengthening
their own norm-supporting behaviour to counterbalance the weakening of norm-supporting by others, and the net outcome will depend
on the changing balance of these tendencies.

Opportunities for normative change are enormously enhanced in
contexts of complex normative intersectionality. If the individuals in
a given social space are all socialised with the same complete set of
norms then the triggers for normative innovation are relatively limited – perhaps new kinds of situation may develop that call for new
norms and perhaps tensions between different norms within the set
may generate new normative thinking. In such contexts, the rate of
normative change might be expected to be rather low. But where there
are not only multiple sets of norms (for the same issue) within the
social space but also large numbers of individuals who are subjected
to pressures to conform with multiple sets, then the scope for normative change would seem to be higher. Individuals who are influenced
by a number of normative circles may find it relatively easy to change
their position on a particular normative question from that endorsed
by one circle to that endorsed by another.[14] By contrast, where a normative change would require the individual to leave a total normative
community and join another, or would require the whole community
to change its beliefs on a question, such changes seem likely to face
greater inertia.

Reactions to normative change, of course, rest on being able to
detect it in the first place. This requires the ability to distinguish normative change from everyday failures of people to support norms
as and when we expect them to and from the dissonance resulting
from exposure to norm-compliant and norm-supporting behaviour
by members of different normative circles. A further source of normative dissonance for the individual arises when people make longer-
term moves between one community and another with a different

[14] Archer makes a similar point in discussing the 'Myth of Cultural Integration'
(Archer 1996 [1988]: ch. 1).

normative environment – from school to work, for example, or from prison to the outside world. In practice, people in modern societies are frequently exposed to all of these types of situations and develop good skills for distinguishing between the different cases. As Giddens puts it,

> The reflexive monitoring of action is a chronic feature of everyday action and involves the conduct not just of the individual but also of others. That is to say, actors not only monitor continuously the flow of their activities and expect others to do the same for their own; they also routinely monitor aspects, social and physical, of the contexts in which they move. (Giddens 1984: 5)

It is only through such continuous monitoring and interpretation of the normative signals they receive from others that actors can cope with the highly intersectional and unstable normative environments that seem increasingly characteristic of the contemporary world.

This section has sought to show that the emergentist account of social institutions is entirely compatible with the explanation of institutional change as well as with the explanation of institutional stability. The account it has given of institutional change rests on two of the foundational principles of critical realist sociology. The first of these is Bhaskar's theory of multiple determination. No theory that sees social institutions as entirely determined by individual behaviour and individual behaviour as entirely determined by social institutions could account for change, since on such an account norms could never alter once they had been stabilised in a particular pattern. It is the recognition that individual behaviour is multiply determined, with social institutions entering only as one of many causal factors, that makes it possible for this model to accommodate behaviour that does not comply with or support the prevalent norms, and this in turn opens up the possibilities for institutional change.

The existence of non-compliant behaviour also opens up the possibilities for doubt and misunderstanding of the prevailing normative environment, and indeed for people to be wrong about that environment. Once we abandon any mechanistic notion that people's beliefs could be instantaneously transformed by changes in the normative environment, the possibility of changes in individuals' normative beliefs rests on a recognition that these beliefs could be out of step with the actual normative environment. Hence this theory of institutional change rests on a second foundational critical realist claim: the ontological distinction between social structures and people's beliefs about them.

Institutions and structuration theory

It is precisely this distinction that is the key point at issue between realist accounts of social structure and Giddens' structuration theory. Nevertheless, readers familiar with structuration theory will have detected some echoes of it in the argument above. This section examines the relation between structurationist and realist accounts of structure, both as a contribution to the critique of structuration theory and in order to clarify the similarities and differences with my own argument. In a parallel to the discussion of agency in chapter 5, this acknowledgement of similarities leads to the suggestion that there may be some scope for synthesis between the structurationist and realist traditions, though one that is premised on a rejection of certain key features of structuration's ontology.

The content of social structure, for Giddens, is *rules* and *resources*, which stabilise social practices and play a key role in their reproduction (Giddens 1984: xxxi). Perhaps the most contentious feature of Giddens' structuration theory is the claim that structure has no existence outside these practices and the minds of the human agents involved in its reproduction: 'Structure is not "external" to individuals: as memory traces, and as instantiated in social practices, it is in a certain sense more "internal" than exterior to their activities in a Durkheimian sense' (Giddens 1984: 25). Giddens' strategy for reconciling structure and agency, then, seems to allow some sort of causal effect to structure, but at the same time to deny a distinct ontological status for structure by seeing it as 'virtual' except in those moments when it appears as a property of human individuals. As Cohen puts it, he seeks to account for the effects of groups while rejecting Durkheim's view that 'social groups are entities *sui generis* with properties of their own' (Cohen 1998: 281–2). He explicitly rejects Durkheim's argument that structure can be seen as emergent and therefore as exercising a causal influence in its own right (Giddens 1979: 50–1). It would seem that he reconciles structure and agency, not as the distinct causal powers of inter-related types of entity, but as different aspects of human individuals.

Archer, like many other critics of Giddens (e.g. Craib 1992) argues that Giddens' *duality of structure* conflates structure and agency as two sides of the same coin rather than two separate but interacting elements:

> To treat 'structure' and 'agency' as inseparable is central to the notion of 'duality' ... There is a decentring of the subject here because human beings only become people, as opposed to organisms, through drawing upon structural properties to generate social practices. There is an equivalent demotion of structure, which only becomes real, as opposed to virtual when instantiated by agency ... If this is the case then its corollary is central conflation, for the implication is that neither 'structure' nor 'agency' have independent or autonomous or anterior features. (Archer 1995: 101; also see Archer 1982)

Archer argues that this *central conflation* of structure and agency 'deprives *both* elements of their relative autonomy, not through *reducing* one to the other, but by *compacting* the two together inseparably' (Archer 1995: 101). This can be contrasted with an emergentist ontology, in which agents and structures are distinct, though inter-related, and each may have causal powers in its own right.

Giddens has been defended by Rob Stones, who disputes the extent of the underlying differences between structuration theory and realism and argues that we should be working towards a productive synthesis of these two essentially compatible approaches, each of which has something useful to contribute to the study of structure and agency (Stones 2001: 177; 2002: 223–4). This argument rests in particular upon a denial of the claim that Giddens rejects the distinction between structure and agency:

> It is a different notion of dualism that Giddens rejects, the kind of dualism that sees structure as always entirely external to agency, in which structure is conceptualized as akin to the walls of a room and agency as akin to the space to move within the room. This kind of dualism is rejected because structuration theory conceptualizes structure as being partly within the agent as knowledgeability or memory traces. So the structure enters into the person (or corporate agent) such that we can say *both* that agency is a part of the person and that social structure is a part of the person. Structure, for Giddens, is something that is conceptualized as inhabiting

people in the sense that it enters into the constitution of the reflexive and prereflexive motivations, knowledgeability and practices of people. (Stones 2001: 184)

This, he believes, constitutes a denial of conflation, with the consequence that Archer ought to be able to accept structuration theory (and that structuration theorists ought to be able to accept emergence) (Stones 2001: 194–5). Indeed, he argues, 'a reliance upon *duality within agents* already runs right through the morphogenetic approach, for example ... within the very idea of structural conditioning' (Stones 2001: 184).

While I sympathise with Stones' desire to synthesise the best from these two traditions, and his recognition of external structure is valuable, this argument still seems to beg the question of the status of 'duality within agents'. I wonder whether this question arises partly because realists and structurationists are using the word *structure* in different senses when they read expressions like 'structure as being partly within the agent'. Raymond Williams' distinction (see chapter 4) again seems potentially relevant: is it possible that realists are reading *structure* here as referring to the thing being structured (the whole building, in Williams' example) and structurationists are reading it as referring to the structure *of* the whole? On the former (*strong*) reading, the idea that the whole structure could exist in someone's head seems utterly incoherent; on the latter (*weak*) reading, the idea that what individuals have in their heads forms part of the structure of a larger social entity is much more plausible.

But the formulations deployed by Giddens and Stones seem at best ambiguous with regard to these two possibilities. Phrases like 'social structure is a part of the person' seem to encourage the strong reading, whereas those like 'structure as being partly within the agent as knowledgeability or memory traces' seem more open to the weak one. This lack of clarity arises, I suggest, partly because of persistent ambiguities with respect to two further distinctions: that between knowledge and the thing known, and that between composition and causation. Both can be detected in Stones' sentence 'Structure, for Giddens, is something that is conceptualized as inhabiting people in the sense that it enters into the constitution of the reflexive and prereflexive motivations, knowledgeability and practices of people' (Stones 2001: 184).

When Giddens argues that 'structure exists, as time-space presence, only in its instantiations in … practices and as memory traces orienting the conduct of knowledgeable human agents' (Giddens 1984: 17), he effectively reduces structure to knowledge. Because he takes knowledge to be part of the individual, it would seem to follow that structure is part of the individual in the strong sense. But this argument entirely neglects the first of the two stages through which norm circles influence behaviour in the account given in this chapter. Individuals do indeed have knowledge (or, more accurately, beliefs and dispositions) that embodies rules and influences their behaviour, but this knowledge is knowledge *of* or *about* or *produced by* the external normative environment faced by the individual. It is our knowledge of the structural influences we face (in this case the endorsing/enforcing practices of the normative circle) that exists as memory traces and not the structures themselves. By collapsing this external normative environment into the individual's knowledge of it, Giddens eliminates the structural moment in the reproduction of normative social practices. But there is an irreducible ontological distinction between (a) the existence of an actual norm circle and (b) any given individual's beliefs about it; a distinction that is lost in Giddens' account, making it impossible, as Archer says, to investigate the relation between the two (cf. Archer 1995: 65–6).

The second ambiguity is to be found in Giddens' frequent use of the term *constitution*, which conflates causation and composition and obscures the distinction between the two. To say that structure 'enters into the constitution' of knowledge is to move smoothly from the plausible *causal* claim that structure (in the sense of our external normative environment) causes our normative beliefs and dispositions to the utterly untenable *compositional* claim that structure is therefore a part of us. Norm circles do have a causal effect on our normative beliefs or dispositions, but, to mirror an argument of John Parker's, the fact that structures are involved in the process of producing knowledge does not mean that these structures necessarily migrate to or inhere in their products.[15] Things that cause effects do

---

[15] In a critique of Giddens and Stones, Parker writes 'the fact that subjectivity is involved in the process of producing outcomes does not mean that this subjectivity necessarily migrates to or inheres in its products' (Parker 2006: 135).

not thereby become parts of the things that they have affected. When I see a bicycle in the street, I do not end up with the bicycle in my brain, I end up with a *memory* of it in my brain. The same is true of my normative environment. If the bicycle knocks me over, this may stimulate a disposition to be careful when I see bicycles. In a very similar way, my experiences of my normative environment may contribute to altering my dispositions. But these dispositions are entirely distinct from the external things that have prompted them.

Despite these concerns over structuration theory's ontology, however, I do see some hope for reconciliation and synthesis, which arises if we can disarticulate structuration theory from Giddens' ontology. This chapter has argued that we cannot explain emergent social institutions without theorising the mechanisms at the level of the individual that combine to generate them. If we read Giddens and Stones as making a contribution to a causal story about these mechanisms, there may be significant value in their *theory* even if we reject Giddens' *ontology*. On this basis, we may be able to find a theory of social institutions that both realists and structurationists could accept.

This chapter, I suggest, has constructed such a theory. In this theory, rules (or their near equivalents, norms) play a crucial role in the mechanism by which norm circles cause individuals to tend to reproduce certain social practices. They exist primarily in the form of knowledge (or its near equivalents – beliefs, or dispositions), a property of the individual concerned that shapes his or her behaviour. This knowledge, however, is a consequence of social interactions that take the form they do because of the existence of social groups that are committed to interacting in support of those rules. These social groups therefore make a causal contribution to determining the actions of the individuals, a contribution that is mediated through the normative beliefs and dispositions of the individuals concerned.

Conclusion

The account of normative intersectionality given in this chapter gives a richer and more nuanced understanding of the complexities of normativity in the contemporary world than earlier understandings of social institutions as congruent with nation-state 'societies'. Yet it does so without discarding the entire classical tradition of thinking about social institutions, unlike many other thinkers who have rejected the association of normativity with 'society'. In doing so, it provides support for the argument that there are social collectivities – norm circles and norm-set circles – that exercise normative causal influences over the behaviour of individuals, influences that are mediated by each individual's understanding of the normative environment within which they live. In a world of normative intersectionality, these influences are neither homogeneous nor hegemonic; the individual must sometimes negotiate a path that balances normative commitments that are in tension with each other. As intersectionality grows, then, it is not only the influence of diverse social forces that increases; so does the need for reflexive individual agency.

This explanation of the power of social institutions provides a strong argument against both methodologically individualist and structurationist ontologies of social institutions. Against methodological individualists, it shows that the normative force of social institutions depends upon the existence of a group that is bound together by certain characteristic relations and that this normative force can not be produced by individuals unless they are organised into this sort of larger whole. And against structurationists, it argues that this normative force depends upon the existence of a real group and not just on *virtual* structure – rules and resources as they are represented in the heads of actors.[16]

Normative social institutions, however, are far from being the only type of social structure, though they are an important one, not only in their own right but also because they are also implicated in other forms of social structure, in a complex hierarchy of inter-relationships. The following chapter will take the next step towards understanding this hierarchy by examining the case of organisations.

[16] It is also a theory that is open to examination in empirical work. As in any case of applying abstracted theory to concrete cases, however, this will inevitably raise a number of further issues, both methodological and conceptual.

7 | Organisations

Contemporary social life is dominated by organisations – states, for example, businesses of all types and sizes, voluntary sector organisations, religious organisations, public enterprises, schools, universities, sports clubs and international organisations such as the United Nations and the World Bank. No serious attempt to explain events in the social world can ignore their influence. This chapter seeks to develop a new account of the structure of organisations that enables us to explain their causal capabilities.

Earlier organisation theorists took it for granted that organisations were social entities with causal influence: March and Simon, for example, had no hesitation in claiming that organisations 'shape the goals and loyalties of their participants' (March and Simon 1993 [1958]: 2). Yet such assumptions have come under fire, from two directions. Methodological individualists claim that the influence of all social entities can be reduced to the influence of the individuals who are their members and that social entities as such have no causal significance over and above that of their aggregated members (e.g. Watkins 1968). More recently, radical social constructionists have claimed that 'organizations are *discursive constructions and cultural forms that have no ontological status or epistemological significance beyond their textually created and mediated existence*' (as described by Reed 2005: 1622). As Westwood and Linstead put it, 'The notion of structure is illusionary, representing only an ideological practice that pretends to stand in the place of the flux of shifting and seamless textual relationships' (as cited in Reed 2005: 1622; Westwood and Linstead 2001: 4–5).

This chapter, by contrast, argues that organisations are structured social groups with emergent causal powers. As a first approximation, we can say, with March and Simon, that organisations are 'assemblages of interacting human beings' (March and Simon 1993

[1958]: 23). Their parts, in other words, are human individuals and the resulting assemblages are real entities.[1] But what kinds of relations between those individuals and what kinds of mechanisms could give these assemblages causal powers of their own? This chapter will argue that organisations in general are the sites of several interacting types of mechanism and that they draw their causal capabilities from this interaction.

On the one hand, the structure of organisations depends on the *roles* that their members occupy and these roles are essentially bundles of norms. Organisations are therefore fundamentally dependent on normative social institutions and thus the causal powers of norm circles. Some theorists have argued, on grounds like these, that organisations simply *are* social institutions (notably Hodgson 2006a: 147; 2006b: 8), but I argue in this chapter that although there are many important and interesting interdependencies between organisations and institutions, they remain different sorts of things. They are different because the roles of members of organisations lead them to interact in ways that result in *further*, non-normative mechanisms, mechanisms that give organisations quite different sorts of causal powers than those possessed by norm circles.

Some traces of the mechanisms at work can be seen more clearly in other, simpler, social forms. The early parts of the chapter develop an emergentist account of two of these simpler forms: *interaction groups* and *associations*. The next section discusses the mechanisms that are characteristic of organisations by considering some simple cases and their implications. Then I consider the relationship between the causal powers of organisations and the individuals who are their members, before going on to look at two issues that introduce greater complexity into the argument: first, the role of authority relations in more complex organisations; and, secondly, the complex ways in which organisations are able to act back upon normative institutions, including those that underpin their own structures.

---

[1] In a parallel argument in economic theory, David Gindis has argued that firms must be seen as real entities with causal significance in their own right (Gindis 2007, 2009). There is already a significant literature on the critical realist contribution to organisation studies. A useful collection is Ackroyd and Fleetwood (2000).

Interaction groups

We can take a first step towards understanding the ontology of organisations by considering what Erving Goffman called *interaction situations* (Goffman 1990 [1956]). In an interaction situation, two or more people interact in a manner that is shaped by their conventional understandings of the situation and of the appropriate way to behave in situations of this type. These are often relatively short-lived interactions, with no necessary commitment of the parties to each other, or to longer term persistence of the interaction. Such interactions come about whenever two or more people recognise that they are in a situation where their behaviour is expected to be guided by certain conventions specific to that kind of situation. The vast majority of social interactions would seem to conform to this pattern. This section will argue that, in at least some interaction situations, the participants may form a group with emergent causal powers and hence it will refer to the group of people involved in an interaction situation as an *interaction group*.[2]

Consider the case of queuing.[3] As Mouzelis points out, the queuing norms we are accustomed to in the West are not universally observed (Mouzelis 1992: 125–6, n. 5), so this example is somewhat culturally specific. Nevertheless, there are many situations in some contemporary societies in which individuals spontaneously form queues. Typically this occurs when there is a physical point from which a service is being provided to one person at a time (or a series of such points), all of the available service points are in use and more than one person is waiting to access the service. Examples of such service points would include checkouts or tills in shops, ticket windows in railway stations and public toilets. When there is more than one person waiting for such a service point, they will commonly form a line, ordered by the time at which the individuals joined it (as a result of each new person joining the line at the back), with the understanding that the first person in the line will take the next turn to access the

---

[2] Goffman sometimes refers to *interaction entities*, though as far as I am aware he does not ascribe causal powers to them (e.g. Goffman 1983: 7; 1990 [1956]: 246). Some other authors have suggested that there is an emergence process at work here (e.g. Brante 2001: 185–6; Sawyer 2005: 198, 210–14).

[3] Goffman touches on queues as interaction situations (Goffman 1983: 14).

service when a point becomes available and the rest will then move up a place.

A queue, I suggest, is an interaction group, whose formation is prompted by two main sets of factors. First, the participants understand queuing and are committed to observing the norms it entails (roughly, that they should behave as specified in the paragraph above).[4] Secondly, the situation itself is one in which queuing is appropriate and is recognisable as such by the participants (this is sometimes aided by the physical setting – props such as signs saying 'queue here', or ropes marking out an area in which to queue). The situation differs somewhat depending on whether the individual is the first to arrive after all the service points become busy, or the second (is that first person queuing or not?) or whether they arrive when there are already at least two people there, in which case the existence of a queuing situation is more obvious. Nevertheless, anyone familiar with the institution of queuing will recognise any of these variations and will tend to respond appropriately.

When individuals do not conform with these norms in situations where others expect them to, they are likely to face strong negative sanctions, particularly from those who are already participating in the queue, but often also from those staffing the service points concerned. A queue may be an interaction group, but *queuing* as such is a normative social institution, endorsed and enforced by the usual normative mechanisms. There is, in other words, a norm circle for queuing and the power of the norm circle tends to influence individuals to form queues, to observe the norms of queuing within the queue and to endorse and enforce queuing norms in queuing situations. These norms also help us to make sense of the situation and of the behaviour of other actors within it.

Norm circles thus play a substantial causal role in generating queuing behaviour. But I have also suggested that queues themselves, as groups of people who are interacting with each other in the ways defined by queuing norms, may be an interaction group with emergent

---

[4] I have spelled out the institution of queuing in detail that may seem superfluous to those (most of my readers, I imagine) to whom it is entirely obvious and taken for granted. It is just such taken-for-granted norms on which all social interaction rests, as Garfinkel has shown, though I do not accept his view that such norms are independent of wider social structures (Garfinkel 1967).

causal powers. What causal role does the queue itself play, beyond the causal contribution of the institution of queuing and the contributions of the participants as individual agents? One contribution would seem to be towards our understanding of the situation. When we see a queue, this makes a contribution to our realisation that this is a queuing situation (the causal consequence is that 'the existence of a queuing situation is more obvious', as I put it above). Furthermore, the existence of the queue contributes causally to our decision as to *where* to queue. When we perceive that a queue exists already, we know that we should join it at the back, rather than, for example, starting a new queue of our own, or trying to join the existing queue in the middle. This (small but essential) causal contribution of the queue results from its consisting of a certain type of parts (people) organised by certain relations (standing in line adjacent to a service point), giving it the emergent property of being recognisable as an instance of queuing.

As a consequence, the queue also has the more interesting emergent causal power to serialise access to the service concerned in a manner that substantially reduces the potential conflict and stress that might otherwise be generated in such situations. The norms of queuing may produce the queue, but it is the queue itself that serialises access to the service. The group of people concerned would not have this effect if they were not formed into an actual queue. The way the members of the queue interact is a product of their normative beliefs and thus of the norm circles that produced them, but the interactions in the queue itself produce a *further* causal mechanism that gives the queue the power to serialise access to the resource.

We could perhaps say that queues are *instantiations* of the institution of queuing, which provide a site for the enactment and reinforcement of the norms concerned. What then, is the ontological relationship between the interaction group and the *norm circle* responsible for the institution that it instantiates? At any given moment, an interaction group is composed of parts that are the people who participate in it, and the properties of the interaction group as a whole depend on those parts, including the properties of those parts and the relations between them. In particular, the existence and properties of the interaction group depend upon a specific set of properties of the people concerned: their beliefs about the relevant norms. These beliefs are the outcome, in part, of the *previous* causal influences of the norm circle's propagation of the norms concerned. Thus the interaction group is *causally* dependent on the prior impact of the norm circle on these beliefs, but this does not entail that the norm circle itself is *part* of the interaction group, nor that the interaction group is *part* of the norm circle: the two structures are ontologically distinct, although they share some of their parts – the individuals who are members of both.[5] Even when all the members of the interaction group are members of the norm circle (as we might expect), this does not make the interaction group as such a part of the norm circle, since each is structured by a different set of relationships. As we shall see, a similar relationship exists between institutions and organisations and is indeed fundamental to understanding the ontology of organisations. There is, however, an intermediate step between interaction groups and organisations, which we must consider first: *associations*.

Associations

I define an *association* as a group of two or more people who have a continuing commitment to the group as such and not just to any normative institutions that the group may happen to instantiate. Perhaps the key respect in which associations differ from interaction groups is that as a result of this commitment the group can persist beyond the duration of a single interaction situation. Its members are likely to have a sense of the group's continuation as a group even when they are not engaged in interaction with each other and they will tend to engage in repeated interactions. One implication is that there is a degree of stability in the membership of the group over a period of time, although associations may allow some turnover of membership.[6]

As with most such distinctions in the social world, there is something of a grey area in the distinction between interaction group and association. We can illustrate this with the example of dating. In some cultures, two people with a romantic interest in each other may agree

---

[5] The distinction that is being drawn here is similar to the distinctions that Mouzelis makes between paradigmatic and syntagmatic structures, and between institutional and figurational structures (Mouzelis 1995: ch. 6).

[6] Except in the case of two-member associations – Simmel's *dyads* – in which the association must necessarily come to an end if one member leaves, although some kinds of dyads may be capable of growing into larger groups (Simmel 1950: 122–5).

to go out on a date, say, for a meal in a restaurant. A date is an interaction situation and its participants form an interaction group, governed by certain (culturally specific) norms; say, for example, that they should take an interest in each other, converse in a friendly way and share information about themselves and their feelings, which they would not normally reveal to strangers. Such an interaction situation need not imply any commitment to a longer-term relationship; the participants may decide, for example, that they are not suited to each other and never date again.

On the other hand, they may both feel encouraged in their interest in each other and agree to date again. This is where our grey area appears. Dating more than once does not necessarily commit them to being 'a couple'; they may still feel they are getting to know each other before making such a decision, for example, and one or both may feel they could still go on a date with someone else without being in any way disloyal. At some point, however, if the relationship develops well, the participants may decide that they are indeed a couple, with a continuing commitment to being so, and at this point we could certainly say that they form not just an interaction group but an association.

There is a variety of reasons why individuals might feel committed to a group, but in general we can say that such commitment is likely to arise when the member feels that the group gives them some continuing benefit or meets some continuing need that they have.[7] In informal associations, these may include, for example, emotional support, or identity definition/affirmation. An interesting case of the latter has been documented by Mary Bucholtz in a study of a group of 'nerd' girls in a US high school (Bucholtz 1999). The group that Bucholtz observed were close friends who banded together to reaffirm a positive 'nerd' identity for themselves, at least in part as a defence against the denigration of such identities by the prevailing 'jock' and

---

[7] The strength of members' commitment to an association may vary. March and Simon suggest that some of the factors influencing this strength of commitment include the extent to which goals are perceived as shared among members of a group, the frequency of interaction between an individual and the members of a group, and the number of individual needs satisfied in the group (March and Simon 1993 [1958]: 85). Although March and Simon are discussing organisations, their argument would seem to apply equally well to associations in general.

'burnout' cultures in the social context of the school. They met frequently, for example in the school grounds during break times, and even named their group and identified themselves as its members in the school yearbook.

The significance of associations for this chapter is that I claim they are social entities with emergent causal powers. In the case of Bucholtz's nerd girls, for example, she documents a fascinating case in which they negatively sanction the linguistic behaviour of a peripheral member of the group (referred to as Carrie) when she employs a word drawn from the sort of 'cool' youth culture that is rejected by the group (Bucholtz 1999: 219). Now in one respect, this is a classic case of norm enforcement, conducted by members of a wider norm circle, but the impact of this norm enforcement on Carrie is potentially greater than it would be if done by someone outside the group. To the extent that Carrie is committed to the group, her tendency to accept the normative standards endorsed by the group is increased. She is more likely to be influenced by their norm-supporting behaviour than someone else would be who experienced exactly the same behaviour from exactly the same individuals but had no desire to maintain membership and status within the group. This additional impact is a causal impact of the association as such (which Bucholtz refers to as a *community of practice*) (Elder-Vass 2008a).

Such impacts need not be confined to conformance with constraining norms. Consider the hypothetical case of a group of teenagers who meet frequently in a local park to skateboard together and who value skateboarding performance as part of their group identity. We might expect the members of the group to be more likely to turn up at the park when the group is expected to be there, more likely to learn new skateboarding skills and more likely to try to skateboard to the best of their ability, all at least partly in order to improve their standing within the group. Perhaps the case that is most clearly distinguished from constraining normativity is the last one here: the suggestion that the skateboarders would try harder in order to improve their standing. This effect might well be produced even if members of the group explicitly endorsed the 'cool' norm of not trying too hard. Status is achieved by being good at skateboarding, which requires trying hard, even though the explicit normative environment negatively sanctions trying hard, and the most skilled members of the group may reconcile these pressures by learning how to try hard while appearing not to. All of these are effects of the causal influence of the group.

Associations, in other words, exert a causal influence over the activities of their members: a case of *downward causation*. This is an emergent causal power, produced by a mechanism that depends upon the parts of the entity – the members of the association – and the relations between them. The mechanisms that are responsible for the causal powers that associations have, beyond those of interaction groups, depend upon that class of relations that distinguishes associations from interaction groups: the various types of commitment of the members to the group. At one level these mechanisms are similar to those involved in normative social institutions: dispositions and beliefs about the incentives an individual faces in their social environment are produced by the individual's experience of that environment and influence subsequent behaviour in ways that respond to that experience. The difference is that the incentives to which an individual responds in an association exist only because the association exists and are produced within it. To the extent that the interactions that occur within the association generate a degree of consensus about the status of an individual within that association (including whether or not they are considered a member) and to the extent that such consensus affects the behaviour of the other members towards the individual concerned, then these interactions generate an incentive for the individual to seek higher status within the association. To the extent that such status within the organisation concerned *matters* to the individual, or in other words to the extent that the individual is committed to the association, these incentives will affect his or her behaviour. The specific effects depend upon the sorts of behaviour that are incentivised in the association, which will vary from case to case.

The causal power of organisations

In general, organisations are a type of association: they are groups of people who have a continuing commitment to the organisation as such. However, organisations tend to be more complex than the simple sorts of association discussed so far in this chapter, in at least two significant dimensions. First, they tend to be strongly structured by specialised *roles*; and secondly, they are marked by significant *authority* relations between at least some of these roles. This section will examine the significance of roles for the causal power of organisations and a later one the significance of authority relations.

Any organisation, I argue, is an entity composed of a group of human individuals, structured by a set of relationships between them (although I shall suggest below that they may also sometimes have non-human parts). These relationships are formalised in the *roles* or *social positions* occupied by the people in the organisation.[8] Role descriptions implicitly or explicitly specify norms that define how an incumbent of the position concerned must relate to other members of the organisation and also how they must relate to outsiders when acting on behalf of the organisation. Some of these norms may be written down in formal job descriptions but roles may also be defined partly by less formal sets of expectations that other members of the organisation have of their incumbents.

In the terms of this book's emergentist ontology, roles are not entities; rather, roles define relations between people. Roles, therefore, are not composed of parts (though we may think of them as bundles of relations), but instead are occupied by actual people. Hence, in contrast to some traditional accounts of the ontology of organisations, I argue that organisations are composed of people and not roles. People are their parts, and roles the relations between them. While it is sometimes argued that roles are more permanent than people in organisations, this does not make roles things that can be parts. Furthermore, organisations are far from unique in having parts that can be replaced and relational structures that may be more persistent than the identity of the parts. Human bodies, for example, can survive the steady replacement of the individual cells that are their parts, while still maintaining the relations that constitute their physiological structure. Likewise, organisations can survive the replacement of the human individuals that are *their* parts, while maintaining the roles that constitute their relational structure.

Roles must be occupied by incumbents who adopt their characteristic behaviours before they can contribute to the causal influence of the organisation. Consider the case of a group of singers, such as a barbershop quartet, who sing unaccompanied music in close

---

[8] Although I equate *role* with *position* here, sometimes the concept is used in somewhat different ways in the literature (Biddle 1986: 68–9). For a useful overview of role theory, see Crothers (1996: 84–92).

harmony. Each singer has a different role in the group, defined both in general terms (lead, tenor, baritone and bass) and by the specific part they must sing in any given song. When the singers perform these roles, the group as a whole gives a musical performance that would be impossible for the individuals to produce in isolation or without being coordinated in this kind of organisation. The ability to produce such a harmonised performance is therefore an emergent causal power of the group – the organisation. The parts of the group are the singers and the relation between them that underpins the production of the performance is a commitment to coordinate their singing according to certain rules. Their ability to do this depends in turn on certain properties of the individuals concerned (most obviously the quality of their singing voices) and a causal history that has brought and kept them together as a group.

Before we look more closely at the kind of mechanism at work here, consider another example: Adam Smith's famous discussion of pin or nail production, in which a group of workers each performing specialised roles is able to produce substantially more than the same group of workers, each producing pins individually (Archer 1995: 51; 1996: 686; Smith 1970 [1776]: 109–10). This capability to produce more is what Archer calls 'the relational resultant of their *combined productive activity*' (2000b: 467): it is an emergent causal power of the organised group and not causally attributable to the individual workers.

In a critique of Archer, Anthony King has argued that although such capabilities cannot be ascribed to the individuals alone, it is not structures or entities that are responsible for them, but rather *social relations* (King 2004: e.g. p. 17). For King, it is not structure but social relations that are causally effective:

The interpretivist tradition is no way arguing that this new division of labour can be understood through dis-aggregating the division of labour back to its molecular constituents – the individual craftsmen or individual readers. This approach fully recognizes the qualitative novelty of this situation but that newness resides precisely in the new relations between individuals. (King 1999a: 213)

Thus he recognises the same facts of the case as Archer and I do. Where we differ is on the question of whether these facts entail that the group as such has causal powers in its own right. King denies that the combination of people plus relations, or people plus inter- action, constitutes a higher-level entity with causal effects of its own (King 1999b: 272). But the *redescription principle* developed in chapters 2 and 3 applies to these cases. If the people concerned were not organised into such organisations, these powers would not exist; and the people plus the relations *are* the higher-level entity, so to say that the people plus the relations have a power is the same thing as to say that the higher-level entity has the power.[9] Thus in Smith's pin factory, for example, if we say that the productive cap- acity of the organisation depends on *both* the workers *and* the rela- tions between them that exist when they are organised as they are in this organisation, this is necessarily equivalent to saying that the productive capacity is a causal power of the organisation and not of the workers.

The mechanisms that produce these powers depend on the inter- actions between members that occur when they perform their specialised roles; let me call this *coordinated interaction*. We must dis- tinguish between two sets of mechanisms here. The first, normative, set is essential to the successful functioning of organisations because it has a causal tendency to produce role-implementing behaviour by the members of the organisation. Without role observance by incum- bents, organisations could not function, but the causal power of the norm circles involved is *only* a power to secure such observance. A further set of mechanisms is required to produce the causal powers of organisations themselves. These are the mechanisms that depend on coordinated interaction and at a concrete level these mechanisms vary from case to case. The quartet's causal power to produce harmonious music, for example, depends on the members' singing notes that have certain tonal and temporal relations to each other. The pin factory's productivity is high because each worker is able to focus on a specific role and the output of that worker is designed as an appropriate input to the role of the next worker on the production line. In each case, it is not simply a commitment to cooperate by performing agreed roles that produces the final product, but a specific coordinated process of interaction.

---

[9] We have debated this question in Elder-Vass (2007a), King (2007) and Elder-Vass (2007e).

Just as in the case of queues, then, organisations depend profoundly on normative institutions, but the mechanisms that generate the causal powers of organisations as such are different from the mechanisms through which norm circles influence our normative beliefs. The way the members of the organisation interact is a product of their normative beliefs, and thus of the norm circles that produced them, but the coordinated interactions within the organisation itself produce a *further* and non-normative causal mechanism that gives the organisation its causal powers.

This distinction between normative and coordinated-interaction mechanisms offers an opportunity to reassess the distinction that Lopez and Scott make between *institutional* and *relational* structure (Lopez and Scott 2000). Although chapter 4 suggested that relational structure may be compared to structure-as-relations in general, another way of reading these terms is to see them as referring to the kind of distinction I am making here. Institutional structure, in this view, refers to the potential of norm circles to induce conformity to the norms concerned. Relational structure, then, would refer to the kind of coordinated-interaction mechanisms that produce the harmony of the quartet or the productivity of the pin factory.

Another parallel can be found in the work of Margaret Archer, who distinguishes between cultural emergent properties and structural emergent properties (Archer 1995: 172–83). Normative social institutions, for Archer, would fall into the former category and the powers of organisations arising from coordinated-interaction mechanisms would fall into the latter. In addition to her discussion of the division of labour discussed above, she has also, for example, analysed the causal significance of different ways of organising educational systems under the category of structural emergent properties (Archer 1979: ch. 1).[10]

Whatever labels we may choose to apply to them, when we seek to identify the causal powers of organisations we must recognise the interaction between normative mechanisms and coordinated-interaction mechanisms. These are two separate classes of mechanism conferring two separate classes of causal powers. In the case of

---

[10] Despite these correspondences there are also some significant differences between our ways of analysing both kinds of structure (see Elder-Vass 2007a, 2010a).

coordinated interaction, there is a sense in which the members of the organisation work together like the parts of a machine to produce a collective effect.

Indeed, there is no necessity that it is only human individuals that interact to produce these effects. The barbershop quartet may depend only on human individuals to produce its sound (at least in a synchronic sense and assuming an appropriate environment – one with air to breathe and vibrate, for example). But the pin producers need their tools; in a sense the power of the pin factory to produce pins at a certain rate is a power of an entity that includes both the workers and their tools. If this is so, then the organisation here is a kind of hybrid entity: an entity that includes both people and other material things as its parts,[11] and that depends on relations between both people and those other things to produce its emergent properties.[12]

There is perhaps a grey area between organisations that include only people as their parts and those that also include other material things, since it can be difficult to decide which non-human material things are essential parts of an organisation. But it does seem clear that some organisations do not depend essentially on such non-human parts while others do. We might perhaps say that Smith's pin factory *uses* tools rather than their being part of the organisation; but such claims become increasingly difficult to sustain as we look at increasingly mechanised factories. When the worker merely presses a button to stop and start the line and perhaps alters its set-up from time to time from a computer terminal, it becomes increasingly difficult to sustain the argument that it is the workers as a group that are causally responsible for the output, rather than the workers and machines taken together as a complex interacting entity.

Whether or not an organisation includes non-human parts, however, the relations between their human members (and those between humans and the non-human parts) are specified (at least partly) in the roles occupied by those individuals.

---

[11] We may call the people *members* of the organisation, and both people and non-human entities its *parts*. I owe this terminological usage to a discussion with David Gindis.

[12] This is one of the productive ways in which sociology must respond to the actor network theorists' desire to break down the barriers between human and non-human actors, though they sometimes take this desire in unproductive directions (Elder-Vass 2008c).

Individuals in organisations

In discussing role performance, we must distinguish between the behaviour of an individual in general and her behaviour 'in the role'. Thus the chief executive's actions are part of the organisation's actions when she is representing the institution in the terms defined by her role (e.g. when making an announcement at a corporate event). But they are not when she is acting outside the role, such as in a private capacity (e.g. when going for a swim), or when acting in some other role as part of some other organisation (e.g. when speaking as a candidate for election under the banner of a political party).

When a role incumbent does act in the role, she adopts behaviours that have been specified by the organisation, as a result of acquiring a normative belief or disposition: the belief that role incumbents ought to act as specified by the norms that make up their role. The role incumbent, that is, is altered as an individual as a result of accepting the role in the organisation and thus we have a case of what was described in chapter 2 as *intrastructuration*. In such cases, we can say that the higher-level entity, in this case the organisation, acts *through* the individual; those properties that the individual acquires by occupying their role are essentially properties of the organisation localised in the individual. And in such cases, the behaviour of the role incumbent in the role is part of the behaviour of the organisation. As Göran Ahrne puts it, 'When organizations do something it is always individuals who act. They do not act on their own account, but on behalf of the organization' (Ahrne 1994: 28). Now, a methodological individualist might argue that this reduces the behaviour of the organisation to that of the individuals and there is no need for the organisation at all in this explanation. However, the role incumbents have the effects that they do when acting in these roles only because they are organised into this organisation. If there were no organisation there would be no such roles and the people would behave differently. Hence the emergent causal powers of the organisation cannot be eliminated from the explanation of this behaviour.

Similarly, if there were no organisation, then those with whom the role incumbents interact would treat them differently. Customers, suppliers and others who interact with an organisation always do so through the human individuals who occupy roles within it, but the way they interact with these individuals is conditioned by their understanding that the role incumbents represent the organisation concerned, that they act on its behalf. Thus the existence of the organisation also affects how these external individuals behave towards its members. Much the same is true within the organisation: role incumbents only accept and follow instructions from their managers to the extent that those managers have, through their role incumbency, the right to make such a request. In this case, the organisation has a downward causal effect on the employee's behaviour that has operated through a fellow role incumbent; but it is nevertheless an effect of the organisation because the manager too is operating as a role incumbent and only has the authority to give an instruction because he or she operates as a representative of the organisation.

Even when a role incumbent is acting 'in the role', however, and thus on behalf of the organisation, this does not mean that their behaviour is entirely determined by the organisation or the role specification. The causal powers of the individual and of other factors also continue to co-determine such behaviour (cf. Archer 1995: 184). Although the organisation has a causal effect on the role incumbent, this effect, like any causal influence, does not fully determine a necessary outcome. Individuals choose to occupy the role, and can choose to leave it, and they also make decisions about how to perform it (see chapter 8 for an illustration). When individuals become parts of organisations, they do not lose the powers they have as individuals, but those powers are channelled and constrained as a result of the relations those individuals now have with others in the organisation.

This helps us to explain the otherwise problematic category of 'mega-actors', introduced by Nicos Mouzelis. These are individuals 'whose economic, political or culturally based social power makes the consequences of their decisions widely felt' (Mouzelis 1991: 107). Such actors can be influential in one of two distinct ways. First, they may have substantial influence in their capacity as private individuals. Thus, for example, a wealthy and prominent private art collector who patronises a particular style of art may have a significant effect on social tastes and through this, for example, on the art-buying behaviours of both other private individuals and of organisations such as public galleries and business corporations.

Secondly, and more relevantly to the current argument, individuals may be immensely influential by virtue of the way in which they perform their roles in organisations. Such roles can be performed well or badly, because role specifications do not completely describe how they are to be performed. Role specifications constrain acceptable behaviour in a role and they may provide criteria for standards of performance, but they also provide resources that are available to the role and leave open many alternative ways of performing the role. This is one of the crucial ways in which social roles differ from role equivalents in the structure of natural objects: they provide the opportunity for flexible behaviour within the social position by its incumbents and such flexibility enhances the possibilities for the individual role incumbent to have an exceptional impact, whether in the form of spectacular success or dangerous failure. Hence, for example, an exceptionally capable chief executive may contribute to the establishment of a dominant business corporation with a major impact on society. And, of course, mega-actors need not become so as a consequence of their own exceptional abilities. It is enough to be in a role that gives one personal influence over a powerful organisation. A president of the USA, for example, will inevitably be a mega-actor simply because of the combination of the president's personal discretion in performance of the presidential role with the immense power of the US government. The president's actions in this role, unlike those of the wealthy private art collector, will be part of the actions of the organisation to which the role belongs, yet the role enables its occupant as an individual to affect the behaviour of the organisation in a potentially influential way.

Thus far, I have given an analysis of organisations that addresses three of the five elements required for a full analysis of a case of emergence – it has identified the components of an organisation (people and sometimes non-human parts), the relations that constitute them into the organisation (roles) and how this gives the organisation emergent properties not possessed by its parts (role-coordinated-interaction mechanisms). A full analysis, then, still requires an account of the morphogenesis and morphostasis of organisations. Such an account is mostly beyond the scope of the present chapter, but there is one aspect that is worth examining: the relationship between role incumbency and organisational morphostasis.

The morphostasis of an organisation requires (a) that it has incumbents for all essential roles; and (b) that those incumbents act within the expectations for their roles. There is no necessity that these requirements will continue to be met. Being a role incumbent, for example, is purely contingent. A role incumbent may choose to leave the role (in most contemporary organisations) and if they do so then any downward influence of the organisation on the former role incumbent will cease. But organisations can survive the replacement of particular role incumbents and they can therefore provide for their morphostasis by replacing role incumbents who leave essential roles. Similarly, role incumbents may fail to perform according to the definition of the role, which could undermine the performance and ultimately even the continuing existence of the organisation. This can be dealt with by managing their performance (e.g. by further training or by disciplinary threats), or by removing and replacing the incumbent. Any organisation that is unable to deal with either of these sorts of problem is likely to fail and dissolve – although there are also many other problems that could lead to such a result and a successful organisation must have morphostatic processes in place to manage these too.

Authority and organisations

It is the mechanisms arising from role specialisation that distinguish organisations from the simplest forms of association, although even quite simple associations may depend on an element of role specialisation. If, for example, the skateboarders discussed earlier had been football (soccer) players instead, then roles such as 'the person who brings the football' or 'goalkeeper' might exist within the group. And roles may also be found in interaction groups: the roles of 'first in queue' and 'last in queue' are significant in queues, for example. There is perhaps a sense in which such interaction groups are short-lived organisations. As organisations become more complex, however, they diverge increasingly from the informality and internal egalitarianism characteristic of many simpler social groups. In particular, more complex organisations are characterised by the attachment of authority to specific roles.

Some writers have therefore argued that it is authority relations between roles that are the significant differentiator between organisations and simpler social forms. Weber, for example, argues that 'by no means every closed communal or associative relationship is an organization. For instance, this is not true of an erotic relationship or of a kinship group without a head. Whether or not an organization exists is entirely a matter of the presence of a person in authority '(Weber 1978 [1922]: 48–9). Weber illustrates the argument with a list of such persons: 'the head of a family, the executive committee of an association, a managing director, a prince, a president, the head of a church' (Weber 1978 [1922]: 48). The inclusion of executive committees in his list somewhat modifies his argument – it is not 'a person in authority' that is decisive, but the vesting of authority within some person or group within the organisation.

Nevertheless, I will suggest, it is because authority relations make *role specialisation* more powerful that organisations are potentially more powerful than simpler associations. Authority relations themselves are a variety of role specialisation: the holders of certain roles in the organisation have, as part of their role, authority in certain respects over the holders of other roles. Hence, in some respects at least, the combination 'role specialisation plus authority relations' is simply a more developed variety of role specialisation. Roles that confer authority on their holders effectively confer some part of the power of the organisation as a whole on certain role occupants.

This is not to say that authority in organisations is *entirely* a product of role specifications; other factors may co-determine the possession of authority. In particular, the possession of capital of various kinds may be a significant factor. Most obviously, the owner-managers characteristic of small businesses acquire their authority primarily from their ownership of the business and their role is dependent on this primary source. Even in large businesses, authority is to some extent dependent on, and delegated from, the ownership of share capital. Other individuals may acquire a degree of authority, or augment authority that is derived from their role, as a result of possessing superior knowledge or skills (educational capital, or cultural capital as Bourdieu would say), or in some cultural contexts as a result of holding an elevated social position outside the organisation (social capital). Furthermore, the *acceptance* of authority relations by those who are subject to them may sometimes be due to a *lack* of capital or of alternative opportunities. This is central to Marx's understanding of wage labour: workers have little choice but to accept alienating authority relations, since in the absence of capital of their own, they must sell their labour power to survive and *all* the opportunities available to them require them to accept such authority relations. For such participants in organisations, their continuing commitment to the organisation and their role in it may be entirely instrumental.

These influences on authority, however important they may be, are distinct from those that are intrinsic to organisations and if we are to isolate the mechanisms of organisations *as such*, as opposed to particular organisations or organisations of particular types, we must focus on those that arise from the general structure of organisations. Here it is roles that are of paramount importance and the differences in authority that they produce. The incumbent of role *A*, for example, may have the authority to allocate work of certain types to the incumbents of role *B* and to reward or penalise them depending on how well the work is performed. Meanwhile the incumbents of role *B* may be required to carry out the work allocated by those in role *A*. The roles themselves, in such cases, define a pattern of authority, but they also connect it to a pattern of control over incentives that tends to enforce the authority relations embedded in the roles.

Ultimately it is the authority vested in those holding managerial roles (whatever its source) that makes roles so strongly binding in organisations. The structural significance of such authority roles is that they make it possible to coordinate the activities of other role incumbents at quite a detailed level and hence make it possible for the organisation as a whole to achieve much more than would otherwise be possible. In other words, organisations can use hierarchical control to generate the benefits of coordinated interaction.

But this still does not entirely capture the power that arises from combining authority relations with role specification. Part of the power of organisations is that they can combine highly regulated task-focused roles, where the role and its expected behaviours are specified in detail for a variety of types of task, with far more flexible roles charged in very general terms with ensuring the coordination of the others: in other words, managers, who provide what March and Simon call the 'central coordinative system' of organisations (March and Simon 1993 [1958]: 23). Most significantly of all, the management role includes the development of the role specifications themselves and their continuing elaboration in response to the goals, performance and circumstances of the organisation.[13] It is this that

---

[13] Of course, different managers have different degrees of freedom from task constraints. Generally it is more senior managers and those in more

gives organisations the potential flexibility to adapt and to develop increasingly effective types of coordinated interaction.

Organisations and institutions

Although the causal powers of organisations depend on coordinated-interaction mechanisms, these in turn depend on the relations between the members of the organisation that are defined by their roles. Roles are normative constructions and the norms involved are therefore emergent properties of norm circles. These are effective because of the beliefs they produce in individual members of the organisation about the normative environment that they face within it. Organisations thus depend profoundly on normative social institutions and this section will examine some of the relationships between these two types of structure.

Like interaction groups, organisations can also instantiate wider norms and depend upon the norms that they instantiate. Businesses, for example, may instantiate various legal norms regarding the formation of limited liability companies and when organisations instantiate institutions in this way they are constrained by the corresponding set of rules, whether or not these are legally enforceable. However, the relation between organisations and institutions is more complex than that between interaction groups and institutions, for a number of reasons.

Most significantly, organisations can to some extent mould the normative environment faced by their members and thus shape their beliefs about their responsibilities and obligations. They can, for example, preferentially favour some norms over others, not only in official role descriptions but also in attempts to shape an organisational culture. And like simpler associations they can use the commitment of members to the organisation (whatever its source) as a lever to influence their conformance with these norms. When a manager, in particular, presses a worker to conform with a particular norm, they act on behalf of the organisation and bring the authority (and potential sanctions) that their own role endows them with to bear in support of that norm.

---

strategy-oriented roles that have most flexibility to drive changes in role specialisation, whereas more junior and more task-oriented managers are more likely to be focused on managing role performance.

Broadly speaking, the norms defining any role in an organisation can be divided into two groups: those that are specific to the organisation concerned and those that are backed by a wider norm circle. Let us call the former *local* role norms and the latter *general* role norms. A company with a unique process for manufacturing pins, for example, may define a role as 'Stage 1 Pin Assembler' that includes a local role norm such as 'Perform process x then pass the part-assembled pins on to a Stage 2 Pin Assembler'. Even such a role, however, is likely to include a selection of much more general role norms, such as 'work an eight-hour shift, five days a week' or 'always wear protective eyewear when at your work station'. And less unique roles, such as 'bricklayer', 'lecturer' or 'treasurer' may be defined by almost entirely general role norms, though the particular selection of norms included in the role specification may be locally distinctive.

The norm circles for local role norms will be confined to the organisation concerned (or to a subset of its members) whereas those for general role norms will be much wider. But in most cases the proximate endorsement and enforcement of both kinds of role norms is dominated by those holding superior and complementary roles within the organisation. As March and Simon put it, 'Not only is the role defined for the individual who occupies it, but it is known in considerable detail to others in the organization who have occasion to deal with him' (March and Simon 1993 [1958]: 22). When those others stand in a relation of authority to the individual, their support for the norm is particularly powerful. Role specialisation only works because role norms are endorsed and enforced by the proximate norm circles, predominantly within the organisation, of the role incumbents.

The ability of organisations to shape the norms that are supported by norm circles is particularly clear in the case of local role norms, which are developed entirely within the organisation and by staff acting on behalf of the organisation. They not only shape norms, however, but also norm circles themselves: they can influence the membership of the norm circles supporting role norms by making the endorsement and/or enforcement of those norms part of the roles of certain other positions. It is these powers to shape norms and norm circles that make it possible for managers to adapt and develop the role specialisation that is the source of the organisation's coordinated-interaction based powers.

In shaping roles, an organisation may draw on wider social institutions by adopting practices drawn from the wider normative culture that forms part of the organisation's social context, but the influence of this wider normative culture is far from being entirely under the organisation's control. As well as being encouraged by the organisation to conform with their roles, its members are also simultaneously members of norm circles that are much wider in extent and that influence their performance in the role. These may be of positive value to the organisation, for example when members bring a commitment to values such as honesty, working hard, punctuality and politeness from the wider culture to their work in the organisation, as described most famously by Max Weber (Weber 2001 [1930]). But they may equally well undermine the purposes or functioning of the organisation, for example in cultures that encourage nepotism or corruption, or in the case of capitalist business organisations, cultures that are hostile to putting profit before the welfare of employees. It is precisely because organisations depend upon normativity to drive role performance and because the performance of the organisation is so dependent on role performance that they are so vulnerable to such cultural issues. We must therefore question Habermas' assertion that 'Organizations ... make themselves independent from lifeworld contexts by neutralizing the normative background of informal, customary, morally regulated contexts of action' (Habermas 1987: 309). While they may *seek* to neutralise elements of the external normative environment by generating a countervailing internal environment, they cannot entirely eliminate the effect of that external context on their own members, let alone the many external parties with which most organisations interact.

Still, we must also recognise that organisations influence not only the norms that comprise their internal role specifications but also norms for the wider social world. Indeed, they may not only shape or modify norms, but even bring normative institutions into existence or destroy them. Most obviously, states (a particularly complex form of organisation, but a form of organisation nevertheless) produce laws and develop apparatuses to enforce them and organisations of many kinds pressure states to introduce laws that constrain us in many different ways. But organisations do not only generate norms that constrain us; many of their most substantial contributions to the modern world come in the form of norms whose observance enables us to access social resources that otherwise would not exist. Thus, for example, post offices have produced ways of sending letters and parcels; software companies have produced more efficient ways of typing documents; governments and financial institutions have produced ways of earning a pension after we retire. Such resources depend upon the non-normative powers of the organisations concerned, but those organisations also provide us with norms that guide us in how to make use of them.

Organisations, then, are distinct from normative institutions and the norm circles that are causally responsible for them, but there is a complex web of causal inter-relationships between these two types of social structure. The consideration of simple norm circles and basic organisations such as barbershop quartets helps us to identify the basic types of mechanism at work, but the story rapidly becomes much more complex once we start to examine how these mechanisms interact in practice.

Conclusion

This chapter has sought to provide an ontological framework that allows us to see how organisations can be causally effective and thus to provide a basis for theorising about how organisations work. Many contemporary organisations are enormously complex, but the chapter began by considering simple cases that illustrate the mechanisms at work in them. Interaction situations illustrate the concept of groups that are governed by normative institutions and yet have a presence and causal significance in their own right. Simple associations show how commitment to a group can provide it with enhanced normative influence. Simple organisations introduce role specialisation, which is itself dependent on norms, but which can also endow the group concerned with causal powers derived from coordinated interactions. More complex organisations enhance both their control over their members and their flexibility through adding authority relations to simpler forms of role specialisation.

Organisations, then, depend on normative mechanisms to produce the role specialisation upon which they depend, but role-coordinated interaction between their members (which may include non-human material things) provides a further class of mechanisms, a class that confers non-normative causal powers on the organisations concerned.

There is a vast range of such organisational powers, corresponding to the vast range of ways in which coordinated human action may be productive.

The relationship between organisations and institutions, however, is much more complex than these synchronic mechanisms might seem to indicate, primarily because organisations have the power to influence their own normative environment. By specifying roles, they set norms for members of the organisation; by including the enforcement of norms on other members of the organisation in the roles of supervisory staff, they influence the composition of norm circles; but they can also sometimes influence their external normative environment.

Organisations, then, have real emergent causal powers that materially affect social events. While there is much more to be said about the ontology and theory of organisations, this chapter has said enough to suggest how the causal powers of organisations work at a relatively abstract level. Hence we now have retroductive accounts of the causal powers of human individuals (from chapter 5) and of several important types of social structure: norm circles (from chapter 6), interaction groups, associations and organisations (this chapter). While there may be many other types of social structure at work in contemporary society, it is not the objective of this book to itemise these exhaustively. Instead, it seeks to show how the emergentist model of causal powers can be applied to the social world. If this is to be successful, we must be able not only to retroduce specific types of social structural power, but also to show how those powers interact to produce social events: to apply our understanding of those powers to provide retrodictive explanations of such events. This is the subject of the next chapter.

8 | *Social events*

The last three chapters have focused on the identification of particular causal powers and the mechanisms that drive them – what Bhaskar calls *retroduction* (Lawson 1997: 24). But this focus may leave the argument seeming vulnerable: these powers and mechanisms may seem too simple to explain the chaotic complexity of our social world. And in each case they may seem to neglect a vast range of factors that tend to interfere with the operation of such basic mechanisms. This chapter, however, will reintroduce some of that complexity, by turning to the equally important question of analysing how those powers or mechanisms interact in the causation of individual actual events – *retrodiction* (Lawson 1997: 221). The realist model of social ontology does not seek to eliminate this complexity from the picture, but rather to abstract from it in the process of identifying the mechanisms at work so that we can use our understandings of these mechanisms as building blocks to construct explanations of actual events. This is the significance of what Bhaskar calls the *multiple determination* of actual events (discussed in chapter 3). If we wish to explain particular events, we need to understand much more than one particular causal power; we need to understand the many causal powers that interact to produce the event and how they affect each other.

By examining how the causal powers studied in the previous chapters interact to produce some illustrative examples of social events, this chapter puts the ontology developed in this book to work. Hence it shows how the pieces fit together to provide us with an ontological framework with empirical relevance and starts to give some indications of the methods we might use in applying it to particular cases. The first part of the chapter discusses an extended example of a hypothetical micro-social event. The second part considers macro-social events by examining how this approach could be applied to some examples from the sociological literature.

A micro-social interaction

This section examines some of the many causal forces at work in a simple hypothetical example of micro-social interaction. In it a customer goes into an electrical shop and purchases a television from a salesperson, who arranges for it to be delivered to the customer's home a few days later.[1] While this may reasonably be considered a single social interaction, it consists of a series of steps and actions by the participants. However, few of the individual actions in this sequence would make sense (in either causal or interpretive terms) if they were considered in isolation from the process as a whole. For simplicity of exposition, the customer will be considered to be male and the salesperson to be female, but most of the issues raised would be the same whatever the genders of the participants (at least in cultures that allow women to occupy such roles). The example is loosely based on my own knowledge and experiences of the retail environment and therefore reflects various cultural specificities, but this is unavoidable when we deal with specific cases. The discussion will focus primarily (but not entirely) on explaining the behaviour of the salesperson in this process and will be ordered roughly in the order of the sales process itself.

Typically the first stage in this process will be the *approach*, in which the salesperson greets the customer and engages him in conversation. In doing so, the salesperson initiates an interaction situation. Indeed, the discussion between them may well instantiate a number of different interaction types. Both parties may regard it, for example, as an instance of the 'polite conversation' interaction situation, but also as an instance of the 'salesperson assisting customer' situation, and there may be a set of interaction norms pertaining to both types of situation. Indeed, the salesperson may deliberately frame the interaction in such a way as to encourage the customer to accept her definition of it (Goffman 1990 [1956]: 15), since some such definitions may be more conducive to successful selling. She may seek to frame the conversation as an instance of 'friendly conversation' as opposed to 'formal conversation', for example, thus hoping to invoke a sense

[1] This example also featured in an exchange in the *Journal for the Theory of Social Behaviour* (Elder-Vass 2007a, 2007e; King 2007; Porpora 2007; Varela 2007).

of obligation to her on the part of the customer. Some customers may resist this if, for example, they believe that a more confrontational definition of the situation will help them negotiate a better price. There may thus be a negotiation over the definition of the situation, which influences the outcome of the purchase process.

Even in this negotiation, of course, other causal influences may be at work. The salesperson, for example, may have been trained to shape conversations with customers towards the 'friendly conversation' model, in which case by doing so she will have been influenced by a normative context, but one that has itself been shaped by the causal power of the organisation itself. Furthermore, the customer may also bring different normative expectations that influence their own contribution to the negotiation of the definition of the situation.

The establishment of the interaction situation, then, is the outcome of a causal process in which different types of causal powers interact. Once it has been established, the interaction group itself has a causal influence, since its existence prompts the customer and salesperson to adopt the corresponding norms. Indeed, others may also be affected. Other customers and other sales staff, for example, may avoid interrupting the conversation because they recognise the existence of the interaction group and a norm that such interactions should not generally be interrupted.

The style in which the salesperson conducts this conversation will also be influenced in other ways by various norm circles of which she is a member. She may speak with an accent, for example, that was absorbed unconsciously into her *habitus* as she grew up, but that reflects prevailing linguistic norms in a particular community that she reproduces without being aware of doing so. Alternatively, she may speak with an accent that she has consciously modified in an attempt to distance herself from those linguistic norms. In either case, the linguistic norm circles concerned will have influenced the accent with which she speaks. That accent may, for example, affect the customer's perception of her professionalism and reliability, and therefore his inclination to buy, or his willingness to engage in friendly conversation.

The salesperson's style may also be affected by other norm circles. Particular shops, for example, may develop particular styles of dealing with customers. Anthony King documents a case in which the staff of a shop treated a customer with considerable rudeness and aggression, a style that was clearly encouraged in a cycle of endorsement and performance by both the manager and the other staff in the shop, who formed, in my terms, a norm circle for this style of behaviour (King 2007: 216–17). In other shops or businesses or retail cultures staff are systematically encouraged to behave in other styles – with respect, perhaps, or in a friendly manner. This may be the product of a very local norm circle, perhaps just the staff in the shop concerned, or of one that is fostered by the larger organisation as a matter of policy, or perhaps an external norm circle that is prevalent in a wider cultural milieu.

In some other respects, the salesperson's behaviour throughout the process will be shaped by the organisation that owns the shop and the television and employs the salesperson. That behaviour is in certain respects determined by her incumbency of the sales assistant role. She believes that she *can* sell the television and that she *should* sell the television because of her occupancy of the role. I do not mean to deny that the sales assistant exercises her individual agency and I shall examine shortly how her own causal powers appear in the process. But as long as she occupies the salesperson's role, certain behaviours are expected of her, such as agreeing to sell what the customer asks to buy (assuming it is in stock, etc.), taking payment and arranging delivery. No doubt she will have been taught these behaviours by *individuals* and no doubt she understands that *individual* managers will discipline or dismiss her if she fails to enact them adequately. Yet all of these people act in these ways towards her purely because they too are enacting roles. Neither they, nor the sales assistant herself, would behave in these ways if they were not part of the organisation as a whole. Although these influences on her behaviour are a result of the salesperson's recognition that she faces a particular *normative* environment, this normative environment is produced by the organisation, acting through its role incumbents (particularly her managers). Hence the salesperson's performance of the role is (downwardly) causally influenced by the organisation.

As the sales process progresses, the question arises of exactly what product it is that the customer will buy. In what is sometimes known as the *match* phase of the sales process, the salesperson seeks to identify the customer's needs and a product that will meet them. Sometimes, as Porpora points out, the organisation may encourage the salesperson to try to sell the customer a more expensive television by paying

her a commission on sales (Porpora 2007: 196). While there may be
no rule stating that she *must* try to do this, this is nevertheless a normative structure, in which certain types of behaviour are endorsed,
in this case through financial incentives, by a norm circle. Such a
norm circle might include the organisation's sales managers, if they
are responsible for introducing the incentive, but to be effective such
incentives must be backed up with messages to the staff informing
them of these incentives and encouraging them to respond to them,
and whichever other staff communicate those messages will also form
part of the norm circle. Of course, as Porpora also notes, the salesperson may find such 'selling up' unethical – but this is still a case
in which her action is normatively influenced, in this case by norms
of ethical treatment of people absorbed from some wider normative
community, for example a religious community of which the sales
assistant is a member.

Within this matching process the salesperson may also be influenced by material objects; the shop may have a computer system, for
example, that tells her what stock is available of the different televisions in the range, which may influence what she tries to sell. Or
she may have personal experience of the advantages or disadvantages
of different types of television, which she uses in recommending one
model rather than another. In such cases, these material objects have
themselves exerted a casual influence over her behaviour, though in
the case of the computer system it may do so as an agent of the organisation, just as human employees may do so.

Finally, let us assume that the salesperson *closes* the sale: she
secures the customer's agreement to purchase a television. Now, when
the sales assistant sells the television, she does not do so on her own
behalf. She does not own the television – the organisation does. She
sells it in her capacity as a part of that organisation. In other words, it
is the organisation that sells the television, though it does so through
the sales assistant, who is one of its parts. The causal power of the
organisation to sell a television is in effect delegated to the salesperson, who exercises that causal power on the organisation's behalf.
Just as we accept that human beings are causally responsible for the
behaviour of their parts when it is directed by their decisions, so we
must accept that organisations are causally responsible for the behaviour of their members or employees when that behaviour is motivated
by organisational policy and roles.

Furthermore, the customer would not hand over his money to this salesperson unless he believed that she had, through her role incumbency, the right on behalf of the business she represents to sell the television he expects in return. Although he is served by an individual person, he knows that she does not own the television and will not deliver it to him personally but he takes her to be an authorised representative of a reputable business against which he would have legal redress should the television fail to arrive. In other words, while some aspects of the customer's behaviour towards the sales assistant may be oriented to her as an individual – he may greet her and chat about the weather, for example, before buying the television – others are oriented towards her as a part of an organisation. The customer only purchases the television from her because he takes her to be acting as part of the organisation that owns it and so his behaviour as an actor external to it is causally influenced by the existence of the organisation as such.

No doubt many other factors could be added to this account, but it is already clear that even in this relatively simple case of microsocial interaction our salesperson is subject to a substantial range of causal influences on her behaviour. The organisation that employs her, the interaction group formed between her and her customer, a broad range of norm circles and even material objects like televisions and computers exert their influence on what she does and how she does it. But does this leave her with no control over her own behaviour? Not at all. The individual still has the opportunity to choose – for example, whether to perform the role at all and to make decisions about *how* to do so. Indeed, there may be conflicts between the pressures on her that mean she *must* choose between them in deciding how to perform her role.

To see how this works we need to return to the action-determination process outlined in chapter 5 and the process through which norm circles influence individuals discussed in chapter 6. None of the causal influences listed in the last few paragraphs operate directly and physically upon the salesperson's actions. All of them are mediated through their effects on her beliefs and dispositions. The linguistic norms with which she grew up may have become embedded in her dispositions without her ever consciously choosing to speak in a particular way. Many of the other norm circles discussed above will have shaped her beliefs about the normative environment she faces as a result of her experience of endorsing and enforcing behaviour and led to decisions on her part to behave in particular ways, decisions that then become embedded in dispositions to conform (or not) with the norms concerned. Even her experience of physical objects such as computers and televisions influences her by becoming embedded in knowledge that she may draw upon in the process by which her action is determined. All these influences, in other words, operate upon her by shaping her mental properties and in particular her beliefs and dispositions.

If the account of action determination outlined in chapter 5 is correct, such beliefs and dispositions may be drawn upon in a non-conscious process that determines her actions. Where there is no conflict between them, she may go on to act on the basis of these dispositions without further conscious deliberation. She may produce her usual accent and her usual friendly greeting, for example, without consciously deciding what to say or how. But other actions may require some deliberation. If, for example, the customer asks a question, she may have to consider how to reply. More significantly, though, there will be cases where different pressures on the salesperson pull in conflicting directions and in such conditions she may have to make decisions about which way to go. Thus, for example, the pressures that Porpora identifies – sales incentives on the one hand and ethical concerns about pushing customers towards costly alternatives they do not need on the other – may come into conflict with each other. In such cases, the salesperson will have to consciously choose whether to sell up or not.

King has suggested that this model of structure and agency commits us to ontological dualism (King 2007: 217). Dualists, he argues, 'need to explain how structure imposes upon individuals without reducing them to "cultural dopes". Dualistic theories often find it difficult not to oscillate between voluntarism and determinism in describing this relationship' (King 2006: 469). But the ontology outlined here does not commit us to this sort of dualism.

On the one hand, it does *not* entail reducing the individual (e.g. our salesperson) to a 'dope', devoid of any influence of her own on the transaction, as some theories of structure might do. Her actions are influenced by a great many causal powers, some of them social structural powers, but these influences are mediated in an action-determination process in which she as an individual retains the capability of influencing the outcome through her decisions. Her behaviour is therefore multiply determined by the interacting causal powers of the following: (a) the organisation; (b) a number of distinct norm circles; (c) the interaction group formed by herself and her customer; (d) material things; and (e) the individual herself. The influence of organisations, norm circles and the interaction group is mediated through the individual's beliefs about the normative environment that she faces and the dispositions she has formed due to unanalysed environmental pressures. Where these are in conflict with each other or with other elements of the situation the assistant faces, she as an individual must make decisions on how to resolve these difficulties: decisions on how to enact her role.

Nor, on the other, does this ontology commit us to voluntarism, since those decisions are themselves causally influenced by the set of dispositions and beliefs that the individual has acquired from her past social experience, itself causally influenced by many varieties of social structure.

Micro-social explanations

As I have suggested already, one strength of this kind of explanation of a social event is that it reintroduces the complexity that is abstracted from when we focus on identifying individual causal mechanisms. We cannot give a realistic account of the interactions of causal mechanisms that produce even quite a simple social event without reintroducing this complexity.

In some senses, this style of explanation can be compared with the explanatory style that has been popularised in recent years by actor network theorists. For them, any given event is to be explained as a coming together of the influences of a wide and unpredictable network of actors, both human and non-human; and when any given actor acts it is in effect the whole network that acts through them. As Bruno Latour puts it, 'Action is not done under the full control of consciousness; action should rather be felt as a node, a knot, and a conglomerate of many surprising sets of agencies that have to be slowly disentangled' (Latour 2005: 44). And more poetically, 'An "actor"… is not the source of an action but the moving target of a vast array of entities swarming toward it' (Latour 2005: 46).

Perhaps the most substantial difference between the account given here and that of the actor network theorists, however, is that they are highly resistant to the idea that social structures may be included in this network of entities. Despite occasional heavily quali-fied acknowledgements that structural sociology may sometimes be of value (e.g. Latour 1996: 200; 2005: 1, 226–7), Latour consist-ently encourages us to substitute explanatory references to individual actors in place of references to social structure. He even entitles one chapter 'How to keep the social flat' (Latour 2005). One part of his argument is that instead of taking social structures for granted, we should trace the associations between actors that produce what we take to be the effects of social structures. This part is entirely con-sistent with my argument in this book: we cannot give a full account of the workings of social structures unless and until we can explain how it is that these structures are produced by associations between actors. But although Latour sometimes writes as if he were just defer-ring the moment at which structure is recognised, he never seems to finally arrive at this moment. In the sociology that results, 'there is no society, no social realm, and no social ties, *but there exist transla-tions between mediators that may generate traceable associations*' (Latour 2005: 108–9). In the end, then, Latour denies the causal powers of social structures.[2] But the central argument of this book is that we cannot understand what is occurring in even the simplest social events without recognising the vast range of causal contribu-tions made by social structures – which also act through individual human actors.

The reintroduction of complexity that occurs when we seek to explain individual micro-social events in this way, however, is a weakness as well as a strength. Even the simple example discussed above could be extended in many different directions to include many more causal factors that have an impact on the interaction. Many of these causal factors are mediated through beliefs and dispositions of the actors concerned that they may be unaware of or unwilling to reveal, with the result that real empirical cases face further obstacles to uncovering reasonably complete explanations. However far we extend the analysis and however carefully we investigate the motiv-ations of the participants there will always be some factors that we have missed and perhaps some significant ones.

---

[2] For a fuller discussion of the relation between actor network theory and critical realism, see Elder-Vass (2008c).

All explanations must therefore necessarily neglect many of the causal powers that contribute to the event being explained. A good explanation will seek to focus selectively on the most relevant causal factors and there are at least two important criteria of relevance: first, the aspect of the event that we are seeking to explain, and secondly, which powers make the most significant contribution to this aspect of the event. In practice, we do not seek to explain all aspects of an event, even as simple an event as selling something in a shop. Instead, there are specific things we want to know – why did the salesperson not try to sell a more expensive television to the customer, for example, or why did she speak to him in a particular accent and what effect did this have on the outcome? Whichever aspect we focus on there will be causal factors we can decide to ignore because they have little explanatory significance for it, though we cannot necessarily prejudge which factors these will be.

Of course, this leaves open a whole range of further methodological considerations. In particular, how can we tell which were the most significant causal factors for any given outcome? This is not a question to which we can give a general answer on ontological grounds; the answer will always depend on the nature of the processes at work and how they interact with each other.

Explaining individual events, then, is challenging in the social sciences, and always involves some subjective decisions about how far to follow the causal chains and which ones to prioritise. But this does not mean that we can never do it: there may be occasions when one or a few causal factors predominate so strongly that we can reasonably treat them as the primary cause(s). Perhaps the salesperson decided not to try to sell a more expensive television because she knew the customer and knew he could not really afford one. Perhaps she decided not to do it because of a recent conversation in which someone she respected criticised the practice. In such cases we may be able to give quite definite answers to the causal question; but it is always a contingent empirical question whether this will be the case.

The social sciences are not necessarily any worse off than the physical ones in this respect. If we want to explain why a bridge collapsed, for example, there may be a huge range of factors that contributed – the weight of traffic on it at the time, metal fatigue arising from the weight of traffic it has handled in the past, the wind, the chemical deterioration of its materials, shortcuts taken in the manufacturing process and flaws in the design, to list just a few of the possible factors in such a case. Even in cases with no human involvement at all there may be an equally wide range of factors at work. The natural sciences rely on just the same process of selectivity in identifying causes for particular events.

From micro to macro

Sociology, however, is not only concerned with the explanation of individual micro-social events; it also has macro-explanatory interests. The terms *micro* and *macro* derive from Greek words meaning *small* and *large*, respectively. In economics, they are used uncontroversially to refer to two different well-defined areas of the subject. Microeconomics studies individual markets and macroeconomics studies aggregate variables such as the rates of unemployment, inflation and interest in whole economies. But in sociology the distinction between micro and macro is more ambiguous. *Micro*-sociology, on the one hand, is fairly universally thought of as the study of individual social interactions between small numbers of people, but the criteria that distinguish this from the *macro*-social are much less clearly agreed. Münch and Smelser, for example, list seven alternative senses of the distinction (Münch and Smelser 1987: 356–7). Often *micro* is equated with individual agency and *macro* with social structure, so that the micro–macro distinction collapses into the debate over the relation between structure and agency, but this understanding of the concept has been criticised by both Mouzelis and Giddens (Giddens 1984: 139; Mouzelis 1991: 32).

Without seeking to legislate over our use of these terms, let me try to bring some temporary order to this debate by suggesting that we can usefully distinguish between three different dimensions in which we could distinguish the macro-social. We may have *macro-actors*, events with *macro-consequences* and *macro-events*, which may be further divided into *collective macro-events*, *statistical macro-events* and *historical macro-events*.

Macro-actors can be equated directly with social entities with causal powers. Although I draw on Mouzelis' work in this section I define macro-actors differently than he does; he makes having macro-consequences the criterion of being a macro-actor and hence includes powerful individuals (his *mega-actors*) as well as collective entities in the category (Mouzelis 1991: 107). I suggest, however, that we must distinguish these two senses of *macro*. In my sense of *macro-actor*, the term refers to what Mouzelis calls collective entities. Most obviously, organisations such as states, corporations and trade unions are macro-actors, but so are norm circles and perhaps there are other types of structural macro-actors too. As we have seen, these always act *through* individual humans, but nevertheless in causal terms we can say that when they do it is ultimately the larger social entity that is acting. Much of the argument of this book is concerned with showing how it is that such entities can indeed be social actors; macro-actors, as I use the term, are social structures.

Secondly, as Mouzelis points out, some human individuals – his mega-actors – can have macro-effects even when acting in their own right (Mouzelis 1991: 107). Here an example might be the speculative activity of George Soros, which made a major contribution to forcing the British pound out of the European exchange rate mechanism (ERM) in 1992. Soros was a micro-actor in the sense that he was acting as a human individual, not on behalf of some larger organisation; but his action had large-scale consequences – it drove the pound out of the ERM, affected the exchange rate of sterling and thus had effects on millions or billions of economic transactions. Of course, it is not only human individuals that can produce macro-effects; macro-actors may also do so and are perhaps more likely to. When a state introduces a new tax regime, or declares war, or privatises a public service, for example, millions of subsequent social events and millions of people may be affected. The next section will briefly consider an event in which macro-actors interacted to produce macro-consequences: the signing of the treaty of Yalta in 1945.

Thirdly, some events may be considered *macro-events*, not because of their consequences (though they may also have macro-consequences) but because they are composed of an aggregation of micro-events. Thus, for example, if I withdraw my savings from a troubled bank, this is a micro-event, but a 'run on the bank' is a macro-event composed of many such withdrawals by different people. Macro-events may be divided into *collective*, *statistical* and *historical* macro-events.

In collective macro-events, a macro-actor acts, but through many of its parts at once and not just through a single one of its parts. Thus, for an army to charge, many soldiers must run forward at once and it is only when many micro-events of the required kind occur together that the macro-event occurs (these are therefore laminated events that include micro-social events at a lower level, in the terms of chapter 3). In such cases, the macro-actor still acts through its parts, but it does so by acting through many of its parts at once, unlike the cases we have considered so far, in which a macro-actor may act through a single individual.

Statistical macro-events, by contrast, are not actions of macro-actors but simply aggregations of micro-social events in which the actors are *not* parts of some common whole that acts through them. The divorce rate in a particular country, for example, is a statistical macro-event, since there is no single actor producing all of the divorces concerned; each is an independent micro-social event and their aggregation into a summary statistic is an artefact of the statistician. This does not mean, however, that we cannot offer explanations of such macro-statistical events, and such explanations need not be a simple aggregation of the explanations of the micro-events. To say, for example, that there was a run on the bank because lots of individuals decided to withdraw their savings and each of these decisions was the consequence of the interaction of many causal factors, tells us very little. Macro-explanations become useful when they abstract from some or most of the factors that contributed to each individual case. Thus, there may be some common factor that influenced all or most of the people who withdrew their savings. In such cases we can attribute the run on the bank to this common factor and dismiss all of the non-common factors that contributed to the many individual decisions as irrelevant to the macro-explanation.

Such macro-events may also be caused in part by structural factors that are not apparent in individual cases but nevertheless have a significant impact. Thus, for example, in explaining global warming (at one level a statistical macro-event, though perhaps also a historical one), we might trace this back to many micro-social events in which individuals and organisations used fossil fuels, but explain the frequency with which they did so in terms of the inability of unregulated markets to deal with the true costs of externalities. This may be a crucial causal factor even though it is more or less hidden to those whose actions lead, in the aggregate, to global warming. Such mechanisms point us towards further types of social structure that have not been theorised in this book, but which must be included in a more comprehensive account of the causal powers of social structure.

Statistical macro-events have a particularly important place in the history of social structural explanations and the last part of this chapter will examine the *locus classicus*: Durkheim's analysis of suicide rates.

Finally, historical macro-events are similar to statistical macro-events in some respects. They are aggregations of micro-social events in which the actors are not necessarily parts of some common whole, but in which the set of micro-social events collectively constitute a change or episode of historical significance – the French Revolution, for example, or the Watergate scandal. The construction of such aggregations as a single macro-event is once again an artefact, but it may not be an artefact of an academic observer; the people involved may themselves see this as a coherent macro-event. These are perhaps the most complex kind of macro-social events, but the explanatory issues they raise are essentially similar to those involved in explaining the other kinds of events discussed above, so I will not consider them further in this chapter.

Macro-actors and macro-consequences

The issues raised by macro-actors and macro-consequences may be briefly illustrated with an example used by Mouzelis: 'the face-to-face encounter between Churchill, Roosevelt and Stalin at Yalta in 1945 led to crucial decisions which, among other things, shaped the post-war map of Europe and profoundly affected the lives of millions of people' (Mouzelis 1995: 18). As Mouzelis points out, this event had wide-ranging consequences at least partly because 'the interacting individuals [occupied] a powerful institutionalised social position' (Mouzelis 1995: 18). It is important, however, to separate these two considerations: the nature of the actors and the consequences of their interaction. These same actors may have done many other things in their roles as leaders of powerful states, which had relatively minor consequences.

In some respects, the positions of these leaders are similar to that of any other individual who acts on behalf of a collective social entity, such as our television salesperson. The salesperson acts on behalf of the retailer in agreeing to sell a television and when she does so the organisation exercises its causal powers through her, though she also exercises some influence over the process. In the same way these world leaders acted on behalf of the states they represented, which exercised their causal powers through them, even though they also exercised some personal influence over the process. The salesperson is taken as a legitimate representative of the retailer by the customer who acts as they do because of this belief. In the same way these world leaders treated each other as the legitimate representatives of the states concerned and acted towards them as they did because of this belief. In both cases, then, the individuals acted on behalf of an organisation and were treated by the other parties as doing so, and in both cases any explanation of how these individuals acted would have to include an analysis, not only of their own motivations as individuals but also of the whole array of social structural forces operating upon and through them. At Yalta, then, it was states and not only individuals that were acting.

Equally significant, however, are the differences between the cases. As occupants of roles carrying enormous authority within the states concerned, Churchill, Roosevelt and Stalin may have been less constrained by detailed role descriptions than our salesperson (particularly so in the case of Stalin, who had dispensed with the constraints imposed on leaders by a democratic political system), with more control over both the projects of the organisation concerned and the strategies they could adopt in pursuit of them. Furthermore, what Mouzelis calls situational factors (Mouzelis 1995: 104–7) could have enhanced their opportunities for reflexive input to the process of negotiation: this was not a routine interaction that could easily follow a heavily norm-regulated process (although standard diplomatic protocols governed some aspects of the interaction) but in many respects a unique historical event where the most important decisions could not be shaped by established norms.

Perhaps the most significant difference, however, is that in this case the *organisations* concerned had enormous power. Between them the three states had military and/or political control over much of the world. This control depended upon a complex set of relationships that had arisen in turn from a series of historical (morphogenetic) processes – not only the military progress of the war itself, but also the historical legacy of British and Russian imperialism. It was the enormous causal powers possessed by these three governments as a result of these relationships and this history that created the *potential* for an agreement between them to have momentous effects. And it was as an agreement between *states* that it had these effects, not as an agreement between these three individuals.

The Yalta agreement, then, must be seen as an agreement between *macro-actors*, not because the individuals concerned were particularly important, but because it was an agreement between collective entities: the three states concerned. But it was also a social event with *macro-consequences*. It led to the re-drawing of several European state boundaries and to the division of Europe into areas under Soviet and Western control. Hence, as Mouzelis puts it, it 'profoundly affected the lives of millions of people' (Mouzelis 1995: 18, cited above). We must, however, exercise some caution in making such claims.

First, according to the model of causation advocated in this book, it is not events but the causal powers of things that cause subsequent events, so the claim that an event can have macro-consequences needs to be explained. This is straightforward enough if we recognise that events are changes in things. It is not an event as such that causes subsequent events, but if the first event brings about an important change in the powers of things to cause subsequent events then we can reasonably say that it has had causal consequences. The Yalta conference, for example, created a disposition amongst the leaders of the states concerned to act in conformity with the agreement, a disposition that then contributed to many subsequent events, such as orders issued by these leaders to their military commanders.

Secondly, according to this model of causation, events are never determined by single causes. Although the conference at Yalta produced dispositions to act in certain agreed ways and these rippled out into military orders and no doubt in many other directions, other factors continued to interact with these causal influences in the determination of individual events. Stalin, for example, chose not to implement the agreement to conduct free elections in Poland after the conclusion of the war, by which time he could afford to ignore the disapproval of the Western powers over how the Soviet Union acted in Eastern Europe. Nevertheless, Mouzelis' conclusion remains true; though the Yalta agreement was only one amongst many causal factors that shaped post-war Europe, it seems reasonable to agree that it made a crucial contribution to the demarcation of the spheres of influence of the Soviet Union and the Western powers and was therefore a significant causal influence on millions of subsequent social events. This encounter was thus not only an encounter between macro-actors but also one with macro-consequences.

Collective macro-events

There is an analytic distinction between macro-actors, macro-consequences and macro-events. In a macro-event, many micro-events are compounded in one of three ways, which I have labelled *collective*, *statistical* and *historical*. This section will focus primarily on statistical macro-events, but let me begin with a few brief comments on collective macro-events.

The concept of a collective macro-event was illustrated above with the case of an army charging in a battle. Now, like the contribution of a politician to an international negotiation, this is an action of a macro-actor, in this case the army, and it seems likely to be an action with macro-consequences. It may, for example, make a substantial difference to whether many hundreds or thousands of soldiers live or die and there may be further consequences arising from its effect on the outcome of the battle, the war and thus the long-term balance of power between the states concerned. Unlike the contribution of the politician to the negotiation, however, this is *also* a macro-event, as it is composed of many distinct micro-social events in which many distinct individuals act. Still, this does not raise many new methodological issues. Each soldier taking part in the charge acts for just the same kinds of reasons as the salesperson selling a television: they are following the norms that define their roles as a result of a prior process of normative conditioning, driven by the causal power of the organisation to which they belong and embedded as a result in their beliefs and dispositions. The strength of conditioning required to lead people to risk their lives to conform with their role norms is no doubt greater than in the case of the salesperson's role and in fact modern armies devote a great deal of effort to this process. But if we examined the motivation of each soldier and produced a retrodictive explanation of why they participated in the charge, we would find the same sort of mix of causal powers at work. And if we compared these analyses for each soldier, we would be likely to find a strong common factor: their disposition to follow the order to charge arises from the power of a set of norm circles that have in turn been shaped by the power of the organisation to which they belong: the army. If this is so, we can give an explanation of this macro-event in terms of the causal powers of an interlinked set of social structures, while recognising that these causal powers have been mediated through their effects on the many individual soldiers involved. Because the mechanism through which this occurs is identifiable (as should be clear from the previous two chapters) this is an explanation, I suggest, in which the roles of both structure and agency have been recognised and reconciled.

There is one methodological issue that arises here, however, and it is one that we also find in considering statistical macro-events: alongside this common factor, there will be many varied non-common factors that influence the decisions of the various soldiers. One, for example, may feel a debt of loyalty to the army for giving them a worthwhile life; another a desire to make some family member proud of them; another a fear of the consequences of desertion. And indeed they may also have many different doubts about the decision to charge. But if we are to give an explanation of the macro-event, we will have to abstract from all the unshared motivations that contribute to the many personal decisions (negative as well as positive) and identify the factors that are collectively decisive. I do not propose to examine *how* to do this; it is a non-trivial task that requires both theoretical and empirical work and the work required will vary from case to case. My point is that this is a further methodological issue that arises when we consider macro-events.

Statistical macro-events: Durkheim and suicide

The paradigmatic sociological consideration of this issue is Émile Durkheim's work on suicide rates (Durkheim 1952 [1897]). The suicide rate in a given country in a given year is a statistical macro-event: it summarises a large number of individual micro-events, but not micro-events that combine to produce a specific action of a macro-actor. Durkheim uses statistical analysis to show that we can abstract from a great many factors that have sometimes been suggested as influencing rates of suicide. Whatever impact these factors may have on particular individuals contemplating suicide, when we come to consider the macro-event, they are of no significance to the explanation.

Although Durkheim is often dismissed as a positivist, there are significant elements of a realist approach even in this, his most positiv-
istic work (see Keat and Urry 1975: 80–91).[3] Most significantly, he
does not content himself with finding statistical correlations between
suicide rates and other 'social facts'; instead he seeks to identify the
mechanisms that are responsible for those correlations. Consider his
famous discussion of egoistic suicide and its empirical relation to religious affiliations (Durkheim 1952 [1897]: 152–216). His empirical
analysis shows that Protestants are more likely to commit suicide than
Catholics. A positivist could rest content with this correlation and
say that Protestantism is a cause of suicide. Durkheim, by contrast,
asks why Protestants are more likely to commit suicide and goes in
search of a mechanism.[4] He finds it in the fact that Protestantism does
not bind its adherents to such a comprehensive body of beliefs and
practices. The Protestant is allowed and indeed encouraged to be 'the
author of his faith', interpreting the Bible himself – but the Protestant
is allowed to do so because his religion has overthrown many of the
traditional beliefs that continue to be endorsed and enforced by the
Catholic Church (Durkheim 1952 [1897]: 158–9). Hence,

if religion protects man against the desire for self-destruction, it is not that
it preaches the respect for his own person … but because it is a society.
What constitutes this society is the existence of a certain number of beliefs
and practices common to all the faithful, traditional and thus obligatory.
The more numerous and strong these collective states of mind are, the
stronger the integration of the religious community, and also the greater its
preservative value. (Durkheim 1952 [1897]: 170)

Indeed, the generality of this mechanism is confirmed for Durkheim
by evidence that integration into the family also tends to discour-
age suicide and he argues that the same applies to political society
(Durkheim 1952 [1897]: 208). Hence, Durkheim believes, the frequency of a certain group of suicides, those he calls egoistic, can be

---

[3] My argument implies that even Keat and Urry understate the realist element
of Durkheim's analysis of suicide.
[4] One implication is that quantitative techniques are entirely compatible with
realism as long as we are cautious about how we use them. Correlations are
not causes but possible pointers to mechanisms, and further work is required
in order to hypothesise those mechanisms (Manicas 2006: 89, 97).

explained by the degree of integration within the social group whose suicide rate is being measured: the extent to which, and the strength with which, the group regulates the behaviour of its members. Here we have a case of one social fact, the rate of suicide, being explained by another, the degree of social integration – precisely the form of explanation he advocates in his methodological works.

Critics have often asked, however, just how Durkheim's explanation of the rate of suicide relates to the causation of *individual* acts of suicide (see Berk 2006).[5] Unless there is a clear mechanism by which lack of integration can influence the decisions of individuals, it is hard to see how it can influence the suicide rate as a whole. Although Durkheim's account of this mechanism is rather loose, the core of his argument is that individuals with low degrees of social integration lack a sense of meaning, purpose, belonging and obligation to others, which he labels 'excessive individualism' (Berk 2006: 70–1; Durkheim 1952 [1897]: 209–12). While it seems plausible to argue that this removes some potential obstacles to suicidal impulses, it is more difficult to see how excessive individualism constitutes a positive reason for committing suicide, as Durkheim argues. And at the level of the individual, the removal of obstacles to suicide (or even excessive individualism, if it constitutes a positive reason for suicide) across an entire social group does not constitute an adequate explanation of why some people commit suicide and others do not. Durkheim seems to resist introducing matters of individual psychology into his account, perhaps because in seeking to explain suicide rates in sociological terms one of his objectives is to assert sociology's independence from psychology (Lukes 1973: 215–16). The consequence, however, is that he ends up relying on the unexplained assumption that some individuals just happen to be more 'suicide prone' than others (Lukes 1973: 217).

I suggest, however, that Durkheim's problem can be solved without relinquishing the causal significance of the social structures involved. The key to doing so is once again the model of multiple determination advanced by Bhaskar, in which any single event is always the outcome of multiple interacting causal powers (see chapter 3). This is somewhat alien to Durkheim's explicit discussions of cause. He argues, in particular, that all events of the same type must have the same cause

---

[5] Other criticisms of his argument are summarised in Lukes (1973: 217–22).

and so, for example, 'if suicide depends on more than one cause, it is because, in reality, there are several kinds of suicides' (Durkheim 1964 [1894]: 129; also see Durkheim 1952 [1897]: 277). The implication would seem to be that each case of suicide falls into one of these kinds and is caused by the single type of cause responsible for all suicides of that kind. As Keat and Urry point out, this is incompatible with the realist understanding of effects as arising from 'the complex interrelations between mechanisms, structures and background conditions' (Keat and Urry 1975: 85).

Once we recognise multiple determination we can argue that any individual's act of suicide is produced by the interaction of a number of causes. We might expect that their personal circumstances, their personality and their social context will all be relevant. They might, for example, have suffered some emotional, positional or financial loss, or a series of them, that lead them to question whether life is worth living. Some individuals may feel less optimistic or secure than others, whether as a result of some genetic predisposition or as a result of their life history, or some combination of the two. And some will be less strongly integrated into a set of norm circles that might otherwise have given them a sense of both meaning and belonging, as well as regulating their behaviour. Any of these factors might individually make an individual more likely to commit suicide, but none of them alone would causally determine such an outcome.

Each individual therefore possesses a set of dispositions and beliefs that have been influenced not only by the kinds of social factors identified by Durkheim, but also by other social factors, by biological and psychological factors and indeed by historical contingency. And in the end suicide is an intentional act. Individuals are not physically compelled to commit it by social or other forces but choose to do so in an act of individual agency, but one that is shaped and influenced by the set of beliefs and dispositions they have acquired. Ironically, despite his more explicit methodological statements, Durkheim sometimes seems to advance arguments that fit more plausibly into this kind of framework. He argues, for example, that the different types of suicide are sometimes combined (Durkheim 1952 [1897]: 287–9) and (very briefly) that personal temperament and circumstances may play a role (Durkheim 1952 [1897]: 294).

Given such a framework for explaining suicide, we can say that each individual decision to commit it is produced causally by a complex set of contributing factors that may vary significantly from case to case. Nevertheless, we can also say that if we compare two social groups that are similar in other respects, a difference between the two groups in one of the factors that tends to encourage suicide would tend to increase the suicide rate in one relative to the other. And this gives us a plausible interpretation of Durkheim's argument: some Protestants, for example, who are in other respects equally likely to commit suicide as corresponding Catholics, will commit suicide even though the corresponding Catholics do not, because the nature of their religion leads them to be less socially integrated and thus to have a reduced sense of meaning, belonging and obligation to others. This does not mean that the lower rate of social integration *alone* causes these individuals to commit suicide, as Durkheim's argument might sometimes seem to imply, but rather that in a population with a given mix of other pressures encouraging and discouraging suicide, a reduction in social integration – in the influence of norm circles – will be enough to push some people over the boundary that separates them from suicidal intent.

We can, in other words, give explanations of some statistical macro-events in terms of the causal powers of social structures while recognising that each of the component micro-social events is multiply determined by many interacting causal powers, including individual agency and indeed biological and psychological causal factors, as well as the powers of social structures. Ascribing causal powers to social structures can therefore be entirely compatible with recognising the causal powers of individual human agency even in the kinds of cases discussed by Durkheim.

Social facts, then, *can* sometimes be explained in terms of other social facts. But this does not mean, as Durkheim argued, that they *must always* be explained *only* in terms of other social facts. The charge of an army is also a social fact, but the idiosyncratic individual decision of its commanding general may be as important a causal factor as the normatively established and organisationally driven discipline upon which the charge also depends.

Conclusion

This chapter has illustrated some of the ways in which the causal powers of social structures interact both with each other and with other kinds of causal powers to produce social events, both micro and macro. In the earlier chapters, which were focused on identifying individual structures and the mechanisms that generate their causal powers, we could abstract from a great deal of complexity. As soon as we shift, however, to the retrodictive explanation of particular events, we must come to terms with the massively complex causal interactions that characterise our social world.

For a full explanation of any actual social event, we must recognise the importance of the *multiple determination* of actual events. In principle, we need to identify all the powers that are interacting to produce the event and how they affect each other. Once we turn to retrodiction, we cannot invoke only social structural powers; we must bring back in the person and indeed a range of other entities that may have influenced the event concerned. In practice, however, retrodiction faces enormous challenges. It depends, for example, on retroductive accounts of the entities and mechanisms to which we attribute causal powers, which may be difficult to disentangle from other entities when there are complex inter-relationships between them. And even when we have a coherent view of some of the causal powers involved, we can never exhaustively identify all of the causal factors contributing to even a relatively simple social event.

Without a realist ontology of causal powers, it might perhaps be tempting to believe that the resulting complexity is so great as to defeat any possibility of causal explanation in the social world. But the ontology of causal powers gives us a framework in which it becomes possible to combine retroduction and retrodiction to produce causal explanations, even in the face of this complexity. As Peter Manicas quite rightly points out, much the same situation confronts the natural sciences, but natural scientists are generally happy to focus on explaining the causal mechanisms at work in complex events without necessarily following through the full details of a retrodictive explanation (Manicas 2006: 1). The best we can hope for in most cases is to identify the key causal powers at work in a given case and the key interactions between them. Such identifications, like all knowledge, will always be fallible. This chapter has tried to show how the ontological approach developed in this book gives us tools to tame these problems, though it cannot eliminate them – they are built into the nature of our social world and indeed our universe.

9 | Conclusion

This book has argued that social structures have causal powers and sought to explain how this can be the case. This concluding chapter will summarise the argument, draw out its implications for the question of naturalism and discuss some of the issues that need to be addressed in further work.

The causal power of social structures

The claim that social structures have causal powers depends on a realist philosophical ontology of causal powers as relationally emergent properties of things (discussed in chapters 2 and 3). In this ontology, the world in which we live is understood to be populated by entities, or things, each of which is in turn composed of other such entities. At one level down from the entity we find a set of its parts, but each of these is also an entity composed of parts and this hierarchical structure continues all the way down to the most fundamental components of our world, whatever they may be. The concept of emergence is essential to our understanding of these structures and their causal powers because it enables us to see how the entities at each level can have causal powers of their own, despite being in a sense 'nothing more' than a collection of lower-level parts.

Relational emergence theory argues that entities may possess emergent properties, which are produced by mechanisms that in turn depend on the properties of the entity's parts and how those parts are organised. This organisation allows the parts to interact in ways that are specific to entities of the type concerned and this process of interaction is the mechanism that gives the entity a causal power. One implication is that it may be possible to produce an explanation of how those parts, organised in that way, produce such a property at the higher level. This, however, does not mean that relational emergence is compatible with the *eliminative reduction* of these higher-level properties, as it might seem to be. Those parts would not be related in that way if they were not organised into an entity of the relevant kind, and therefore the collective power they have when organised into such an entity is a power of the higher-level entity and not of the parts. Even though it may be possible to explain relationally emergent powers, we cannot *explain them away*.

The relational concept of emergence, then, has the twin benefits that it provides a justification for treating the emergent properties of higher-level entities as causally effective in their own right, while at the same time allowing us to explore the ways in which these properties are produced as a consequence of the properties of the parts and the way in which they are organised to form this particular sort of higher-level entity.

These emergent properties are, I have argued, identical with the *real causal powers* described by Roy Bhaskar in his theory of causation and this book has made use of his argument that each particular case of *actual causation* is the outcome of the interplay of a variety of such real causal powers. Actual events, then, are co-determined by the causal powers or emergent properties of the entities that are significantly involved in the production of those events.

The arguments of chapters 2 and 3 therefore provide a general ontological framework that can be applied to entities and their properties at any level of the emergence hierarchy. It is this framework that underpins the argument that social structures and human individuals are entities with emergent properties, which can interact to co-determine social events. These arguments also provide a methodological framework for examining the relationship between a whole and its parts (outlined in chapter 4), on which I have drawn in considering the relationship between social structure and its human parts and that between human beings and their biological parts. The implication of this framework is that if we wish to explain the emergent properties of any entity, we must consider the following: (a) its parts; (b) the relations between those parts that are characteristic of this particular type of entity; (c) the set of morphogenetic causes that have produced the entity in its current form; (d) the set of morphostatic causes that stabilise the entity and ensure its continued survival; and (e) the mechanisms by which its parts and relations produce the specific properties of the entity.

One implication is that in the case of human individuals, our causal powers of agency are emergent from our biological constitution. The properties and powers we have depend synchronically on the material parts of which we are composed and the relations and interactions between them. But this does not mean that human *actions* are purely determined by biological forces. Like any other events, they are co-determined by a variety of interacting causes from a variety of ontological levels. The mechanisms through which human action is determined provide opportunities for our action to be influenced both by the social structures in our environment, but also by our own uniquely human powers of conscious reflexive thinking and indeed by biological factors. This is possible because all these factors can diachronically affect our beliefs and dispositions by affecting the neurological networks that underpin their emergence (altering our neurological structure and therefore our emergent mental properties). These altered beliefs and dispositions then feed into a process of action determination that may proceed without our conscious awareness.

Human beings, then, are entities with emergent causal powers, but like other such entities they do not have the power uniquely and totally to determine subsequent events. Rather, social events are always the outcome of many interacting factors, of which our input is only one. In providing an explanation of *how* human individuals can be causally effective (rather than merely taking this for granted), the argument of this book therefore also shows how this causal effectiveness can be reconciled with the causal effectiveness of *other* entities that affect social behaviour.

In particular, this book has stressed some of the many ways in which human causal powers interact with social structures in the causation of social events. If we are to place social theory on a sound ontological footing, we need to investigate the whole range of possible social structures, identify where the boundaries lie between the different types, establish which really do have emergent causal powers and investigate how those causal powers emerge. But there is an essential precursor to such an exercise: to demonstrate that the concept of emergence can apply to any social structures at all. To achieve this we need only show that at least *one* type of social structure is indeed emergent. This book has gone further and made the case for two major types of social structure: normative social institutions and organisations (as well as touching on the causal powers of less formal associations and interaction groups).

Normative social institutions, chapter 6 argued, are produced by the causal power of social groups that I call *norm circles*. A norm circle is an entity whose parts are the people who are committed to endorsing and enforcing a particular norm. Operating through its members, such a norm circle has the causal power to influence people to observe the norm concerned. Those individuals become aware that they face a normative environment (and not just some specific individuals) that will sanction their behaviour and this tends to create a disposition in them to conform with the norm concerned – although like any causal influence this one may be offset by countervailing influences. A particularly significant feature of norm circles is that they may be profusely intersectional: any given individual will belong to a large number of norm circles and, although these may tend to cluster, there is no necessity that they should all be congruent with each other and no necessity that they should all share the same membership. In complex contemporary societies, normative intersectionality is widespread.

Such intersectionality is fostered by the second major type of social structure considered here: organisations. Chapter 7 sought to show that organisations are also entities with emergent properties. Their parts are (at least primarily) human individuals, related to each other by a set of practices that are specific to the particular roles that each individual adopts within the organisation. While those roles are themselves normative structures, supported by norm circles that are to some extent shaped by the organisations themselves, they lead to further interactions between the members of the organisation concerned that can in turn produce further causal powers for the organisation as such. When they interact in these normatively coordinated ways, the individuals that make up an organisation behave differently than they would do if they were not parts of it and (whether individually or collectively) they have different effects on the world than they could have as individuals outside the organisation. The effect of this behaviour must then be seen as a causal effect of the organisation itself and not of the individual *qua* individual. Indeed, the implication is that when an individual acts on behalf of an organisation (or indeed a norm circle), then it is the organisation (or norm circle) that acts and not just the individual. In such cases, the social structure acts *through* the individual.

Organisations, then, *are* causally effective in their own right and a relational emergentist account shows us how this can be. However, this should give no succour to methodological collectivists, because the emergentist account developed here also recognises that social structures do not entirely *determine* human behaviour, but only *co-determine* it in conjunction with the causal powers of a great many other entities from a variety of levels of the emergence hierarchy, including human individuals themselves. Furthermore, this account encourages us to analyse *how* the emergent properties of organisations can be explained as an outcome of lower-level interactions. Such explanations are entirely compatible with the rejection of methodological individualism.

Social structures, then, are entities or things with causal powers. To say so, however, is to invite charges of reification or hypostatisation: the error of treating an abstraction as if it were a real thing. But if, as I have argued, groups of people are real and they do compose higher-level entities with emergent powers, arising from the ways in which the members of the group interact, then they *are* things in the sense that is significant for a causal powers ontology. As Durkheim puts it, social structures 'are things by the same right as material things, although they differ from them in type' (Durkheim 1964 [1894]: xliii). When we are employing *reification* to mean treating something as a thing then, as Bhaskar points out, it cannot be an error to reify something which really *is* a thing (Bhaskar 1975: 50).

Reification, however, is sometimes also taken to imply that in treating something as a thing we commit ourselves to the belief that it is static or unchanging and to a denial of the causal significance of its parts or of the agents that contribute to its causal significance. But neither of these is true of the argument of this book and neither, in any case, reflects an accurate understanding of the nature of *things*. Social structures, like many other things, are far from static and like other things with causal powers, their causal powers always depend on the interactions between their parts. Social structures are indeed things, but they are dynamic things whose powers depend on the activities of people.

For and against naturalism

At one level, this book advocates a form of naturalism, in the sense that it applies the same philosophical ontology to the objects of the social and natural sciences. The general theory of emergence describes a world in which the emergence of social entities depends on the same sort of structural relations as the emergence of natural entities and indeed they contain natural entities as their lower-level parts. The approach to method outlined in chapter 4 is also a naturalistic *methodology*: it applies equally well to the social and the natural world. But much more needs to be said about the question of naturalism. On the one hand, some of the sources of resistance to naturalism need to be confronted, but on the other, we must recognise that naturalism itself needs to be problematised and qualified.

Despite these naturalistic elements, the emergentist approach advocated here also retains what might seem to be an anti-naturalistic element. In recognising that entities at different ontological levels have different sorts of properties that must be studied in different sorts of ways, it implies that at least some of the methods of the social sciences will differ from the methodologies of other sciences. Thus, for example, we need an interpretive element in the social sciences that we do not need in, say, physics.[1] This particular difference seems to distinguish sharply between the natural and the social sciences and thus to have *anti-naturalistic* implications.

However, other methodological differences between the sciences do not neatly follow the boundary between the natural and the social sciences. The natural sciences are by no means homogeneous in their methods, for the same reason as has been identified above: the disciplines of the natural sciences differ in their objects of study and these objects differ in their structures and properties (see chapter 1). In a sense, then, the methodology of the natural sciences themselves assumes that *methods* of study will differ between the disciplines, with the consequence that it is consistent with that methodology to employ different methods in sociology from, say, biology, just as it is consistent with that methodology to employ different methods in, say, astronomy and meteorology (Benton 1985: 190–2). Once we recognise this, the very concept of anti-naturalism is in danger of unravelling. If that concept rests on the assumption that all natural sciences share the same methods, then it is based on an empirical error. But if

[1] Note that the interpretive method is entirely compatible with a causal approach to the social sciences, as Weber, for example, argued (Weber 1978 [1922]: 4) (see also Sayer 2000: 17–18).

we assume that the natural sciences have diverse methods, then the suggestion that the social sciences are fundamentally different from the natural sciences because their methods differ is internally contradictory. The concept of anti-naturalism just will not bear the weight that is often placed upon it.

Nevertheless, it remains useful to examine similarities and differences between different groups of sciences and there is room for debate over the specific ways in which social entities are like and unlike other kinds of entities. Perhaps the biggest obstacle in recognising the similarities between social and other entities is the role that we ourselves play in them and the resulting temptation towards a causal variety of anthropocentrism: the temptation to see intentional human agents as the unique possessors of causal power in social interactions.[2]

Such beliefs might generate resistance to at least two major claims of this book. First, the argument that human behaviour is to be explained within the terms of just the same philosophical ontology as the behaviour of other natural entities. This flies in the face of extreme human exceptionalisms that see human behaviour as uncaused, or as caused by some process that is so radically unlike other natural processes as to be beyond the scope of a causal powers theory. To be more precise, the book argues that when individuals act, that action is the direct and immediate product of non-conscious brain processes and that conscious intentionality is itself a naturally caused phenomenon that acts as an input into this process, but only as one of many such inputs. This means that human individuals do sometimes make choices that affect their actions but it does not mean that they have free will in the controversial philosophical sense of making *uncaused* choices. We are choosing beings, but choosing is itself a natural process and one that is governed causally like any other. If this is the case, the sense we have of free will arises from the fact that we are the being doing the choosing, not because that choosing is uncaused.

Secondly, there might be anthropocentric resistance to the idea that institutions and organisations act in and through the actions of human beings. When I mark an exam paper, for example, and assign a mark, I do so as an arm of my university, not as an individual. The

---

[2] This position often seems to be taken implicitly; it is taken explicitly by Harré and his followers (Manicas 2006: 72–5, 115; Varela 2002; Varela and Harré 1996).

marking may rely on a number of my own personal causal powers, but it is the university that has the power to assign a mark and I do so on its behalf. Just as when I use my own arm to lift a bag it is me (as well as my arm) that is doing the lifting, so in the marking case it is the university (as well as me) that is doing the marking. But it is much easier to think of the action of an arm as 'really' an action of a human being than it is to think of the action of a human being as 'really' an action of an organisation or a norm circle. Just as anthropocentrism might lead us to question the causal ordinariness of human beings with respect to their parts, it might lead to questioning the causal ordinariness of human beings with respect to the wholes of which they themselves are parts. Yes, I am the one who thinks and writes comments and a number on a piece of paper, but it is the university acting through me that assigns an official mark to the exam script. We have no difficulty in accepting similar arguments when they are made for other kinds of things, but the causal myopia that afflicts us when our own causal contribution is centre stage may make it difficult to see that just the same argument applies to our own human actions.

Once we have cleared away such erroneous objections to naturalism, however, we must turn to examining some of the genuine differences between social structures and non-social ones. The fact that their parts – us – can store beliefs and dispositions that reflect our experience and decisions is an enormously significant difference. Even though it does not license anthropocentric denials of causal power to social structures, this does introduce a whole new level of complexity into the process by which they work. Because the influence of social structures such as norm circles is mediated through their effects on our stored beliefs and dispositions, there can be a temporal gap between sociological influence and individual action: a gap that has been central to realist accounts of social structure, such as those of Archer and Bhaskar. It also, however, makes possible an equally significant but largely neglected dimension of difference between social and non-social structures: the possibility of spatial disarticulation.

The spatial disarticulation of social structures

As a general rule, the entities studied by the natural sciences depend on relatively fixed spatial relationships between their parts, either static arrangements or stably dynamic relationships, such as an elliptical orbit, or the physiological structure of a body. Similarly, such entities generally have clear spatial boundaries that distinguish their internal parts from their external environments.

But social entities do not depend on these sorts of spatial fixity. Some, such as households, schools and cities, usually assume a set of relations that is spatially constrained by particular physical contexts, such as a house, a school building and yard, or the physical layout of the city, but even these have considerable room for spatial diversity of inter-relationships within these contexts. Thus, for example, school children move around within the school and they may go off site for sports activities or educational visits, all while they are still within the confines of the 'pupil' role.

Other organisations may have even looser spatial relationships. In a business corporation, for example, some of its activities may be focused on specific sites, such as office blocks or factories, but others may be much more far-flung, such as sales representatives visiting clients or buyers attending trade fairs. It is this inherent flexibility of spatial relationships that makes possible the unlimited extension of social entities across space and thus the phenomenon of 'globalisation'. More generally, it has been possible for social entities that developed in relatively localised spatial contexts to spread much more widely in space *without becoming new kinds of entity*. Thus, social entities do not depend on structural adaptation to increase their spatial reach or alter their spatial distribution, with the result that such changes can occur relatively quickly and easily.

All this is possible because social structures, or at least some varieties of them such as norm circles and organisations, do not depend on spatially specific physical relations between their parts to produce the mechanisms that give them their causal powers. Unlike non-social entities, they depend instead on the beliefs and dispositions of the human agents who are their parts to produce these mechanisms. The effectiveness of these beliefs and dispositions in regulating the interactions between these human parts is *not* dependent on those people being in specific spatial relations to each other. Such structures, we may say, can be *spatially disarticulated* – they can operate in the absence of any specific set of spatial relations between their parts.

This spatial flexibility does leave social theorists with one problem. When entities depend on spatial relations for their causal powers, it is usually relatively straightforward to identify their parts. But this is not necessarily the case for social structures. Perhaps the most striking example is provided by norm circles. While we may plausibly say that there is an actual set of people committed to endorsing and enforcing a particular norm, those people may be scattered unpredictably in space. Actually tracking down all the members of a typical norm circle in the contemporary world would probably be impossible.

But the problem may be still worse for organisations. Chapter 7 took it for granted that we knew which groups of people were the members of an organisation, but is this necessarily the case? Consider the case of a business corporation. We might assume that a corporation's parts are its employees, but in legal terms we could argue that it is really a company's shareholders that are its parts; and if we took some sort of dependence relation as the criterion of membership we might even argue that a company's customers should also be included in its parts. I cannot offer a decisive criterion for drawing such boundaries, though it seems most plausible to me to argue that it is the employees who are the parts of an organisation, on the grounds that they are committed to acting on behalf of the organisation. The point I want to make here, though, is that these questions only become significant because of the spatial disarticulation of the organisation: without clear spatial boundaries it becomes more difficult to determine the *ontological* boundaries of an entity.

Spatial disarticulation, however, also makes possible some crucial positive qualities of social structures. Above all, it makes possible intersectionality. Because individuals can be parts of a social group without being located inside some spatial boundary or in some specific spatial relationship with other members of the group, it becomes possible for them to be part of more than one social group. Thus, for example, I can be part of a university, part of a married couple, part of the British Sociological Association and part of a great many other social systems all at the same time (cf. Cilliers 1998: 7; Parsons 1966: 1; 1969: 354). This is quite different from the situation of most natural entities. Because of the physical boundedness of most natural systems, any entity that is part of one natural system cannot be part of another, except yet higher-level systems of which the first one is itself a part. An atom, for example, can only be part of one molecule at a time. It could, of course, via being part of the molecule also be part of a cell and via the cell also be part of a human being, but the molecule can be part of only one cell and the cell part of only one human being. A person, however, can be part of many different social structures by virtue of playing multiple different roles. To an extent, it is even possible for human beings to play multiple roles at the same time and in the same action. Thus, for example, if a manager in a business promotes a fellow member of a secret society whose principles include mutual assistance, they will, in a single action, be acting simultaneously 'in the role' of manager and society member.

The consequence of this is to introduce a unique dimension of complexity to the social sciences. By virtue of their overlapping membership of multiple social entities, human beings are subject to (possibly conflicting or contradictory) downward influences from a variety of different organisations and norm circles in which they are expected to play a part. If this were not the case, then normativity would indeed take the form that sometimes seems implicit in crude accounts of monolithic closed societies: everyone in a society would be committed to and subject to exactly the same set of norms. Such societies could fight for dominance but never mingle and interact in the way that real human groups do.

On occasions, any individual's role performance in one role is likely to be affected by the influence of other social structures (Biddle 1986: 82–4; Goffman 1990 [1956]: ch. 4). Indeed, as chapter 7 has suggested, the ontology of organisations *depends* on such intersectionality: managers, for example, perform their role as part of an organisation at least partly by acting as part of the proximal norm circles for the role norms of their staff. None of the complex structures of interaction between norm circles and organisations examined in that chapter would be possible if it were not for intersectionality and thus the spatial disarticulation of social structures.

The unique ways in which human behaviour is produced, then, are central to the differences between social entities and others, not because they force us to adopt a non-causal interpretive social science, but because they make possible the development of higher-level collective entities that are spatially (and indeed temporally) disarticulated and ontologically intersectional.

An agenda for research

This book has offered a framework for theorising about social structure and started to show how we might go about filling in that framework by analysing different types of structure. What it has not done is developed a *complete* theory of social structure, even at the level of retroducing the entities and mechanisms that constitute the various kinds of structure. While it has looked at two important types of structure in the shape of norm circles and organisations, there are certainly many more kinds of social structure and variants on these two kinds whose influence must also be understood. Indeed, the process of theorising these influences may also feed back into our understanding of those structures that have been discussed here.

This book has, for example, paid little attention to the roles of language, discourse, culture and knowledge. Yet all these play roles in forming our dispositions and beliefs and these in turn play a key role in forming normative institutional structures. In recent decades, this role has been stressed by social constructionists and indeed sometimes treated as if it undermines traditional understandings of structure and agency. In the most extreme formulations of this tradition, language and discourse are taken to shape both individual behaviour and everything that we understand as 'the social', making conceptions of structure and agency redundant.

For realists, such attributions of causal significance to language, discourse, culture and knowledge demand an investigation into *their* ontological structures and the identification of the mechanisms by virtue of which they can be causally effective. Such analysis has been conspicuously absent in most constructionist work and where it has been done the problem of causality has often been left unresolved. Here I have in mind the work of Foucault on discourse, which is examined carefully in *The Archaeology of Knowledge* (Foucault 2002 [1969]), while still leaving the source of the causal influence ascribed to discourse as something of a mystery (Dreyfus and Rabinow 1983: xxiv, 70, 81, 83).

I intend to address this by developing a social ontology of language, discourse, culture and knowledge that is based on the philosophical ontology outlined in the early chapters of this book. All these, I expect to argue, are themselves dependent on normative structures; all are products of the powers of different varieties of norm circles; and all interact with agents and other structures in complex ways that can ultimately be analysed using the tools of retroduction and retrodiction. If this is the case, then we may be able to recognise that language, discourse and the like do have causal significance and thus that there is some value in social constructionist arguments, while also recognising the importance of two realist arguments; first, that this causal significance can only be explained in realist terms and secondly that this causal significance is entirely compatible with, and interacts with, the causal powers of agents and other structures.

It is not only in the area of normative or lifeworld structures, however, that more work remains to be done. In analysing the ontology of organisations, this book has only begun to address the range of other structures whose causal powers arise from *non-normative* mechanisms, although they may also depend indirectly on normativity, as organisations do. Most strikingly, there is a need to analyse the mechanisms of what Habermas calls 'systems', notably the mechanisms behind money, markets and capital. The price mechanism, for example, steers the behaviour of participants in market systems, contributing to systematic macro-effects, including production and investment decisions, profits, losses, bankruptcy, growth, unemployment, poverty, the degradation of the environment and the satisfaction of our material needs. No social theory could claim to make sense of the contemporary social world without some recognition of the central role of such mechanisms. Unlike Habermas, I do not see these as governing an empirically distinct domain of social life. Rather, I suggest, systemic mechanisms interact with lifeworld mechanisms in almost all domains of social life. Any event that involves an economic transaction, for example, will be multiply determined by both systemic and lifeworld mechanisms. The example of selling a television discussed in chapter 8 amply illustrates the role of *lifeworld* mechanisms in such events, but there is much more to be said about the role of *systemic* mechanisms. While both orthodox economics and heterodox political economy have cast useful light on these mechanisms, neither has yet placed them in the kind of emergentist ontological framework that is developed here.[3]

There is also a need to theorise power more comprehensively. Both the ways in which structure and agency contribute to the possession of power and the ways in which power influences our social structures have been given relatively little attention here, focused as this book is on identifying structural mechanisms at the most abstract level.

[3] The work of Tony Lawson represents an important step in this direction (Fullbrook and Lawson 2009; Lawson 1997, 2003).

Likewise the fascinating relations between knowledge and power highlighted by Foucault need to be brought into this synthesis in ways that recognise the ontological foundations of both.

Even if all the above could be addressed, however, this would only take us as far as a fairly abstract ontology of the causal powers of social structures and a theory of the mechanisms behind them. Such an analysis could make a major contribution to placing the social sciences on a firmer ontological footing, but would still need to be filled out at a more empirical level. This would require substantial work on both the retrodiction of specific social events, showing how these social powers interact to produce them, and also the morphogenetic analysis of concrete structures, showing how they have come about historically. As the argument of chapter 4 implies, any social ontology must ultimately be validated by empirical application. Only a series of such applications could offer strong confirmation of the ontology and we could reasonably expect the process to throw up challenges requiring modification of the ontology itself.

There is much more to be done here than could ever be done in a single book, or even by a single researcher. The prospect is made a little less daunting if we recognise that a great deal of existing work in the social sciences is at least potentially compatible with the ontological framework that this book has begun to outline and could therefore be employed in the process of filling out this framework. But there can be no doubt that if the research programme sketched out above is to progress, it will depend on a dialogue between many voices. Indeed this book is already part of such a process, in which not only critical realists but a range of thoughtful social scientists of many different theoretical persuasions are engaged. It does not initiate this dialogue but does seek to nudge it in a different direction, by offering a coherent justification of the claim that social structure is best understood as the emergent causal powers of specific social entities. This, I argue, is a significant step towards the larger goal of putting the social sciences onto the firm ontological foundation that is sadly absent today.

References

Ackroyd, Stephen and Fleetwood, Steve (eds.) 2000. *Realist Perspectives on Management and Organisations*. London: Routledge.

Adams, Matthew 2006. 'Hybridizing habitus and reflexivity', *Sociology* 40: 511–28.

Ahrne, Göran 1994. *Social Organizations*. London: Sage.

Anderson, Benedict 1991. *Imagined Communities*. London: Verso.

Archer, Margaret 1979. *Social Origins of Educational Systems*. London: Sage.

1982. 'Morphogenesis versus structuration', *British Journal of Sociology* 33: 455–83.

1995. *Realist Social Theory: The Morphogenetic Approach*. Cambridge: Cambridge University Press.

1996. 'Social integration and system integration: developing the distinction', *Sociology* 30: 679–99.

1996 [1988]. *Culture and Agency*. Cambridge: Cambridge University Press.

1998. 'Realism and morphogenesis', in M. Archer, R. Bhaskar, A. Collier, T. Lawson and A. Norrie (eds.), *Critical Realism: Essential Readings*, pp. 356–81. London: Routledge.

2000a. *Being Human: The Problem of Agency*. Cambridge: Cambridge University Press.

2000b. 'For structure: its reality, properties and powers: a reply to Anthony King', *Sociological Review* 48: 464–72.

2003. *Structure, Agency, and the Internal Conversation*. Cambridge: Cambridge University Press.

2007. *Making Our Way Through the World: Human Reflexivity and Social Mobility*. Cambridge: Cambridge University Press.

forthcoming. 'Routine, reflexivity and realism'.

Ball, Philip 2000. *H₂O: A Biography of Water*. London: Phoenix.

Bedau, Mark A. 1997. 'Weak emergence', *Philosophical Perspectives* 11: 375–99.

Benton, Ted 1985. 'Realism and social science', in R. Edgley and R. Osborne (eds.), *Radical Philosophy Reader*, pp. 174–92. London: Verso.

206

Benton, Ted and Craib, Ian 2001. *Philosophy of Social Science*. Basingstoke: Palgrave.

Berger, Peter L. and Luckmann, Thomas 1971 [1966]. *The Social Construction of Reality*. Harmondsworth: Penguin Books.

Berk, Bernard B. 2006. 'Macro–micro relationships in Durkheim's analysis of egoistic suicide', *Sociological Theory* 24: 58–80.

Bertalanffy, Ludvig von 1971. *General System Theory*. London: Allen Lane.

Bhaskar, Roy 1975. *A Realist Theory of Science*. Leeds: Leeds Books.

1986. *Scientific Realism and Human Emancipation*. London: Verso.

1993. *Dialectic: The Pulse of Freedom*. London: Verso.

1998. 'Critical realism and dialectic', in M. Archer, R. Bhaskar, A. Collier, T. Lawson and A. Norrie (eds.), *Critical Realism: Essential Readings*, pp. 575–640. London: Routledge.

1998 [1979]. *The Possibility of Naturalism*. London: Routledge.

Biddle, Bruce J. 1986. 'Recent developments in role theory', *Annual Review of Sociology* 12: 67–92.

Blau, Peter M. 1976. 'Parameters of social structure', in P. M. Blau (ed.), *Approaches to the Study of Social Structure*, pp. 220–53. London: Open Books.

Blau, Peter M. and Schwartz, Joseph E. 1984. *Crosscutting Social Circles*. Orlando, FL: Academic Press.

Blitz, David 1992. *Emergent Evolution*. Dordrecht: Kluwer.

Bohman, James 1999. 'Practical reason and cultural constraint: agency in Bourdieu's theory of practice', in R. Shusterman (ed.), *Bourdieu: A Critical Reader*, pp. 129–52. Oxford: Blackwell.

Boogerd, Fred C., Bruggeman, Frank J., Richardson, Robert C., Stephan, Achim and Westerhoff, Hans V. 2005. 'Emergence and its place in nature: a case study of biochemical networks', *Synthese* 145: 131–64.

Bourdieu, Pierre 1984. *Distinction: A Social Critique of the Judgement of Taste*. London: Routledge & Kegan Paul.

1990a. *In Other Words*. Cambridge: Polity.

1990b. *The Logic of Practice*. Cambridge: Polity.

2000. *Pascalian Meditations*. Stanford, CA: Stanford University Press.

Bourdieu, Pierre and Wacquant, Loïc J. D. 1992. *An Invitation to Reflexive Sociology*. Chicago, IL: University of Chicago Press.

Bouveresse, Jacques 1999. 'Rules, dispositions, and the Habitus', in R. Shusterman (ed.), *Bourdieu: A Critical Reader*, pp. 45–63. Oxford: Blackwell.

Brante, Thomas 2001. 'Consequences of realism for sociological theory-building', *Journal for the Theory of Social Behaviour* 31: 167–95.

Broad, C. D. 1925. *The Mind and Its Place in Nature*. London: Kegan Paul.

Brubaker, Rogers 1993. 'Social theory as habitus', in C. J. Calhoun, M. Postone and E. LiPuma (eds.), *Bourdieu: Critical Perspectives*, pp. 212–34. London: Polity.

Bucholtz, Mary 1999. '"Why be normal?": language and identity practices in a community of nerd girls', *Language in Society* 28: 203–23.

Buckley, Walter 1967. *Sociology and Modern Systems Theory*. Englewood Cliffs, NJ: Prentice-Hall.

1998. *Society: A Complex Adaptive System*. Amsterdam: Gordon and Breach.

Bunge, Mario 1996. *Finding Philosophy in Social Science*. New Haven, CT: Yale University Press.

1999. *The Sociology–Philosophy Connection*. New Brunswick, NJ: Transaction.

2003. *Emergence and Convergence*. Toronto: University of Toronto Press.

Campbell, Donald T. 1974. ' "Downward causation" in hierarchically organised biological systems', in F. J. Ayala and T. Dobzhansky (eds.), *Studies in the Philosophy of Biology*, pp. 179–86. London: Macmillan.

Catlin, George E. G. 1964. 'Introduction to the translation', in E. Durkheim, *The Rules of Sociological Method*. New York: Free Press.

Chaiken, Shelly and Trope, Yaacov 1999. *Dual-Process Theories in Social Psychology*. New York: Guilford Press.

Cilliers, Paul 1998. *Complexity and Postmodernism*. London: Routledge.

Cohen, Ira J. 1998. 'Anthony Giddens', in R. Stones (ed.), *Key Sociological Thinkers*. Basingstoke: Macmillan.

Cohen, Jack and Stewart, Ian 1995. *The Collapse of Chaos*. New York and London: Penguin.

Collier, Andrew 1989. *Scientific Realism and Socialist Thought*. Hemel Hempstead: Harvester Wheatsheaf.

1994. *Critical Realism*. London: Verso.

Collins, Patricia Hill 1998. 'It's all in the family: intersections of gender, race, and nation', *Hypatia* 13: 62–82.

Collins, Randall 1981. 'On the microfoundations of macrosociology', *American Journal of Sociology* 86: 984–1014.

Coole, Diana 2005. 'Rethinking agency: a phenomenological approach to embodiment and agentic capacities', *Political Studies* 53: 124–42.

Corning, Peter A. 2002. 'The emergence of "emergence": now what?' *Emergence* 4: 54–71.

Craib, Ian 1992. *Anthony Giddens*. London: Routledge.

Crenshaw, Kimberle 1991. 'Mapping the margins: intersectionality, identity politics, and violence against women of color', *Stanford Law Review* 43: 1241–99.

Crossley, Nick 2001. 'The phenomenological habitus and its construction', *Theory and Society* 30: 81–120.

Crothers, Charles 1996. *Social Structure*. London: Routledge.

   2002. 'History of social structural analysis', in S. C. Chew and J. D. Knottnerus (eds.), *Structure, Culture, and History*, pp. 3–41. Lanham, MD: Rowman & Littlefield.

Davidson, Donald 2001. 'Actions, reasons, and causes', *Essays on Actions and Events*, pp. 3–19. Oxford: Clarendon.

Dean, Kathryn, Joseph, Jonathan and Norrie, Alan 2005. 'Editorial: new essays in critical realism', *New Formations 56*: 7–26.

Dennett, Daniel 2003. *Freedom Evolves*: London: Allen Lane.

Dreyfus, Hubert L. and Rabinow, Paul 1983. *Michel Foucault: Beyond Structuralism and Hermeneutics*. Chicago, IL: University of Chicago Press.

Dupre, John 2001. *Human Nature and the Limits of Science*. Oxford: Clarendon Press.

Durkheim, Émile 1952 [1897]. *Suicide*. London: Routledge & Kegan Paul.

   1964 [1894]. *The Rules of Sociological Method*. New York: Free Press.

   1974 [1898]. 'Individual and collective representations', *Sociology and Philosophy*, pp. 1–34. New York: The Free Press.

   1984 [1893]. *The Division of Labour in Society*. Basingstoke: Macmillan.

   2001 [1912]. *The Elementary Forms of Religious Life*. Oxford: Oxford University Press.

Edwards, Jason 2003. 'Evolutionary psychology and politics', *Economy and Society* 32: 280–98.

Elder-Vass, Dave 2005. 'Emergence and the realist account of cause', *Journal of Critical Realism* 4: 315–38.

   2007a. 'For emergence: refining Archer's account of social structure', *Journal for the Theory of Social Behaviour* 37: 25–44.

   2007b. 'A method for social ontology', *Journal of Critical Realism* 6: 226–49.

   2007c. 'Reconciling Archer and Bourdieu in an emergentist theory of action', *Sociological Theory* 25: 325–46.

   2007d. 'Re-examining Bhaskar's three ontological domains: the lessons from emergence', in C. Lawson, J. Latsis and N. Martins (eds.), *Contributions to Social Ontology*, pp. 160–76. London: Routledge.

2007e. 'Social structure and social relations', *Journal for the Theory of Social Behaviour* 37: 463–77.

2008a. 'From speech community to intersecting linguistic circles', *SociolinguistEssex*. Colchester.

2008b. 'Integrating institutional, relational, and embodied structure: an emergentist perspective', *British Journal of Sociology* 59: 281–99.

2008c. 'Searching for realism, structure and agency in actor network theory', *British Journal of Sociology* 59: 455–73.

2010a 'The emergence of culture', *Kölner Zeitschrift für Soziologie und Sozialpsychologie*.

2010b. 'Realist critique without ethical naturalism or moral realism', *Journal of Critical Realism* 9.

Emirbayer, Mustafa 1997. 'Manifesto for a relational sociology', *American Journal of Sociology* 103: 281–317.

Emmeche, Claus, Koppe, Simo and Stjernfelt, Frederik 1997. 'Explaining emergence: towards an ontology of levels', *Journal for General Philosophy of Science* 28: 83–119.

Fleetwood, Steve 2001. 'Causal laws, functional relations and tendencies', *Review of Political Economy* 13: 201–20.

2008. 'Institutions and social structures', *Journal for the Theory of Social Behaviour* 38: 241–65.

Fodor, Jerry A. 1974. 'Special sciences (or: the disunity of science as a working hypothesis)', *Synthese* 28: 97–115.

Foucault, Michel 2002 [1969]. *The Archaeology of Knowledge*. London: Routledge.

Freeman, Walter J. 2000. *How Brains Make Up Their Minds*. London: Phoenix.

Frisby, David 2002. *Georg Simmel*. London: Routledge.

Fullbrook, Edward and Lawson, Tony 2009. *Ontology and Economics: Tony Lawson and His Critics*. London: Routledge.

Garfinkel, Harold 1967. *Studies in Ethnomethodology*. Englewood Cliffs, NJ: Prentice-Hall.

Gell-Mann, Murray 1995. *The Quark and the Jaguar*. London: Abacus.

Giddens, Anthony 1979. *Central Problems in Social Theory*. Basingstoke: Macmillan Press.

1984. *The Constitution of Society*. Cambridge: Polity.

1993. *New Rules of Sociological Method*. Cambridge: Polity.

Gilbert, Margaret 1990. 'Walking together', *Midwest Studies in Philosophy* 15: 1–14.

Gindis, David 2007. 'Some building blocks for a theory of the firm as a real entity', in Y. Biondi, A. Canziani and T. Kirat (eds.), *The Firm as an Entity*, pp. 266–91. Abingdon: Routledge.

2009. 'From fictions and aggregates to real entities in the theory of the firm', *Journal of Institutional Economics* 5: 25–46.

Goffman, Erving 1983. 'The interaction order', *American Sociological Review* 48: 1–17.

1990 [1956]. *The Presentation of Self in Everyday Life*. London: Penguin.

Goldstein, Jeffrey 1999. 'Emergence as a construct: history and issues', *Emergence* 1: 49–72.

Gribbin, John R. and Gribbin, Mary 1999. *Almost Everyone's Guide to Science*. London: Phoenix.

Groff, Ruth (ed.) 2008. *Revitalizing Causality: Realism about Causality in Philosophy and Social Science*. London: Routledge.

Habermas, Jürgen 1987. *The Theory of Communicative Action*. Boston, MA: Beacon Press.

Harré, Rom and Madden, Edward H. 1975. *Causal Powers: A Theory of Natural Necessity*. Oxford: Blackwell.

Hartwig, Mervyn (ed.) 2007. *Dictionary of Critical Realism*. Abingdon: Routledge.

Heer, David M. 2003. 'Social structure', in W. Outhwaite (ed.), *The Blackwell Dictionary of Modern Social Thought*. Oxford: Blackwell.

Hempel, Carl G. 1968. 'Explanation in science and in history', in P. H. Nidditch (ed.), *The Philosophy of Science*, pp. 54–79. Oxford: Oxford University Press.

1998. 'Two basic types of scientific explanation', in M. Curd and J. A. Cover (eds.), *Philosophy of Science: The Central Issues*, pp. 685–94. New York: W. W. Norton.

Hodgson Geoffrey, M. 2006a. *Economics in the Shadows of Darwin and Marx*. Cheltenham: Edward Elgar.

2006b. 'What are institutions?' *Journal of Economic Issues* 40: 1–26.

2007. 'Meanings of methodological individualism', *Journal of Economic Methodology* 14: 211–26.

Holland, John H. 1998. *Emergence: From Chaos to Order*. Oxford: Oxford University Press.

Honderich, Ted (ed.) 1995. *The Oxford Companion to Philosophy*. Oxford: Oxford University Press.

Horgan, Terence 2002. 'From supervenience to superdupervenience', in J. Kim (ed.), *Supervenience*, pp. 113–44. Aldershot: Ashgate/Dartmouth.

Hume, David 1977 [1748]. *An Enquiry Concerning Human Understanding*. Indianapolis, IN: Hackett.

Humphreys, Paul 1997. 'How properties emerge', *Philosophy of Science* 64: 1–17.

Jary, David and Jary, Julia 2000. *Collins Dictionary of Sociology*. Glasgow: HarperCollins.

Jenkins, Richard 2002. *Pierre Bourdieu*. London: Routledge.

Kadushin, Charles 1968. 'Power, influence and social circles', *American Sociological Review* 33: 685–99.

Kaidesoja, Tuukka 2007. 'Exploring the concept of causal power in a critical realist tradition', *Journal for the Theory of Social Behaviour* 37: 63–87.

    2009. 'Bhaskar and Bunge: a comparison and evaluation of their theories of social emergence', *Journal for the Theory of Social Behaviour* 39: 300–22.

Kauffman, Stuart A. 1995. *At Home in the Universe: The Search for Laws of Self-Organization and Complexity*. London: Viking.

Keat, Russell and Urry, John 1975. *Social Theory as Science*. London: Routledge & Kegan Paul.

Kim, Jaegwon 1992. ' "Downward causation" in emergentism and non-reductive physicalism', in A. Beckermann, H. Flohr and J. Kim (eds.), *Emergence or Reduction?*, pp. 119–38. Berlin: de Gruyter.

    1993. 'The non-reductivist's troubles with mental causation', in J. Heil and A. R. Mele (eds.), *Mental Causation*, pp. 189–210. Oxford: Clarendon.

    1997. 'The mind-body problem: taking stock after forty years', *Nous* 11: 185–207.

    1998. *Mind in a Physical World*. Cambridge, MA: The MIT Press.

    1999. 'Making sense of emergence', *Philosophical Studies* 95: 3–36.

King, Anthony 1999a. 'Against structure: a critique of morphogenetic social theory', *Sociological Review* 47: 199–227.

    1999b. 'The impossibility of naturalism: the antinomies of Bhaskar's realism', *Journal for the Theory of Social Behaviour* 29: 267–88.

    2000. 'Thinking with Bourdieu against Bourdieu: a "practical" critique of the habitus', *Sociological Theory* 18: 417–33.

    2004. *The Structure of Social Theory*. London: Routledge.

    2006. 'How not to structure a social theory: a reply to a critical response', *Philosophy of the Social Sciences* 36: 464–79.

    2007. 'Why I am not an individualist', *Journal for the Theory of Social Behaviour* 37: 211–19.

Kitcher, Philip 1998. '1953 and all that: a tale of two sciences', in M. Curd and J. A. Cover (eds.), *Philosophy of Science: The Central Issues*, pp. 971–1003. New York: W. W. Norton.

Klee, Robert L. 1984. 'Micro-determinism and concepts of emergence', *Philosophy of Science* 51: 44–63.

Laszlo, Ervin 1972. *The Systems View of the World*. Oxford: Blackwell.

Latour, Bruno 1996. *Aramis: Or the Love of Technology*. Cambridge, MA: Harvard University Press.

2005. *Reassembling the Social*. Oxford: Oxford University Press.

Lawson, Tony 1997. *Economics and Reality*. London: Routledge.

2003. *Reorienting Economics*. London: Routledge.

Lewes, George Henry 1874–9. *Problems of Life and Mind*. London: Trubner.

Lloyd Morgan, C. 1923. *Emergent Evolution*. London: Williams & Norgate.

Lopez, Jose and Scott, John 2000. *Social Structure*. Buckingham: Open University Press.

Loyal, Steven and Barnes, Barry 2001. ' "Agency" as a red herring in social theory', *Philosophy of the Social Sciences* 31: 507–24.

Lukes, Steven 1973. *Émile Durkheim: His Life and Work*. London: Allen Lane.

McCall, Leslie 2005. 'The complexity of intersectionality', *Signs* 30: 1771–800.

McLaughlin, Brian P. 1992. 'The rise and fall of British emergentism', in A. Beckermann, H. Flohr and J. Kim (eds.), *Emergence or Reduction?*, pp. 49–93. Berlin: de Gruyter.

Manicas, Peter T. 2006. *A Realist Philosophy of Social Science*. Cambridge: Cambridge University Press.

March, James G. and Simon, Herbert A. 1993 [1958]. *Organizations*. Cambridge, MA: Blackwell.

Marras, Ausonio 2006. 'Emergence and reduction: reply to Kim', *Synthese* 151: 561–9.

Marx, Karl 1978 [1852]. 'The Eighteenth Brumaire of Louis Bonaparte', in R. C. Tucker (ed.), *The Marx-Engels Reader*, pp. 594–617. New York: W. W. Norton.

1978 [1859]. 'Preface to a contribution to the critique of political economy', in R. C. Tucker (ed.), *The Marx-Engels Reader*, pp. 3–6. New York: W. W. Norton.

Mayes, G. Randolph 2005. 'Theories of explanation', *Internet Encyclopedia of Philosophy*, URL: www.iep.utm.edu/explanat/

Merton, Robert K. 1968. *Social Theory and Social Structure*. New York: The Free Press.

Meyering, Theo C. 2000. 'Physicalism and downward causation in psychology and the special sciences', *Inquiry* 43: 181–202.

Mihata, Kevin 1997. 'The persistence of "emergence", in R. A. Eve, S. Horsfall and M. E. Lee (eds.), *Chaos, Complexity, and Sociology*, pp. 30–8. Thousand Oaks, CA: Sage.

Mill, John Stuart 1900. *A System of Logic*. London: Longmans.

Mouzelis, Nicos P. 1991. *Back to Sociological Theory*. Basingstoke: Macmillan.

　1992. 'The interaction order and the micro-macro distinction', *Sociological Theory* 10: 122–8.

　1995. *Sociological Theory: What Went Wrong?* London: Routledge.

　2000. 'The subjectivist-objectivist divide: against transcendence', *Sociology* 34: 741–62.

Mumford, Stephen 2008. 'Powers, dispositions, properties or a causal realist manifesto', in R. Groff (ed.), *Revitalizing Causality: Realism about Causality in Philosophy and Social Science*, pp. 139–51. London: Routledge.

Münch, Richard and Smelser, Neil J. 1987. 'Relating the micro and macro', in J. C. Alexander, B. Giesen, R. Münch and N. J. Smelser (eds.), *The Micro-Macro Link*, pp. 356–87. Berkeley, CA: University of California Press.

Nagel, Ernest 1998 [1974]. 'Issues in the logic of reductive explanations', in M. Curd and J. A. Cover (eds.), *Philosophy of Science: The Central Issues*, pp. 905–21. New York: W. W. Norton.

Newman, David V. 1996. 'Emergence and strange attractors', *Philosophy of Science* 63: 245–61.

Parker, John 2000. *Structuration*. Buckingham: Open University Press.

　2006. 'Structuration's future?' *Journal of Critical Realism* 5: 122–38.

Parsons, Talcott 1937. *The Structure of Social Action*. New York: The Free Press.

　1966. *Societies: Evolutionary and Comparative Perspectives*. Englewood Cliffs, NJ: Prentice-Hall.

　1969. *Politics and Social Structure*. New York: The Free Press.

　1976. 'Social structure and the symbolic media of interchange', in P. M. Blau (ed.), *Approaches to the Study of Social Structure*, pp. 94–120. London: Open Books.

Phoenix, Ann and Pattynama, Pamela 2006. 'Editorial: intersectionality', *European Journal of Women's Studies* 13: 187–92.

Pickel, Andreas 2004. 'Systems and mechanisms: a symposium on Mario Bunge's philososphy of social science', *Philosophy of the Social Sciences* 34: 169–81.

Porpora, Douglas 1998. 'Four concepts of social structure', in M. Archer, R. Bhaskar, A. Collier, T. Lawson and A. Norrie (eds.), *Critical Realism: Essential Readings*, pp. 339–55. London: Routledge.

2002. 'Social structure: the future of a concept', in S. C. Chew and J. D. Knottnerus (eds.), *Structure, Culture, and History*, 43–59. Lanham, MD: Rowman & Littlefield.

2007. 'On Elder-Vass: refining a refinement', *Journal for the Theory of Social Behaviour* 37: 195–200.

Postone, Moishe, LiPuma, Edward and Calhoun, Craig J. 1993. 'Introduction', in C. J. Calhoun, M. Postone and E. LiPuma (eds.), *Bourdieu: Critical Perspectives*, pp. 1–13. London: Polity.

Potter, Garry 2006. 'Reopening the wound: against God and Bhaskar', *Journal of Critical Realism* 5: 92–109.

Prigogine, Ilya and Stengers, Isabelle 1984. *Order Out of Chaos: Man's New Dialogue with Nature*. London: Heinemann.

Read, Rupert J. and Richman, Kenneth A. 2007. *The New Hume Debate*. London: Routledge.

Reed, Michael 2005. 'Reflections on the "realist turn" in organization and management studies', *Journal of Management Studies* 42: 1621–44.

Rose, Hilary and Rose, Steven 2001. *Alas Poor Darwin: Arguments Against Evolutionary Psychology*. London: Vintage.

Rose, Steven P. R. 2006. *The 21st-Century Brain*. London: Vintage.

Saussure, Ferdinand de 1986 [1916]. *Course in General Linguistics*. Chicago, IL: Open Court.

Sawyer, R. Keith 2005. *Social Emergence*. Cambridge: Cambridge University Press.

Sayer, Andrew 1992. *Method in Social Science*. London: Routledge.

2000. *Realism and Social Science*. London: Sage.

2005a. 'Class, moral worth and recognition', *Sociology* 39: 947–64.

2005b. *The Moral Significance of Class*. Cambridge: Cambridge University Press.

2009. 'Review of *Making Our Way Through the World*, by Margaret Archer', *Journal of Critical Realism* 8: 113–23.

Searle, John R. 1992. *The Rediscovery of the Mind*. Cambridge, MA: The MIT Press.

1997. *The Mystery of Consciousness*. London: Granta.

Sheehy, Paul 2006. *The Reality of Social Groups*. Aldershot: Ashgate.

Shilling, Chris 2005. *The Body in Culture, Technology and Society*. London: Sage.

Simmel, Georg 1950. *The Sociology of Georg Simmel*. New York: The Free Press.

1955. *Conflict and the Web of Group Affiliations*. New York: The Free Press.

Smith, Adam 1970 [1776]. *The Wealth of Nations*. Harmondsworth: Penguin.

Smith, Thomas S. 1997. 'Nonlinear dynamics and the micro-macro bridge', in R. A. Eve, S. Horsfall and M. E. Lee (eds.), *Chaos, Complexity, and Sociology*, pp. 52–63. Thousand Oaks, CA: Sage.

Sperry, Roger W. 1969. 'A modified concept of consciousness', *Psychological Review* 76: 532–6.

1986. 'Macro- versus micro-determinism', *Philosophy of Science* 53: 265–70.

Stephan, Achim 1992. 'Emergence – a systematic view on its historical facets', in A. Beckermann, H. Flohr and J. Kim (eds.), *Emergence or Reduction?*, pp. 25–48. Berlin: de Gruyter.

2002. 'Emergentism, irreducibility, and downward causation', *Grazer Philosophische Studien* 65: 77–94.

Stones, Rob 2001. 'Refusing the realism-structuration divide', *European Journal of Social Theory* 4: 177–98.

2002. 'Structuration', *Sociology* 36: 222–4.

2005. *Structuration Theory*. Basingstoke: Palgrave Macmillan.

Thompson, John B. 1992. 'Editor's Introduction', in P. Bourdieu *Language and Symbolic Power*, pp. 1–31. Cambridge: Polity.

Tooby, John and Cosmides, Leda 1992. 'The psychological foundations of culture', in L. Cosmides, J. Tooby and J. H. Barkow (eds.), *The Adapted Mind: Evolutionary Psychology and the Generation of Culture*, pp. 19–135. Oxford: Oxford University Press.

Urry, John 2000. *Sociology Beyond Societies*. London: Routledge.

Vaisey, Stephen 2009. 'Motivation and justification: a dual-process model of culture in action', *American Journal of Sociology* 114: 1675–715.

Vandenberghe, F. 2005. 'The Archers', *European Journal of Social Theory* 8: 227–37.

Varela, Charles R. 2002. 'The impossibility of which naturalism? A response and a reply', *Journal for the Theory of Social Behaviour* 32: 105–11.

2007. 'Elder-Vass's move and Giddens's call', *Journal for the Theory of Social Behaviour* 37: 201–10.

Varela, Charles R. and Harré, Rom 1996. 'Conflicting varieties of realism', *Journal for the Theory of Social Behaviour* 26: 313–25.

Wacquant, Loïc J. D. 1993. 'Bourdieu in America', in C. J. Calhoun, M. Postone and E. LiPuma (eds.), *Bourdieu: Critical Perspectives*, pp. 235–62. London: Polity.

Walby, Sylvia 2005. 'No one polity saturates the political space in a given territory', *Sociology* 38: 1035–42.

2007. 'Complexity theory, systems theory and multiple intersecting social inequalities', *Philosophy of the Social Sciences* 37: 449–70.

Watkins, John W. N. 1968. 'Methodological individualism and social tendencies', in M. Brodbeck (ed.), *Readings in the Philosophy of the Social Sciences*, pp. 269–80. New York: Macmillan.

Weber, Max 1978 [1922]. *Economy and Society*. Berkeley, CA: University of California Press.

2001 [1930]. *The Protestant Ethic and the Spirit of Capitalism*. London: Routledge.

Weissman, David 2000. *A Social Ontology*. New Haven, CT: Yale University Press.

Westwood, Robert and Linstead, Stephen 2001. 'Language/organization: introduction', in R. Westwood and S. Linstead (eds.), *The Language of Organization*, pp. 1–19. London: Sage.

Williams, Raymond 1976. *Keywords*. London: Fontana/Croom Helm.

Wimsatt, William C. 2000. 'Emergence as non-aggregativity and the biases of reductionisms', *Foundations of Science* 5: 269–97.

2006. 'Reductionism and its heuristics: making methodological reductionism honest', *Synthese* 151: 445–75.

Winch, Peter 1958. *The Idea of a Social Science*. London: Routledge & Kegan Paul.

Yuval-Davis, Nira 2006. 'Intersectionality and feminist politics', *European Journal of Women's Studies* 13: 193–209.

Index

emancipation, 11
embodied structure, 79, 85
emergence, 4–6, 13–39
   history of the concept, 14–16, 31
   relational, 5, 14, 16–18, 20–3, 38
   strong, 28, 33
   synchronic, 5, 16
   temporal, 5, 16, 46, 67
   weak, 14, 24
emergence level test, 73, 76, 84, 114
emergent properties, 4, 16–18, 45, 66,
   192
emission of light by a star, 59
empirical methods, 73, 177–9
endorsing, 122, 123, 126, 129
entities, 16, 66, 192
events, 7, 44, 47–8, 68
evolutionary psychology, 92
explanatory reduction, 24, 54, 56–8,
   89

feminist social theory, 131
finger pressing a key, 27
Fleetwood, Steve, 22, 117
Fodor, Jerry, 58
Foucault, Michel, 203
framing, 170
free will, 198
Freeman, Walter, 95, 96, 100

Garfinkel, Harold, 147
Gell-Mann, Murray, 58
general role norms, 165
generative mechanism, *see* mechanisms
Giddens, Anthony, 4, 8, 10, 85, 106,
   118, 120, 137, 142, 179
Gindis, David, 145
global warming, 181
globalisation, 82, 120, 200
Goffman, Erving, 146, 170
Groff, Ruth, 43

Habermas, Jürgen, 166, 204
habitus, 99–102, 113, 125, 133, 171
Harré, Rom, 5, 24, 43, 47, 198
heaps, 16, 67
Hempel, Carl, 41, 68
Hodgson, Geoff, 25, 115, 145
Holland, John, 21, 36, 57
Hume, David, 41, 43

hybrid entities, 157, 173

imagined communities, 128
imagined norm circle, 128, 129, 130,
   132
individual representations, 117
institutional structure, 78, 156
interaction group, 146–9, 171
interaction situation, 146, 170
internal conversation, 102
internalisation, 105, 106, 125
intersectionality, 116, 122, 131–3, 136,
   195, 201
intrastructuration, 26–8, 124, 158,
   162, 173
iteration in methodology, 71–6

Keat, Russell, 189
Kim, Jaegwon, 25, 30, 33, 59, 61, 91
King, Anthony, 154, 171, 175
knowledge, 203, 205

laminated entity, 49–53, 62, 66, 72,
   124
laminated event, 50, 62, 181
language, 131, 151, 171, 174, 203
Laszlo, Ervin, 37
Latour, Bruno, 121, 176
Lawson, Tony, 47, 48, 204
level abstraction, 49–53
levels, 19–20, 49–53
liabilities, 47
local complementarity test, 71, 75, 85
local role norms, 165, 172
Lopez, Jose, 77–9, 121, 156

macro-actors, 179, 180, 182–5
macro-consequences, 180, 182–5
macro-events, 180
   collective, 180, 186
   historical, 182
   statistical, 181, 190
Manicas, Peter, 191
March, James, 144, 150, 163, 165
markets, 181, 204
Marras, A., 57
Marx, Karl, 1, 3, 22, 162
mass, 17
mechanism (nineteenth-century school
   of philosophy), 29